arionne
nettles

We Are The Culture

Black Chicago's Influence
on Everything

Lawrence Hill Books
Chicago

Published by Lawrence Hill Books
An imprint of Chicago Review Press Incorporated
814 North Franklin Street
Chicago, Illinois 60610
ISBN 978-1-64160-830-5

Portions of this book's interviews have been previously published by the author in Chicago news media.

Library of Congress Control Number: 2023950680

Typesetting: Jonathan Hahn

Printed in the United States of America
5 4 3 2 1

To my son, Jackson—the sunlight that makes me
want to be a brighter ray in this world.

To my grandmothers—my sugar and my spice.

And to my city, Chicago—the place that
made me and continues to raise me.

CONTENTS

Part IV: "And You Say Chi City?"

Part V: Black Life in Print

Part VI: Black Luxury, Baby

Part VII: Hair That Makes a Statement

Part VIII: Black Representation on the Big and Small Screens

Part IX: The Oprah Effect

Part X: Sports Cool

Part XI: The Arts

INTRODUCTION

From Chicago with Love

Written while listening to "Sunday Candy" by Donnie Trumpet & the Social Experiment

> "I am from the South Side of Chicago. That tells you as much about me as you need to know."
> —Michelle Obama in the documentary *Becoming*

THE FIRST THING I EVER LEARNED, as far as identity, was twofold: I knew I was Black and I knew I was from Chicago. And frankly, those were the only two things that mattered to me.

That's because Chicago is *more* than just the place where I grew up; it's the place that is an integral part of me. I grew up playing in its streets and alleys, roller-skating and biking even over broken concrete throughout my South Side block, where my family had lived for three generations. Everything about this neighborhood, to me, has translated to love, strength, and street savviness.

I went to Chicago public schools, molded by teachers who—along with my family—intentionally instilled a sense of Black pride into me, letting me know that I came from a long line of amazingly smart and creative Black people. And that so many of those Black people had spent time here in this beautiful city, where they created community and cultivated each other's talents.

And I was a city kid: going to city parks after school, spending hours and hours in city libraries, entering city oratory and poetry contests, participating in art fests. So it was not lost on me how Chicago itself is and always has been an epicenter of culture, and how Black Chicagoans have been contributors to that culture.

Chicago is in my DNA. And when a city is part of your identity, it means something different. It means you're very much invested in that city's story, how it's told, and who's doing the telling. And when it comes to what makes Chicago *Chicago*, I've never felt that story was shared enough here—let alone with the rest of the world.

I grew up on the South Side, mostly in Englewood, and went to the very same elementary school as my mama and her sisters and brother. The block that we lived on, Sixty-Eighth and Parnell, was what my family called home for more than fifty years. We were the first Black family on that block, my grandma Bea used to say. She moved to Englewood from the Bronzeville neighborhood because, like many of the Black folks who moved to Chicago in the mid-twentieth century and long before, that was where she found community.

I remember my grandma being a fixture of our community, someone who demanded respect and received it with love. During Chicago summers, whenever I wasn't headed up to Hamilton Park, or Rainbow Beach, or even swimming in the pool at Kennedy-King (the community college closest to us), I would be "working" at her candy store. To me, working meant eating way more than it meant actually helping. With thick red and blue snowball syrup dripping down my hands as they grasped the cold Styrofoam cup filled with shaved ice, I'd leave my post behind the glass counter selling penny candy and nickel cookies whenever my cousins wanted to play, and this happened just way more times than I could count.

But even in those moments of being an overstimulated kid, with scratched-up knees from running through the alleys and streets and skinny walkways of our block, I was never too busy to notice how every single person who stopped by greeted my grandmother. "Hey, Ms. Bea!" they'd yell. "How you doin' today?" It simply did not matter who you were. Whether you thought you were the biggest gangster in the hood or a police officer on patrol, this was Ms. Bea's territory. And she was, in essence, the Queen Bee of the block.

But my grandma's position was one that was hard earned. In 1940, she packed herself up as a teenager and moved to Chicago from

Greenwood, Mississippi, where she'd made a way out of no way. Greenwood is as far back as I can trace my legacy. It's likely that many of us slaved away on the cotton plantations, and later, like my grandma, still worked the same land.

My grandma didn't bring much of anything with her, and after years of scraping and scraping, she was able to buy her own home for her family. Her story, like that of many others, is what makes the city what it is.

When I think about who encompasses the true spirit of Chicago, I think about her: scrappy, bold, making a way out of no way. To me, she was the toughest, most amazing bee in the world. But I also know that even though she was one in a million in my life, so many people here have loved ones just like her. And the reason why is clear: Chicago, a city that has always felt full of opportunity, draws them to it.

In all honesty, that's the true beauty of Chicago: It's tough; it's *always* been tough. But it teaches how you to seize opportunity. How to take advantage of what's in front of you. How to make anything better than you found it. Chicago itself is special in that way, filled with those who know how to make a way, and when given the right opportunity, we make magic.

This book is the story of just some of those magic-makers—some we talk about, but many we don't. It's a celebration of their greatness and what they achieved, because when we look back on their collective contributions, we see that one thing is clear: Black Chicago contributed to *everything*.

When we talk about Black Chicago, though, it's especially important to acknowledge the southern roots that made it all so. During the Great Migration that began over a hundred years ago, more than a half million Black Americans moved from the South to Chicago, and as Black Chicagoans, we know that means this Chicago story is also a great part in the larger story of Black American history and how we also built the country that we know is our own. Black Chicago would not be the powerhouse it is if it weren't for the South, if it were not for Mississippi and Arkansas and Georgia and Tennessee and all of the other places we grew up visiting in the hot summers when we were out of school because "that's where our people are from" and "we still got kin there."

So, southern cousins, this story—it belongs to you too. You are an intricate part of Black Chicago life, and you, too, should be proud of all that has happened here. And because Black people and Black culture are built on community, I hope that you also find the connections in Black culture from pretty much everywhere across the country: in the intellectual confidence of the work of the Harlem Renaissance; in the music industry hustle of Atlanta; in the creativity of film and TV in Los Angeles; and in all the beautifully Black places in between.

Like in all things, as Black people moved to Chicago, we innovated. We drew on the things that were of cultural significance when we lived in the South: the arts, media, everything. And we did it however we felt could best uplift Black people and provide opportunities for our communities.

Although Chicago already had some Black residents prior to World War I, it was around the 1910s when large populations came en masse and moved to the Black Belt on the South Side, an area south of downtown that would become seen as the "Black Metropolis" because it was where so many Black people found refuge when they arrived. Many decades after the start of this migration, the neighborhood's official name changed to Bronzeville, as we pushed against names such as the "Black Ghetto" and "Darkie Town"[1] and instead embraced the beautiful bronze color of our people's skin.

But we also made our way to the city's West Side. It's where my daddy grew up, and so it also has a part of my heart. This side of Chicago Black migration may have started with slower growth compared to its South Side counterpart, but it would have huge spurts in the 1920s and '30s in neighborhoods such as East Garfield Park and the Near West Side.[2] We started new businesses and dove into new industries; we created our own genres of the music we loved; we took our talents to the theater and showed Black life on the stage and, soon, on the screen. Many of us were called "race men and women," who were dedicated to improving the lives of Black people. (You'll often see in this book terms like "race film" or "race record," which are forms of entertainment created for Black audiences specifically.)

And with this, we brought the blues, amplifying what would be one of the city's greatest musical art forms. In 1958, the iconic Johnson Publishing Company, the voice of Black America, launched the Ebony Fashion Fair show, leading to the creation of the first makeup brand for Black skin. For three decades, starting in the 1970s, households across the country were transported to a stage in Chicago as they moved their hips in front of TV screens airing *Soul Train*. And in the 1990s,

Hall of Famer Michael Jordan led the Chicago Bulls to six championships, including two three-peats, making the NBA a must-see attraction worldwide.

It all happened right here, in Chicago. For the past century, Black Chicago's influence has permeated not just the city but, really, what we see as modern-day pop culture, throughout the country and, in some ways, the world.

The innovation of Chicago's Black residents helped this "City of the Big Shoulders" gain its reputation as one of the hardest-working cities in the nation. Yes, Chicago is a gigantic melting pot of different cultures and ethnicities, but these particular contributions gave it so much; they put it on the map. Yet much of what we have contributed to popular culture has gone ignored.

There are many possible reasons for this. First of all, we know that racism has often tried to diminish the value of our influence, make us think that it was too small to be acknowledged or, even worse, that it never happened at all. That affects what is preserved, what is saved, and what is documented. We see this today in everything from stealing dances from Black TikTok creators to crediting Bo Derek—and now, white women like Kim Kardashian—with popularizing cornrows because Derek wore Fulani braids in the 1979 movie 10. (In 2018, Kardashian would wear the braids, which are from a Fulani tribe subgroup called the Wodaabe, and other tribes in Ethiopia and Eritrea, and call them "Bo Derek" braids.)[3] When we see the popularization of the "clean girl aesthetic"—glossy lips with slicked-back hair and large gold hoop earrings—we know that for Black and Brown girls, it's been our signature look for decades.[4]

As a place, Chicago has been key to many of these trends. In fact, the celebration of Black history actually began here in Chicago because the contributions of Black people were being ignored. In 1915, it was Dr. Carter G. Woodson, the "father of Black History," who started the mission to celebrate Black history specifically. He created the Association for the Study of Negro Life and History in Chicago, saying that our accomplishments were being "overlooked, ignored, and even suppressed by the writers of history textbooks and the teachers who use them."[5] Woodson, a master's degree graduate from the University of Chicago and the second Black person (after W. E. B. Du Bois) to receive a doctorate from Harvard, had been prohibited from going to American

Historical Association conferences. Knowing white historians had no interest acknowledging let alone celebrating Black history, he wanted to create something separate to honor that. And in 1926, he launched Negro History Week, which would become Black History Month fifty years later in 1976.[6]

So in this vein, as we ourselves work to draw historical lines from event to event and from person to person, how do we connect these time periods? For me, it means going back to the very beginning—it means going back to the time of slavery. Everything—absolutely everything—stems from slavery: the first Black newspapers were abolitionist papers that called for the end of chattel slavery; the blues stemmed from spirituals sung on plantations; the presentation of hair and clothing were key to survival in getting work after slavery ended.

When we know what Black people had to go through to accomplish such amazing feats, our contributions become even more remarkable: how courageous it is to still write after receiving threats; how monumental it is to create a film with Black people and for Black people that focuses on Black joy; how amazing it is to demand that the world's top designers include Black models in their shows.

These contributions lie within the heart of the very areas we categorize as popular culture today: music, media, fashion, television, film, the arts, sports. But what exactly makes them "popular"? Popular culture is defined in sociology as being the "widely accessible and commonly shared aspects of culture."[7] My interpretation is this: The hype around beloved forms of art and music and fashion is hype for a reason. It is, in fact, the culture of the masses because it's good, because it means more than some frivolous obsession, because it's built on what people care about and is an expression of our growth as a people.

The movie industry isn't just a means of entertainment that is important in its own right; it is also a way to create job opportunities and to combat unfair representations—something Black filmmakers are still fighting for today. Drill music, which started in Chicago, began as the music of a generation frustrated with losing loved ones and being asked to pretend as if that loss were normal. Watching Oprah on a nationally syndicated show during the day was a revolutionary act because not only was she a Black woman who did not have the "traditional look" TV managers pushed on talent, but she also rose to power in her industry, creating an influence greater than what anyone had seen before.

And honestly, if we aren't seeing or hearing the importance of these things, it's because we aren't listening or watching closely enough. It doesn't mean that they aren't important, just that we aren't paying attention.

When Black cultural contributions are finally recognized, it is sometimes too late. We knew some of the largest Black publications were important, but we did not understand their full influence until we no longer had them in their original form. Sure, many such as *Ebony* and *Jet* are in the process of relaunching in the digital age for a new audience, which is exciting. But today, looking back on the power that they once held, I can only imagine what it felt like to walk into the opulent Johnson Publishing Company building and see the physical manifestation of the empire a Black Chicago family built.

On top of what we do know, there's so much that we don't. The Great Migration brought many of us here, sure. But Black folks were making their mark in the Chicago area long before then. In fact, we helped to create it. Black people have been part of Chicago since its incorporation as a town in 1837 and long before that. Jean Baptiste Point DuSable, a Black Haitian man, became the area's first nonnative settler around 1779 after marrying a Potawatomi woman named Kitihawa.

All of this leads me to legacy. It's up to those of us who have that legacy to draw the line, to create that connection, to start telling our stories the way they should be told. And as a Black Chicagoan, as a creative, as an academic, I am excited by the thought of celebrating the culture. It's a beautiful and wonderful idea whenever we can get together and share all the amazing work our ancestors put in—and learn a little something in the process. So this book is part history lesson, part academic celebration of Chicago's Black folks—Black with a capital *B*—a people so incredible that there's no way all our cultural contributions can fit in one book.

So is this the full anthology of Black Chicago culture? Not at all—I'd need a hundred books for that! But this book is a love letter to the city that raised me.

Thank you so much, Chicago.

Part I

BLACK NEWS CANNOT BE SILENCED: THE CREATION OF THE *DEFENDER*

HOMECOMING

Written while listening to "How I Got Over" by Mahalia Jackson

"Many of the people who left the South never exactly sat
their children down to tell them these things, tell them what
happened and why they left and how they and all this blood
kin came to be in this northern city or western suburb or why
they speak like melted butter and their children speak like
footsteps on pavement, prim and proper or clipped and fast,
like the New World itself."
—Isabel Wilkerson in *The Warmth of Other Suns*

WHEN MY GRANDMA BEA arrived in Chicago's chilly spring of 1940, she
didn't even own a winter coat. Seventeen years old, she stepped off the
train and expected to figure things out for herself. Greenwood hadn't
prepared her for this cold, and although the small Mississippi delta city
was home, she was anxious to leave it. Like other places in the area,
Greenwood, incorporated in 1844, was a city that was built on slave labor.
Its moneymaker? Cotton. Lots and lots of cotton.

Because cotton is one of the only commercial products you might
hear about in an elementary schoolbook's short chapter on slavery, it
initially felt cliché to say that fact. But Greenwood was not just a place
where enslaved Black people created significant wealth for their white
enslavers, it was also—as a sign proudly proclaimed—the COTTON CAPI-
TAL OF THE WORLD.

Even after slavery legally ended, Greenwood remained a top producer of the plant, relying on Black labor to power the industry. According to the Advisory Council on Historic Preservation, Greenwood was a major shipper of cotton to New Orleans, Vicksburg, Memphis, and St. Louis during the nineteenth and early twentieth centuries. The city's "Cotton Row" was filled with processing factories and other related businesses.

And to me, this is a significant point. When my grandma said she was "sick and tired of picking cotton" as a teenager, she meant it. What other opportunities were there for a young Black girl to seek in Jim Crow America? Besides domestic work, there weren't many, and with my grandma being as headstrong as she was, doing laundry and scrubbing floors wasn't exactly a safer job than picking cotton—not for her.

When I was very little, my grandma would tell me stories about her life in Greenwood, little tidbits about what happened before she came here. Honestly, my grandma, who at home we called Bea Ma, was my very best friend when I was small. So it's not a stretch for me, as an adult, to believe I became a safe space for her too—a place where she could get out the hard and rough memories that can feel like little pieces of stubborn sand that just never leave us, no matter how hard we try to wash them away.

One day as a teenager in Greenwood, Bea Ma told me, she was working as a maid for a white woman who demanded that, instead of using a mop, my grandma get down on her hands and knees to wash the floor. Anyone who's ever met Bea Ma would tell you: she wasn't one to suffer fools or disrespect. And even as a teenager, I can imagine, she was no different.

"I don't even get down on my hands and knees to scrub my own floor," she'd told the woman. "So I for damn sure ain't doing that for you."

Now, this is when all hell broke loose. The woman called her brother, and a mob of men came to the house—my grandma suspected to lynch her—before the woman's husband came home and stopped them. "This is a child," she remembered him telling them. "She is *a child*."

My mind constantly plays this incident in a loop. Our family's legacy could have ended right there, that day in that woman's house. None of us could have ever been born.

For Bea Ma, Chicago was different. It was a place of more economic opportunity. When she moved here, she worked at what was then the

Dixie Cup Company. Factory jobs like these meant more than just a paycheck. They meant a life other than picking cotton, an alternative to scrubbing somebody else's floors on her hands and knees.

In 2019, my family decided we'd go down to Greenwood together. It was my aunt Elaine's seventieth birthday, and as the matriarch, she'd decided that we'd go and look for records and do all this research. We didn't find anything, really. Records for Black residents were not always accurately kept, and we didn't have any leads on remaining family in the area, so we spent most of the time playing cards in the lobby of the Holiday Inn. But this strange reverse trip back "home" juxtaposes itself in my mind next to these stories: visuals of us shopping with discretionary income at a gift shop, going to a soul food restaurant to eat a meal prepared by someone else, "visiting" the last place fourteen-year-old Emmett Till ever visited before a white mob came and murdered him in 1955—fifteen years after my family moved away.

Emmett's mother, Mamie Till, had also moved up north, but as a child with her family in the 1920s. Her father found work in Argo, Illinois, and Mamie later moved to Chicago as an adult. Emmett had just gone down to Money—about ten miles from Greenwood—to visit family and never made it back home.

Yet, despite the traumatic past, what I felt being there over a half century later was a calm, a strength, a pride in the connection I had with these amazing people who came before me. I walked the streets my grandma had walked when she was a young girl. I touched everything, even reaching down to connect with the earth, grounding myself in the land and knowing that strength can flow from the ancestors that came before us. I wanted to take that strength back home to Chicago with me. These pieces of information work like connected lines in my own memory, threaded together to weave the history of Black Chicago today. It's a reminder that we are who we are because of who we came from, and that our culture is one of collective tenacity.

When my grandma got off that train in 1940, she wasn't expecting to see her cousin Nancy, waiting right there with a coat for her. She thought she was coming up here to make it all on her own. But what she found was a community of Black people living, working, doing for each other. It reminds me of what Gwendolyn Brooks, who also moved to Chicago with her family during the Great Migration, once wrote: "We are each other's harvest; we are each other's business."[1] Like Bea Ma, other people had come to Chicago seeking better lives—armed with a copy of the *Chicago Defender* urging them to do so.

In writing this book, I leaned heavily on the *Defender*, one of the few fully digitized chronicles of Black life I could read in full, spending late nights at my laptop after logging into the Chicago Public Library's website. I love searching through its archives, reading the stories about who got married, who hosted a party, who had a new business.

I still can spend hours getting lost in the pages that tell those stories of being Black in Chicago and how, although it was nowhere near perfect, it was a symbol of hope and wanting more—more than what had been given to us, even though what we deserve is immeasurable. Even though you could read the happenings of Black life around the country in the *Defender*, it was here in Chicago where our voices could be heard.

As a Chicagoan, it was an honor to work there, to add to the chorus of Black voices who have chronicled over a century of events, happenings, and perspectives. I often argue that the *Defender* is one of the most influential newspapers in American history, and being in Chicago was essential to its impact. The *Defender* is the only publication I remember Bea Ma picking up and reading—its writing steeped in a strong Black voice that could be enjoyed by everyone, from those like her who had not made it through high school all the way, to those of us who took on higher education. And those historic pages still have a special place in my heart.

Where would we be without the *Defender*? I'm not sure. But I'm glad that its creator, Robert Abbott, made his way to Chicago. Here is where we start and spend some time getting to know some of the city's early journalists and the culture they helped create.

1

BLACK JOURNALISM PUSHES FOR PROGRESS

"A ship rotting at anchor meets with no resistance, but when she sets sail on the sea, she has to buffet opposing billows. The enemies of the Negro see that he is making progress and they naturally wish to stop him and keep him in just what they consider his proper place."
—Frederick Douglass in *The Reason Why the Colored American Is Not in the World's Columbian Exposition*

THE FIRST BLACK NEWSPAPER in Chicago is one that's unknown to many people. The famed *Chicago Defender*—although a large influence—was not the first to take up the role as the voice of Black Chicago. That title rightfully belongs to the *Chicago Conservator*: a paper that was formed by some of the nation's brightest minds and that influenced journalists and writers who would later help shape news for decades to come.

The full story of how the *Conservator*—and ultimately the *Defender*—came to be goes back to the late 1800s, back to the Reconstruction era, and back to the beginning of Jim Crow. During this time, Chicago became a hub for using newspapers as a medium for activism, Black empowerment, and Black progression. Amazing leaders in journalism such as Ferdinand Lee Barnett, Ida B. Wells, and Robert Sengstacke

Abbott would take the hands dealt to them and spark dramatic change throughout Chicago that spread across the country.

The *Conservator* was founded in Chicago in 1878, and one of its founding editors, Ferdinand Barnett, was an attorney. Originally from Nashville, Tennessee, Barnett was born during slavery in 1852. His father purchased his family's freedom the year Barnett was born, but they feared being unfairly captured and wanted to escape the South. So they fled to Canada for safety.

For decades, it had been a lucrative business to track down, capture, and return a Black person who had escaped slavery back to their enslaver or sell them, especially after some northern states, like Vermont, New Hampshire, and Connecticut, started to abolish slavery. Lawmakers in the South worried that more and more enslaved people could easily find refuge in these places and pushed to pass the Fugitive Slave Act of 1793, giving enslavers the right to search anywhere in the US. The only action a white person needed to take was to sign an affidavit saying the person belonged to them and it would be considered proof.

After the introduction of the Fugitive Slave Act of 1850, even more free Black people faced the same fate. If any Black person was accused of being a fugitive, they had no right to a jury trial or to testify on their own behalf. It also meant that citizens were now bound by law to help in seizing them.

In free states like Illinois, Black people still were not safe. It is true that Illinois also had slavery. Even after 1818—when the legal language was reworded to be a type of indentured servitude, with term limits that could still be extended and renewed—there were still Black Codes that placed restrictions on the Black population to ensure they would not have all of the same rights as their white counterparts. They could not sue or testify against white people, could not vote, could not even gather in groups of three or more people in public, and could not be out without a Certificate of Freedom or else they would be considered a runaway and arrested. And, if arrested for anything and assumed to be guilty of a crime, Black people could be sent to work in salt mines— another form of slavery. County sheriffs could even sell their labor if they said Black people owed a fine.

After the Civil War, when slavery was legally abolished in Illinois as in other states, the Barnetts moved to Chicago. There, Ferdinand went to school and received his law degree from Union College of Law, now

Northwestern School of Law. When he gained admittance to the Illinois bar in 1878, he was only the third Black person to do so. He founded the *Conservator* that same year, and with Barnett at its helm, its focus was naturally on justice, rights, and freedom. It stood out at the time because it didn't sensationalize stories and tried to provide even, fair coverage. These stances were both innovative and progressive. Also that year, he wrote an editorial in the paper titled "Spell It with a Capital" in which he pushed for the capitalization of the word *Negro*. Like today's argument that the *B* in *Black* must be capitalized, Barnett explained that this move was a sign of respect.[1]

As Barnett's law career took off, after four years at the helm of the paper he gave ownership and editorial control to Alexander Clark and Alexander Clark Jr., who continued the focus of their predecessor.[2] There are not many copies of the *Conservator* available; just a few pages of a few issues have been recovered and archived. But in an 1886 editorial archived by the Library of Congress, a *Conservator* writer argues that Black people must support the Black press because it's a way to advocate for equity, push for progress, and educate the masses.[3]

There is not be much writing available by Barnett himself, but he wrote some of his most memorable work in 1893 when he, along with a group of Black trailblazers, set their sights on helping right a wrong that was happening in his own backyard. That year, Chicago was set to host the World's Columbian Exposition. Held in Chicago's Jackson Park, it was supposed to be representative of all of the country's advancements, and it drew in twenty-seven million visitors over its six-month run.[4] Yet, as journalist Ida B. Wells's autobiography, *Crusade for Justice*, explains, every Black American who submitted a petition to participate in the world's fair was denied, which brought Wells to Chicago to join forces with Barnett, famed abolitionist Frederick Douglass, and educator and journalist Irvine Garland Penn.

Born enslaved in 1862, Wells grew up in Holly Springs, Mississippi, then moved to Memphis, Tennessee, with her younger siblings in 1882 after her parents died. Just years after her move, she started work as a journalist, and in 1889, Wells became part owner of the *Memphis Free Speech* newspaper. Her work eventually turned to the problem of lynching when, in 1892, a white mob killed three of her friends, People's Grocery owner Thomas Moss and his employees Will Stewart and Calvin McDowell. Moss, who was successful in his business, was an example of the type of mobility that Black people worked hard toward with their newfound freedom—a type of mobility that many white people resented, which often led to violence, especially during the eras of Reconstruction and Jim Crow.

After the lynchings, the importance of Black journalism became clear: it's a way to get out the real and accurate accounts of racial terror. For Wells, the deaths were the start of the work she'd become most famous for. "This is what opened my eyes to what lynching really was. An excuse to get rid of Negroes who were acquiring wealth and property and thus keep the race terrorized and 'keep the nigger down,'" she wrote in *Crusade for Justice*.[5]

In spite of the danger that surrounded her—from the violence and hate of the recently created and rapidly expanding Ku Klux Klan to the threat of death dictated by the whims of what white people deemed as proper etiquette in how Black people should interact with them; "Black man didn't tip his hat, so I shot him" is a key example[6]—Wells became one of the most notable investigators and crusaders against lynchings the world has seen. She published facts, wrote editorials, and spoke globally about the lynchings that were taking place across the South. She interviewed families and residents, and worked with publications everywhere to share this work: She published statistics in the *Chicago Tribune*, worked with the *New York Age* to publish what she writes is the first inside story of a lynching, and gave an interview to England's *Anti-Caste* magazine that launched her worldwide campaign. She was invited to travel to England and then all over the world. When we think about investigative journalism today, Wells deserves major thanks for doing this dangerous work and using her influence to bring awareness to the cause.

But Wells also had a superpower of mobilizing people. It's why she was pulled into the project of improving Black representation at the world's fair in Chicago. Douglass, a seventy-five-year-old elder at the time, was widely respected. And he respected Wells, whom he called a "brave woman."[7] Her 1892 pamphlet titled *Southern Horrors: Lynch Law in All Its Phases* had a letter introduction by Douglass that said as much. She would publish another pamphlet in 1895 titled *A Red Record: Lynchings in the United States*, which provided statistics around lynchings from 1892 through 1894 and also included Douglass's letter as an introduction.

Douglass had served as US minister to Haiti from 1889 to 1891. Because Haiti was an independent Black nation, it was invited to participate in the World's Columbian Exposition. It erected a building at the fair and pulled in Douglass to represent it. His was the only participation granted to Black Americans. So Douglass's group had brought in Wells to raise money and publish their eighty-one-page booklet, *The Reason Why the Colored American Is Not in the World's Columbian Exposition: The Afro-American's Contribution to Columbian Literature.*[8]

The fair was to mark four hundred years since Christopher Columbus had first arrived in the Americas and undeservingly claimed himself the discoverer of a place that was already inhabited by Indigenous people. It was supposed to be a display of innovation, achievement, and—as its mission said—American progress. But what is honoring a country's progress if not showcasing the achievement of the very people who worked to build it? Not only are Black people key inhabitants of the country, the pamphlet argued, but no celebration of innovation and progress could occur without their contributions.

"The exhibit of the progress made by a race in 25 years of freedom as against 250 years of slavery, would have been the greatest tribute to the greatness and progressiveness of American institutions which could have been shown the world," the pamphlet's preface stated. "The colored people of this great Republic number eight millions—more than one-tenth the whole population of the United States. They were among the earliest settlers of this continent, landing at Jamestown, Virginia in 1619 in a slave ship, before the Puritans, who landed at Plymouth in 1620. They have contributed a large share to American prosperity and civilization. The labor of one-half of this country has always been, and is still being done by them."[9]

According to Wells, ten thousand copies of the pamphlet were distributed, with Wells sitting at the Haitian Pavilion for months, passing it out to visitors from around the world. The pavilion became a hub for Black Americans to speak. And although they were still not allowed to officially participate in the world's fair, fair officials eventually decided to make a Negro Day, officially named "Colored American Day." Wells wrote in her autobiography that she thought it was perhaps created to "appease the discontent of colored people over their government's attitude of segregation." Although this was seen by Wells and others as an insulting offer, Douglass accepted, his feelings being that "he thought it better to accept half a loaf than to have no bread at all."[10]

Even though Wells and Douglass may not have agreed, Douglass used Negro Day and his platform to continue the discussion started in the pamphlet: that Black Americans were also Americans, and when the US treated its Black citizens as less than, it was not living up to its own promises. Instead of blaming Black people for the country's problems, Douglass argued in his speech, "The true problem is a national problem. The problem is whether the American people have honesty enough, loyalty enough, honor enough, patriotism enough to live up to their own Constitution."[11]

Even with the pushback from authorities and the fight for representation, the world's fair became the foundation for relationships that would change Black history—really, American history—as we know it. That was especially true for Wells, who became one of the most prominent voices in media and who did much of that work in Chicago. And after this project was completed, it was love and romance that brought Wells to Chicago more permanently. Wells returned to Chicago in 1895, and soon thereafter she married Ferdinand L. Barnett, founder of the *Conservator*, in a large double parlor of the home where she was staying, decorated with ferns, palms, and roses, as an organist softly played "Call Me Thine Own" from the opera *L'éclair* by French composer Fromental Halévy.

The two became a power couple. Barnett returned to focusing solely on practicing law. In 1896, he became the first Black assistant state's attorney in Illinois. Wells purchased the *Conservator*, and the Monday after her wedding, she took charge of the paper, leading it in a role that would be similar to that of a managing editor. Wells would continue to work in and run the *Conservator* for two years before stepping back to take care of her children. She then sold the publication in 1914, but not before hiring and mentoring Chicago's next Black newspaper leader: Robert Sengstacke Abbott.

2

THE MAKING OF THE MAN

"The first decade was merely a prolongation of the vain
search for freedom, the boon that seemed ever barely to elude
their grasp—like a tantalizing will-o'-the-wisp, maddening
and misleading the headless host. The holocaust of war, the
terrors of the Ku-Klux Klan, the lies of carpet-baggers, the
disorganization of industry, and the contradictory advice
of friends and foes, left the bewildered serf with no new
watchword beyond the old cry for freedom."
> —W. E. B. Du Bois in his book *The Souls of Black Folk*,
> on the decade after Emancipation

WHEN ROBERT SENGSTACKE ABBOTT made his way to Chicago during
the world's fair in 1893, he was a twenty-year-old student enrolled at
the historically Black college called Hampton Normal and Agricultural
Institute, now known as Hampton University. Known as the educational
home of one of its "most distinguished" graduates, Booker T. Washington,
the school was experiencing a time of significant growth when Abbott
arrived in 1892.

Starting in the 1880s and through to the 1890s, Hampton became
a huge trade school. During this era, the school worked to expand the
courses taught there. Classes around skills such as farming, carpentry,
and blacksmithing prepared students for jobs, while also providing them
a method to pay their way through school.[1]

Printing was the skill that Abbott came to Hampton to learn. He also joined one of the school's most talked-about organizations: the Hampton Singers. In the 1870s, Hampton founder Samuel Chapman Armstrong started traveling around the country with a group of singers—some of whom were formerly enslaved—to raise money for the school by singing spirituals and songs once sung on plantations. This was a popular practice seen in the history of HBCUs, like the Jubilee Singers of Fisk University in Nashville, Tennessee.

It was with the Hampton Singers that Abbott traveled to Chicago. And there, on Colored American Day at the World's Columbian Exposition, he heard Frederick Douglass speak about America's promises and—at some point—Ida B. Wells, who would become his future boss.

But the young Robert Abbott, often referred to as a "late-starter"[2] by people who knew him at the beginning of his career, had a long road ahead before he would become the Robert Abbott spoken of today. His life, in fact, had a lot of turns that led him to become a newspaper man. Author Roi Ottley worked with the Sengstacke family to write the only known biography of Abbott in 1955. As he describes in the book, *The Lonely Warrior: The Life and Times of Robert S. Abbott*, Abbott was twenty-seven when he graduated from Hampton, around thirty when he graduated from law school, and thirty-seven when he founded the *Defender*.

Before Hampton would become part of his eventual road to Chicago, Abbott's start was in St. Simons Island, Georgia. Born in 1868, he started life during Reconstruction—just five years after the signing of the Emancipation Proclamation and three years after the end of the Civil War. Not much is known about his biological father, Thomas Abbott, but inside a Chicago Public Library archive collection of the Sengstacke family's documents lives an autobiography written by Robert's mother, Flora Abbott Sengstacke.

Abbott's mother had a hard life. She was born enslaved on December 4, 1847, in Savannah, Georgia. Despite the illegality of doing so, a young Flora taught herself to write by tracing letters on a doorplate, and taught herself to read while watching the white children of her enslaver study their lessons. At nine years old, she was taken from her mother to serve the family's children, only getting to see her on Saturdays when she came to bring Flora her clothes.

She was a bit older, close to eighteen, when slavery finally ended in 1865. While on an errand for her enslaver, a Union soldier told her she was free. After that, she found a job working for the editor of the *Georgia Gazette*. Her job was to carry copies to the printing office and bring the proof back to the editor for correction. "Little did I think then that I was to be the mother of children who would be printers, too," she wrote in an autobiography.[3] She married Thomas Abbott a few years later, but he died while Robert was a baby. She soon met and married Rev. John Hermann Henry Sengstacke, a fair skinned, mixed-race man who had experienced a very different life from his wife. He spent much of his childhood in Germany, where he had been given the best education. He spoke five languages, and he had even worked for the *Savannah Morning News* as a translator until he was fired after they found out he was Black.

As a couple, the Sengstackes were fearless in their attempts at entrepreneurship and other work opportunities: They started their own school and a church close to the city of Savannah, they worked for the American Missionary Association, and they continued to try different jobs. Because, as Flora Abbott wrote in her autobiography, they "were pioneers trying to establish work in a new field."[4] She even became a self-appointed police officer because she wanted to help protect her community.

The lives and ambition of Robert Abbott's parents affected how ambitious he was in starting a newspaper when so many people around him thought he was foolish to do so. Although both his mother and stepfather went through two totally different experiences of being Black in America at the time, they each had their own challenges. Those challenges would later guide Abbott in his work at the *Defender*, and in how he would see his role.

Rev. Sengstacke, for example, was a fierce proponent of information and the press.[5] He passed that belief along to his stepson. "Before I started on my life's work—journalism—I was counseled by my beloved father that a good newspaper was one of the best instruments of service and one of the strongest weapons ever to be used in defense of a race which was deprived of its citizenship rights," Robert would later write about Sengstacke in 1930.[6]

In 1896, Abbott graduated from Hampton with his printer training and returned home to his family, who were then living in a small town called Woodville, just outside of Savannah. There he taught school on a plantation and helped Sengstacke publish the *Woodville Times*. It was a small newspaper that covered science and church culture. Sengstacke had published his first issue in 1889, but the four-column, four-page paper that sold for five cents did not have a racial stance and didn't talk about serious issues that affected Black people.[7]

In 1897, Abbott returned to Chicago to attend Kent College of Law, the second-oldest law school in Illinois. According to Ottley's interviews, people around Abbott told him he wouldn't have a successful career as a Black lawyer because he was dark skinned. He was further deterred from continuing in the field when he wasn't able to get work.

But Abbott had something else to pivot to. While taking law classes, he also worked as a printer and was employed at the *Chicago Conservator*. It's likely that Abbott was able to see firsthand how the Barnetts ran the paper, then helmed by Ida B. Wells-Barnett herself. He would've seen up close the kinds of editorials they ran, the decisions they made, and how they did their business. Because he believed in the power of the press, he wanted to make *this* his life's work—and he had a clear vision of exactly how he'd do that.

3

A GREAT MIGRATION

"Single-handed, Abbott had set the great migration of the
Mississippi Valley in motion. For he had repeatedly cried:
'Come North, where there is more humanity, some justice
and fairness!' He had coaxed and challenged, denounced and
applauded—until finally he decided to launch a full-blown
campaign he called 'The Great Northern Drive.' From then on
things moved fast."

—Roi Ottley in *The Lonely Warrior:*
The Life and Times of Robert S. Abbott

NOT ONLY WAS ABBOTT TOLD he wouldn't be a good lawyer—solely
based on his skin color and not his skill—but many of his friends and
associates told him his idea to start a newspaper was foolish. He wasn't
seen as being eloquent enough to be an editor, and there was no money
in newspapers, they told him. One of Abbott's friends, Oliver A. Clark,
is quoted in Ottley's book as saying, "Mr. Abbott was fairly intelligent,
above average, but his English was poor, sounding much like a southern
dialect."[1]

Abbott's friends also told him that Chicago already had three Black
newspapers by the turn of the century: Barnett's *Conservator*, founded
in 1878; the *Broad Ax* by Julius Taylor, who had moved the popular
paper to Chicago in 1899 from his home in Utah;[2] and Sheadrick B.
"Sandbag" Turner's *Illinois Idea*, founded in 1898 after two previous
publishing attempts in Springfield, Illinois.[3]

Everyone Abbott asked to partner with in launching his own newspaper declined, but he was not deterred, explaining that his plan was already in motion and that he had no desire to stop. Because he wanted his paper to be a defender of Black people, one of his friends, a lawyer named James A. Scott, suggested the name the *Defender*.

On May 5, 1905, Abbott launched the *Chicago Defender* with "borrowed capital and good credit" at the kitchen table of Henrietta "Mother" Lee in her home at 3159 South State Street.[4] The first issue had a print run of three hundred copies and three paid subscribers at a subscription price of one dollar—about thirty-five dollars today. The total cost of the first edition was $13.75, which would be over $400 today.

"I was editor, publisher, printer and newsboy; going out in snow, slush and mud; selling the paper to a reluctant, doubting public," Abbott wrote thirty years later in a reflective piece for the *Defender*. "My friends made fun of me; they ridiculed me and laughed at me. For, they thought it was foolish of me to anticipate success in a field in which so many men before me had failed. But, I went on fighting against what seemed to be insuperable odds; fighting the opposition of my adversaries on the one hand, and the indifference of my FRIENDS on the other. A struggle out of which I emerged victorious though battle-scarred."[5]

Mother Lee was a widow with three children who saw Abbott as a son. She supported him, and when he found success, he later repaid her by buying her a new home and keeping her original house as the paper's first official headquarters.

At the time of the first issue's release, Abbott was thirty-seven years old, and his previous life experiences had been preparation for this role. With the *Defender*, Abbott focused on making a newspaper that would catch the eye of those he wanted to read it. He knew how to appeal to the everyday man while also engaging in discussions with great thinkers. He did what many journalists today also want to do: help people dissect and digest complicated ideas by being concise and clear, and by holding the attention of their audiences.

Abbott's approach worked, as Black people across the country felt connected to the paper. According to a letter archived in the *Journal of Negro History*, a reader in Port Arthur, Texas, wrote in to the *Defender* in 1917 to say, "Permit me to inform you that I have had the pleasure of reading the *Defender* for the first time in my life as I never dreamed that there was such a race paper published and I must say that [it's] some paper."[6]

In a way, Abbott defied his critics. He used his southern roots and his Chicago experiences to create a paper that people saw as both accessible and easily understood, not too highbrow but still on the nose of current events to stir up elevated conversations in circles of influence. It was a newspaper for the Black farmer and the Black banker, and up until this point, there was often a tension between the two: Is a Black leader a W. E. B. Du Bois, focused on creating an intellectual "Talented Tenth," or a Booker T. Washington, focused on skill-building and jobs through the trades?[7] To many people, Robert Abbott fit in neither category, and the *Defender* was a reflection of that.

"I entered the field of journalism with a determination to take the Negro newspaper out of the soap-wrapper class; to give the people a paper which they would not be ashamed to read on the street cars, and which could not be put away like a dime novel in an inside pocket," Abbott said in a clipping from the archives about his start.[8] "I built up the Defender not only by printing all the news, but also by clinging to the idea that success could be achieved by recording contemporary documents and public utterances, and, by contending for social justice, political rights and industrial equity. They told me that it could not be done, exploded the theory that our people would not support adequately a Negro paper, or any Negro business that was national in scope."

In short, Abbott wanted the *Defender* to be a race paper, the voice of his people, with the goal of fighting racism. "American race prejudice must be destroyed," he would often write in the paper, as part of its official platform and stance.[9]

One way Abbott would eventually do this was by encouraging more and more Black people to move from the South, especially to Chicago. Most people know one thing about the Great Migration: that it is responsible for the "up North" movement—or migration—of an estimated six to seven million Black people from the South to areas in the Midwest, Northeast, and West. It started in 1916, and by the time it ended in the 1970s, the demographic spread of the country looked very different. Forty-seven percent of Black people now lived in the North and West, a vast difference from when 90 percent lived in the South in 1916.[10] But not as many people understand the direct influence the *Chicago Defender* had on the Great Migration

Abbott didn't initially encourage migration from the South. Jobs in places like Chicago were not always plentiful, and labor unions that refused to include Black people within its ranks also fought to keep them out of factory jobs. But in 1916, Abbott changed his stance.[11] The threat of lynching incidents was increasing in the South, and the *Defender* printed firsthand accounts of these horrors.

Economically, one of the main ways Black people in the South supported themselves and their families was changing too. The growing presence of the boll weevil, a species of beetle, led to crop infestations and destruction throughout the South. Many Black sharecroppers lost work on plantations or were evicted by white landowners, and for those who weren't, farming cotton became even less profitable. This employment loss happened as work opportunities in cities like Chicago opened up during the First World War, with fewer European immigrants to work the stockyards, steel mills, and factories Black workers had been previously shut out of.

So it was money—the opportunity to make it—and safety that were two of the most commonly mentioned reasons why Black people from the South wanted to move. Abbott started to talk about these things on the pages of the *Defender*, and on May 15, 1917, he kicked off the Great Northern Drive, his campaign to encourage southern Black people to pick up and move north. Abbott was good at convincing people this move was a necessity: He used bold headlines—such as NORTHBOUND HEAR THEIR CRY and GOOD-BYE DIXIE LAND—satirical cartoons, and a direct style of writing to appeal to the masses.

But what did Chicago itself look like at this time? Before the migration, the Encyclopedia of Chicago says, Black people made up only 2 percent of the city's population.[12] But after, a third of Chicagoans were Black—a percentage that has remained around the same to this day.[13] Chicago became the home of the more than a half million Black people who sought a better life.

But it's helpful to look at the Great Migration in two parts when thinking about changes in the labor market: what happened during World War I and what happened once World War II started. And this is true in the movement patterns to Chicago in particular.

Before World War I, the city's very small population of Black folks did come from the South, but as in other places across the country, there was not yet an abundance of jobs. The absence of legal segregation in contrast to the Jim Crow states did not mean that Chicago lacked racial discrimination. There was still a system of racial oppression that made it difficult for Black folks to live and work here.

A city known for immigration, Chicago experienced a large influx of European immigrants starting in the mid-nineteenth century. These white immigrants held what were seen as low-skilled positions in manufacturing. But the supply and demand of labor changed when World War I started in 1914 and the Unites States entered the war three years later.[14]

Immigration from Europe contracted as fewer people were able to travel by the ships now being used for hospitals and for carrying troops and cargo. What little commercial traveling that did occur was dangerous. Plus, the US no longer had an "open door" policy.[15] Congress increased immigration requirements with the passage of the Immigration Act of 1917, and Chicago manufacturers had to look elsewhere for people to work in their factories.

Opportunities for work were also created by those who left their jobs to fight in the war. More than three hundred thousand recruits from Illinois alone joined the military,[16] with thousands from the Chicago area heading to Fort Sheridan and the Great Lakes Naval Training Station for training camp.

"Four million men went into the military, which made for a serious labor shortage," Joseph Gustaitis, author of *Chicago Transformed: World War I and the Windy City*, told Chicago public television station WTTW.[17] "Especially in Chicago, where you had a need for a lot of unskilled labor in places like steel mills and meatpacking houses." So when Black people finally got jobs in Chicago, it was out of industrial necessity, not a desire to provide equal and fair opportunities. But by the time the war ended in 1918, the city's population of Black residents had doubled.

In addition to knowing about job openings, there are other issues involved with moving to a new place—where to live, where to go, what to expect. Abbott also provided these tools people needed, so that they would have information before they uprooted their families and some direction before they arrived. The *Defender*'s Great Northern Drive coverage showed photos of the best homes and schools in Chicago, printed next to images that showed the worst of these in the South. Abbott kept space for job postings—including pay and contact information—plus news about people who had already moved to Chicago and were happy about their relocation. But getting the *Defender* to these southern states required a specific and covert operation—one that also was possible because of a group of Black men who were primarily stationed and living in Chicago.

When a white Chicago businessman by the name of George Pull-man decided to create luxury sleeping cars for his white passengers, he made it a point to hire Black men who were formerly enslaved. Pullman reasoned that these men had experience serving white people before and would be virtually invisible to his customers—white people who were used to ignoring those they considered far less valuable than themselves.

"He was looking for people who had been trained to be the perfect servant, and these guys' backgrounds was, as having been chattel slaves, and he knew that they knew just how to take care of any whim that a customer had," Larry Tye, author of *Rising from the Rails: Pullman Porters and the Making of the Black Middle Class*, told NPR's *Morning Edition*.[18] "He knew they would come cheap, and he paid them next to nothing."

Unlike in today's interconnected world, the Pullman porters served an essential role in the dissemination of information, and their skills did more than make them the "perfect servant." It also made their moves undetectable. Their official job was to wait on white passengers: carry bags, serve meals, shine shoes. But it also gave them the opportunity to listen and move in secret. As their jobs carried them back into the South, they carried with them copies of the *Defender* to distribute to towns along the way, the pages filled with editorials, poems, and infor-mation about jobs. The same ability to move without being noticed that got them hired for the position also made them key participants in the Black migration movement.

All told, Abbott and the *Defender* are credited with moving fifty thousand Black people during this first wave of the Great Migration. But with this explosion of people came new turmoil—turmoil that would also push the *Defender* into an entirely different league of newspapers.

4

NEWS IN TIMES OF TURMOIL: BLACK NUANCE, BLACK PERSPECTIVE

"It looks very much like Chicago is trying to rival the South in its race hatred against the Negro. Especially does this seem so when we consider the bombing [of] Negro homes and the indifference of the public to these outrages."

—Ida B. Wells-Barnett in a letter to the *Chicago Daily Tribune* on July 7, 1919, twenty days before the start of the Chicago Race Riot

THE *DEFENDER*'S COMMONLY KNOWN IMPACT in its early years was definitely a nationwide push for migration. As more and more Black people moved to Chicago, the city's Black Belt became a bustling neighborhood, filled to the brim with people on its tree-lined streets, families and new boarders packed into what are now seen as historic Bronzeville greystones. But this increase would soon cause problems the city's Black communities had not yet seen. And through the events that followed, particularly in the summer of 1919, the *Defender* not only played a key role in information-sharing but also solidified its place as a newspaper of record for Black America.

As more and more Black people arrived in Chicago, racial tensions grew as quickly as the city's changing demographics. The city's Black population more than doubled from 44,000 people in 1910 to 110,000 in 1920.[1] With more people came more competition for jobs in places such as factories—jobs that before World War I were held by the white working class and poor white immigrants. And when the war ended, many white men came home to Chicago and blamed Black migrants from the South for "taking" their jobs while they were away.

In the nineteenth century, working at Chicago's factories and stockyards had generally been rough work: It was dangerous and people often died on the job, according to historian Dr. Elizabeth Todd-Breland. During a 2020 interview about Chicago poverty, she explained, "During its early days, there were already major clashes between workers and capitalists—the employers—because of the exploitation of workers. Many of these in the late nineteenth century were early European immigrant workers who were being exploited, who were being pitted against each other in a sort of race to the bottom on wages and working conditions, and so you see this really long history of the exploitation of the poor and the working poor, and also really strong movements against that exploitation."[2]

Even then, Chicago was a city of strong labor movements, with unions that would protest and strike for improved working conditions. But in the city's major industries like meatpacking and steel, the most dangerous work always went to Black workers, who were also the lowest paid. For years, these Black workers were shut out of efforts to demand better. Most unions still refused to allow Black people to join their ranks. When the unions decided to strike, the Black people who then crossed the picket line to support their families were seen as strikebreakers.

"I think those [labor tensions] honestly were just further exacerbated by the strictly stratified racial hierarchy that was imposed as a significant mass of Black people migrated to the city," Todd-Breland added. "In response, the corporate and political and social hierarchies of the city really imposed a racial hierarchy, and that racial hierarchy was economic as well."

So Black people who had come to Chicago leaving legal segregation behind and seeking better economic opportunities were still being stifled by a racial caste system not too different from the one they had left. Chicago segregation was complicated, because although it was illegal, it was still extremely prevalent. There were unwritten societal rules about where Black people were supposed to live—and there wasn't just Black and white Americans in the mix.

The large populations of European immigrants who had migrated to the US in the early 1900s—coming from non-English-speaking countries such as Italy, Poland, and Russia—were not seen as white at the time. They often came to cities with industrial jobs, like Chicago but also New York City, where they were mistreated and struggled for power, seeing themselves above Black Americans.

It's also important to add that—especially when talking about areas like Chicago that once had large Indigenous populations—US officials had violently forced Native Americans from their homelands by this point. *Chicago* is in fact a name derived from a version of a word in Algonquian, a language spoken by the Miami and Illinois peoples: *shikaakwa*. And yet the very people who were already in Chicago and who were integral in its change to an incorporated city were removed. During the Black Hawk War of 1832 and following the 1833 Treaty of Chicago, US and state officials forced out most of the area's remaining Native American groups.[3] So even in a place like Chicago, a place that Black southerners flocked to as a so-called safe haven, the "Whites Only" mentality of Jim Crow was still there. It just had a different facade.

At the same time economic pressure was intensifying, Black people were also frustrated with the increased inequity throughout the city after the war. For Black veterans returning home, things were tough. After fighting and risking their lives for this country, they were still denied the access and privileges that white residents had. Giving everything seemingly did not give them anything in return.

Because the Black Belt held a majority of the city's Black population, the community started to experience overcrowding and a shortage of housing, and Black families had few options to move elsewhere. Even though they could legally relocate to other parts of the city, unlike in the Jim Crow South, Black families who moved to predominantly white parts of the city often found their homes bombed. In February 1919, a young Black girl, six-year-old Garnetta Ellis, was killed when her family's home was bombed, one of about two dozen Black homes that were bombed between 1917 and 1919.[4] Police solved none of the cases.

The city was on the edge during the summer of 1919. On July 27, the violence began when a Black teen, seventeen-year-old Eugene Williams, and his friends allegedly swam over an invisible line in Lake Michigan that separated the white and Black parts of the beach. A white man named George Stauber, twenty-four, hit Eugene in the head with a rock, drowning him.

When Eugene's friend John Turner Harris was interviewed decades later by historian William M. Tuttle, he explained that a Black officer had tried to arrest Stauber but a white officer intervened and the two began to argue. Eugene's friends then ran to tell other Black people what happened, he said.[5]

What happened after this incident turned into the deadliest week the city had seen. Reports attribute the start of the riots to white gangs of young men in "athletic clubs" who left the all-white South Side neighborhoods of Bridgeport and Back of the Yards to go into the Black Belt. There, the gangs set fire to buildings, pulled Black people from streetcars, and attacked Black people they saw walking. Black people fought back in what the Chicago Race Riot of 1919 Commemoration Riot Project describes as unprecedented numbers.[6]

The violence lasted until August 3, and although the total number of people involved is unknowable, the casualties counted in the aftermath showed a violence Chicago hadn't seen before. Thirty-eight people died, twenty-three of whom were Black and fifteen white, and more than five hundred people were injured.[7] Rioters also torched the homes of about a thousand Black families.[8]

That summer, called the "Red Summer," riots also broke out in other places across the country, including Washington, DC; Knoxville, Tennessee; Longview, Texas; Phillips County, Arkansas; and Omaha, Nebraska. The Chicago riot is estimated to have been the largest of the violent incidents that summer, but in many places, the death count is likely underestimated.

But in times of trouble and confusion, the public needs the press more than ever. Robert Abbott knew this was a time that journalism, his newspaper especially, could inform his readership across the US about the violence, expand the perspectives of Black people, and directly combat any false narratives about Black people that were being spread by white publications. Chicago—and the country—was changing, and the *Defender* was the trusted voice of Black America.

Looking back through history can be difficult. Oftentimes, the perspectives of those who hold power are the only perspectives recorded.

Looking just through the *New York Times* or *Chicago Daily Tribune* archives, for example, tells a one-sided story of American life in the early 1900s, since the only voices on record were those of the white population. For example, the *New York Times'* recent Overlooked project reflects the fact that people like the remarkable Ida B. Wells-Barnett were not deemed important enough for a *Times* obituary when they died.[9]

Today, newspapers across the country are just beginning to come to terms with their past and acknowledging that "mainstream" journalism has often not included non-white voices. But when looking back at how historic events were recorded in those papers, we see that not only did they lack the perspective of those who were often at the receiving end of violence, but they often played a part in inciting that violence as well.[10]

This context is offered not to dive deep into the history of media's failings but to explain why Black media is so essential and how Robert Abbott's *Chicago Defender* was truly an innovation: a newspaper that provided a needed voice nationwide during a time when it was extremely difficult to do so.

Today, the archival help of papers like the *Defender* is essential in understanding events that occurred generations ago. The care that was put into maintaining such an important voice of the Black community is why articles from those periods are still accessible today.

The earliest *Defender* articles available to the public free of charge are on the Chicago Public Library's website and date back to January 1, 1910. It is from these archives that a large portion of information for this section of the book was gathered and many cultural comparisons are made.

For instance, in comparing the coverage of these events in mainstream versus Black publications, we find that many of the differences lie in subtle wording and in who and what the newspapers of the time chose to amplify. In the case of the Race Riot of 1919, many of the basic facts were recorded similarly in both the *Defender* and some of the city's white publications. In fact, the *Defender* reprinted at least one *Chicago Daily News* article at the time: an editorial by former president William Howard Taft, who was then two years from becoming chief justice of the Supreme Court. But so many articles were filled with coded[11]—and sometimes blatant—language that dehumanized and spread racist stereotypes about Black people. Papers like the *Chicago Tribune* would seed their coverage with racist and colorful descriptions of Black people, such as "a crowd of howling Negroes."[12]

On July 28, the day after the riots started, the *Tribune* published an editorial that claimed to be written to support a Black pastor, Rev. John F. Thomas of Chicago's Ebenezer Baptist Church. The story starts off well, discussing how Chicago's Black residents should have good living conditions, and at first glance, it would seem that this piece is understanding of Black Chicagoans' frustrations. But the story takes a quick turn, blaming the riots on both sides, saying, "We have often tried to show that it is the impatience and intemperate conduct of the ignorant of both races which inspires race riots" and that "the problem of Negro advancement is largely his own."[13]

Without the *Defender*, checking facts and understanding the thoughts and complex perspectives of Black people during this time would be difficult. Compared to the *Tribune* editorial, which pushed the narrative that Black people were to blame for not being in a better position, an editorial in the first issue of the *Defender* after the riots explains that although it has "little sympathy with lawlessness, whether those guilty of it be Black or white, but it cannot be denied that we have much in the way of justification for our changed attitude.[14]

"Under the promise of a square deal our boys went cheerfully into the service of the country hoping the aftermath of the struggle would find our people in an improved social and industrial condition," the editorial said. It said that riots in Washington, DC, which had started a week before the riots in Chicago, "was a case of 'teaching us our place'" when a group of white veterans headed to DC's Black neighborhoods with clubs, lead pipes, and lumber, while "Chicago was a case of limiting our sphere to metes and bounds that had neither the sanction of law nor sound common sense. In both cases we resented the assumption."

Before the riots, though, the 1910s was a decade of significance for Black Chicagoans. By then, not only were many Black people doing financially better in Chicago, some—like Abbott—were becoming wealthy. The *Defender* was a success, and in 1918, he bought a mansion at 4847 South Champlain Avenue. Because Abbott had money and was in this position of power within his community when the riots happened, he was able to make some decisions that helped him continue his work and actually made the *Defender* an even larger operation—pushing Abbott to even greater wealth.

By 1919, the *Defender* already had a wide reach. It was being distributed nationwide to readers who would eagerly await the paper. It was important to get the news to them, but even more so with the first issue following the riots. After such tumultuous news in Chicago, news that mirrored violence in other cities across the country, readers needed to know what was happening and they needed to know it from the voices they trusted most.

At the time, like many newspapers, the *Defender* didn't have its own printing press. The newspaper publisher that had been printing the *Defender* every week was located in the Chicago stockyards where much of the labor unrest that sparked this violence had taken place. Because of its location, its owner was afraid to print a Black paper after the riot in fear of backlash from the city's white residents. Thus, Abbott and the *Defender* team had to quickly create a new plan to get their paper printed and out to readers across the US.

In *The Defender: How the Legendary Black Newspaper Changed America* by Ethan Michaeli, the ingenuity of the Defender staff is on full display. They brainstormed who could possibly print the issue for them, and staffer Leslie Rogers came up with a solution. Rogers was a cartoonist at the *Defender* who created many of the cartoons the paper would become famous for, especially when it made its way down south. He was from nearby Gary, Indiana, and had the suggestion to ask the *Gary Tribune* to print the issue. They agreed, and the paper was able to make it to its subscribers just a few days late. But it was only a temporary solution.

Before all of the turmoil, Abbott had already wanted to buy a new headquarters that would be large enough for his own printing press. But now, left in a predicament that had forced him to go to extreme means to get his paper out, he was even more determined to achieve self-sufficiency. In response, he left the former home of Mother Lee, which he'd transformed into a full office, and bought a new building at 3435 South Indiana Avenue, which became the heart of "Defenderland"—Abbott's term to describe the newspaper's geographical reach. This expansion helped widen the *Defender*'s reach even further and helped it become a more sustainable business, one that also employed more writers from across the US, as well as Black Chicagoans in other roles to help maintain the company. The size and scope of the newspaper's operations made it a newspaper that could rival any journalism organization at the time. And it was inspiring.

Abbott would lead the *Defender* until his death in 1940, and for decades he was able to keep it profitable as other publications failed. A count in Ottley's *The Lonely Warrior* says that thirty-two Black newspapers failed during the thirty-five years Abbott was at the *Defender*'s helm.[15] According to Library of Congress records, that count is on the higher side, as some of the papers listed as examples were around in some form at the time of Abbott's death. Abbott himself also had a number of endeavors that were not successful. He created other publications, such as *Abbott's Weekly and Illustrated News*, which was founded in 1933 and ran for only a year.

Nevertheless, the *Defender* kept its status and influence as many Black papers came and went, oftentimes because their leaders had other interests. The Barnetts, for example, sold the *Conservator*. Ida B. Wells-Barnett had left the paper to raise her children after having her second son in 1897, although she continued to write. In 1913, she also briefly had a paper associated with her organization, the Negro Fellowship League, called the *Fellowship Herald*, which she refers to only once in her autobiography as "publishing a little paper."[16] The *Conservator* later went out of business shortly after it was sold in 1914.

In 1912, Abbott had joined Julius Taylor of *Broad Ax*, Sandbag Turner of *Illinois Idea*, and William D. Neighbors, publisher of the *Illinois Chronicle*, to create the Colored Press Association of Chicago—not to be mistaken for the Association of Negro Press, which was later founded in Chicago in 1919 by Claude Albert Barnett (no relation to the Barnetts of the *Conservator*). But he was soon the lone founder left in that group.

Sandbag Turner had already transferred editing duties of the *Illinois Idea* to his wife in 1910 so that he could turn his sights to politics, and he won a seat in the state legislature in 1914.[17] By 1916, his wife was listed in the paper as "Mrs. S.B. Turner," the editor and later publisher of the *Idea*, which published its last issue around 1922, as estimated by the Library of Congress.[18]

In 1931, Taylor ceased publication of *Broad Ax* due to health reasons. He died in 1934.

Neighbors's *Illinois Chronicle* ended in 1921. He was the president of the Illinois Chronicle Company, as listed in the *Defender* and several notices of incorporation.[19] Neighbors was also a successful businessman and real estate developer,[20] and it is possible his greatest efforts were placed there, as indicated in the stories about how he advocated for Black wealth through real estate. Other popular Black newspapers came and went, but left an important mark, such as the *Chicago Whip* (1919–1932) and the *Chicago Bee* (1925–1947).

After Abbott's death in 1940, his nephew John H. Sengstacke took over the *Defender*. Abbott had been training Sengstacke to take the baton and run with it, and had also been working to create the National Newspaper Publishers Association to bring together Black publishers of newspapers when he died; Sengstacke became an NNPA cofounder.

The *Defender* was in print for 114 years before ceasing its print publication in 2019. Although it does not own the *Defender*'s media arm, the Sengstacke family still runs the *Defender*'s foundation, now named the Robert Sengstacke Abbott Foundation, which gives college scholarships and runs the Bud Billiken Parade—the world's largest and oldest Black parade in the United States—which Abbott started in 1929.

Myiti Sengstacke-Rice is the foundation's president and CEO, and also started a bimonthly publication called *Bronzeville Life*, following in the footsteps of Abbott, her great-granduncle; her father, renowned photographer Robert A. "Bobby" Sengstacke; and her grandfather, John Sengstacke.

From 1905 until well into the 1990s, the *Defender* remained an example of how a newspaper could be a vessel for change. And toward the end of that period, the *Defender* was known for such strong journalism that it boasted a diverse staff of people from all over. Journalists from every background clamored to write for its pages. Yet what is likely its largest legacy is a bold one: creating media so strong that it helped change the face of Chicago and that of the nation. As Roscoe Conkling Simmons, nephew of Booker T. Washington, would write about Abbott in the *Defender* in 1949, "Only a few men, as numbers go, created the civilization of the New World. Among the number, large or small, you will have to include, Robert Sengstacke Abbott."[21]

Part II

AND WITH THEM, THEY BROUGHT THE BLUES

CADILLAC BABY'S
SHOW LOUNGE

Written while listening to "I'm Ready" by Muddy Waters

> "When I went to Chicago, I'll put it like this: I was looking for a
> dime and I found a quarter."
>
> —Buddy Guy

My granddaddy was a charismatic man. I mean, with a nickname like Cadillac Baby, he had to be. A smooth talker, a top-hat wearer, a man who never shied away from a mic—he was the face of Cadillac Baby's Show Lounge. And like the name suggests, he was a colorful fixture on that block of Forty-Seventh and Dearborn. He aimed to live up to that hype.

Basically, he was king of what kids today say is "doing the most." At least that's what I said to myself when I interviewed author David Whiteis while researching a story for WBEZ's *Curious City* about Chicago blues.

"At some point in the evening, he would drive his Cadillac right up onto the stage and get out of the car, and bow to the audience, and that was the start of the show," said Whiteis, who is author of the book *Chicago Blues: Portraits and Stories*. "It was quite a flamboyant entrance, and he was a very flamboyant character."[1]

I couldn't stop laughing as the image of my granddaddy, Narvel Eatmon, swirled in my head. I'd seen the pictures of him suited up, dressed to the nines: a hat removed to show his perfectly waved hair, a leg propped up to reveal the smooth shininess of his shoes.

But I didn't really know about this legacy. As years passed, lost stories made it easy to walk past those photos and forget: we, too, were a part of Chicago history.

I wanted to know more. I wanted to save those lost stories, bottle them up in an article, and remind my family that we'd had a piece of an important pie—the music and lifestyle and scene that was the backdrop for our people as we made a new life in the city. And part of our slice in our little corner of the city was about how we expressed ourselves, what we brought with us, and what new opportunity awaited.

Today, neither of my grandparents are here to tell us the story, and decades after the passing of my granddaddy, Narvel, and years after that of my grandma, Bea, their legacy was something we newer generations didn't know much about. So after I opened Whiteis's book about Chicago blues and found my granddaddy's name right smack in the middle, I had questions. I called up my aunt Mary, my mama's oldest sibling, to try to capture the history I didn't want to see lost.

"He was a showman," she said, living up to her title of our family's unofficial historian. "So you know, he had to be a showman to dress up every Saturday night in a top hat and a tuxedo, but he loved it. He loved the notoriety. He loved the 'Cadillac Baby.' You know, he loved all that."

But as is often the case, although my granddaddy was the face of Cadillac Baby's Show Lounge, and later Bea & Baby Records, he in no way built these things alone. While he was putting on a show—top hat and all—it was my grandma, Bea, who was the quiet force who worked to keep things running. Behind the scenes, she was the one who made sure the business stayed afloat.

I'm lucky enough to have spent so much of my childhood with my Bea, the same grandma from Greenwood. About five foot two and not taking mess from anybody, she was always a force to be reckoned with. And, as she informed me when I was a little girl, even back then, you couldn't catch her slipping. "I never drank," she'd say about her days in the lounge. "If someone bought me a drink, I might hold on to it all night to be polite, but I never took a sip."

That was because she didn't partake in any substance that could take away her control or alter her senses. It's how she could stay aware of all the comings and goings of the club. But as the hospitable host she was, she'd always pretend to oblige someone who wanted her to have a drink with them. And even a bumblebee like her knew how and when to turn on the honey to make her guests feel good.

Because I spent so much time as a little girl with Bea Ma, she'd tell me about how all the biggest blues acts would stop through *their* spot when they were in town and all the people she'd known back then. "See, that's Muddy Waters," I distinctly remember her saying one day as we walked hand-in-hand down Sixty-Third and Halsted, passing a record store with Muddy's image displayed in the window. "I knew him." And now, as an adult researching all that they'd done and talking to folks who heard about them, I believe that to be true.

I wish I could've been there to see all the liveliness. But thankfully, the stories my aunt Mary remembers about what it was like in that lounge paint a vivid picture. As a ten-year-old in the 1950s, she was old enough to remember my granddaddy's larger-than-life persona and what it was like in our family's club.

My grandparents owned the building, which was then in the city's Black Belt, living upstairs while running the club downstairs and a store next door. Late at night, my aunts would sneak downstairs like any normal little sneaky kids would do, and they'd take it all in—the performers, the people dancing, the shows. But to really get to be with the music—blues music—was enticing. It was the real star of the show. "Just like the kids are rapping now, we knew the words to these songs," Aunt Mary said. "Because these were the songs we heard and this was the expression of who we were."

For kids like my aunt, the music felt fresh and new and edgy. But it was still grounded in history in a way only the adults could understand. Both my grandparents came from the Mississippi River culture that birthed this new, thriving subgenre of music in a lively city full of Black folks looking for a great time. They met here in Chicago, but both came here determined to create better lives. My granddaddy arrived post–World War II, fresh out of the army, ready to make a name for himself and hustle his way into some real money.

Chicago blues was, in fact, "a hustler's industry." My aunt says my granddaddy paid police officers and did whatever else he needed to do to keep the business going.

"[Cadillac Baby] was a hustler," Whiteis said. "He wasn't a hoodlum, he wasn't a gangster, but he was a hustler. He was out there making that money, and that was the name of the game."

But he also did it for the love of the blues. Musician and blues historian Sebastian Danchin wrote in his book *Earl Hooker, Blues Master* that my grandparents "tried to promote blues music to the best of their ability, genially providing room and board to the penniless artists who dropped in at their lounge."[2]

In addition to their tavern, my grandparents soon opened a recording company, Bea & Baby Records, in 1955. They recorded artists who would grow to become well-known at the time, like Little Mac, Hound Dog Taylor, Homesick James, and Eddie Boyd.

"[Cadillac Baby] cultivated his image as a colorful entrepreneur," Whiteis said. "And over the course of his career, he recorded quite a few Chicago blues artists who later became quite well known: small label, relatively crude technique that wasn't what we call high-quality recordings, but he recorded them, and that was often someone's first break."

So picture it: a Black-owned record label and a Black-owned club, playing Black music in a Black neighborhood for Black patrons. And like my aunt says, "Everybody loved them. Everybody loved Bea and Cadillac."

Chicago's Black Metropolis lived up to its name. And as was the case for my grandparents, it was a place where *many* Black folks could make their own successes. So when they moved to the city in droves during the Great Migration, they didn't just come alone; they came with the blues. Chicago blues meant more than just a kind of music—it was a form of expression that was deeply rooted in what it meant to be Black.

It is true, too, that generations of Black people in Chicago would make an indelible mark in other popular music genres. But right now we're taking a look at what Chicagoans before us brought with them—and that's the blues.

5

MISSISSIPPI MUD MUSIC

"A lot of people's wonderin', what is the blues? I hear lots of people sayin', 'The blues, the blues . . '. But I'm gonna tell you what the blues is."

—Howlin' Wolf

THE BLUES MUSIC ITSELF that made its way to Chicago was indicative of the place where it originated. Lovers of the genre will often hear that blues was born in the Mississippi delta, and it's true. The delta was, at one point, one of the richest cotton-farming areas in the US, with land nurtured by the labor of enslaved Black people. That hard, backbreaking work continued after the Civil War in the form of sharecropping, where Black people would rent land to farm from white landowners and then have to pay them back with large portions of their crops and high interest rates. "Slavery by another name," people still say.

But it's in those fields and in those towns where blues music continued to be nurtured, although its exact origins likely stretch far back past the point where many Black Americans can trace their own family trees. When Black people were enslaved, they sang spirituals about their pain on those southern plantations. And once slavery legally ended, the music—and the hard work—did not.

Blues developed as a way for Black people to express the trials and tribulations of everyday life. They needed an outlet for the economic oppression and violence they faced—and it landed in the blues.

In *American Roots Music*, writer David Evans explains how the music evolved into something new, through creative techniques for instruments like bending the strings on the guitar certain ways and stories about people who became famous. He writes, "The blues singer became his or her song's chief protagonist, dramatizing the self to heroic proportions, still living and acting on the margins of society as defined and structured by the 'white folks,' ready to 'catch the train and ride' if trouble arose or opportunity beckoned."[1]

Like so many things that originated in the hearts and minds of Black folks, by the 1920s, white record companies saw there was money to be made in this form of popular music. Recording technology got better around this time, making it much easier to record and distribute music.[2] Paramount Records was one such label making "race records," which were records marketed to Black consumers that could be anything from blues to gospel to comedy. After the Black-owned label Black Swan Records went bankrupt, Paramount bought it and cornered an estimated quarter of the market in the early 1920s. Yet it is the impact of Black Swan and its owner, Harry Pace, that contributed to this widely known success.

Harry Pace later became part of Chicago's history as an insurance company owner, an attorney, and an activist who fought against racial housing discrimination. He even won the Supreme Court case *Hansberry v. Lee*, which ruled against restrictive covenants that kept Black Chicagoans from buying property in white neighborhoods. But before this work—and before he moved to the city—Pace was one of the country's most influential cultural leaders, a pioneer of this emerging, increasingly profitable Black music industry.

In an interview with NPR, Emmett Price III, executive editor of the *Encyclopedia of African American Music*, explained that Pace recorded musicians who "ended up changing the sound of America."[3] Pace helped launch the recording careers of music legends such as star singer Ethel Waters, who later became the first Black American to star in her own TV show, and composer William Grant Still, who became the first Black American to conduct a major symphony orchestra.

In that vein, once Paramount started to record Black musicians, doing so became a lucrative endeavor for the company. And there was no blues musician of the time more popular than Charley Patton, who became known as the "Father of the Delta Blues." Patton was a mixed-race Black man born sometime around 1890. He grew up near Ruleville, Mississippi, on a former plantation where he would perform and develop his style. But Patton had something special. He wasn't limited to one kind of blues; he did it all. The Rock & Roll Hall of Fame, where he was honored as an early influencer in 2021, says Patton's songs showed "the pain of field hollers," "the joy of vaudeville," "the humor of ragtime," and "the righteousness of gospel."[4]

Patton was also the quintessential showman, playing his guitar under his legs or on his knees or behind his head or back. Because of this talent, he continually booked performances wherever Black people gathered for a good time. That stretched across the US and especially to Chicago, where Patton traveled annually.

But he spent most of his life in the delta. Patton had been in the blues game for an estimated twenty-two years by the time he started his recording career. In 1929 Paramount released one of his first recordings, "Pony Blues," an upbeat song that was perfect for dancing and became so popular that Paramount quickly set up additional recording sessions. Between that year and his death in 1934, Patton would record nearly seventy records.

Patton's death was not reported in newspapers—not even in the *Defender*. And his name may not be easily recognized today. But Patton's influence can be measured through the musicians who came after him. In many ways, he was a mentor, and those who idolized him became the very people who brought the blues to Chicago, popularized it, and made it into a style of its own.

Howlin' Wolf, real name Chester Burnett, is an artist who is well known in and out of blues circles and in popular culture: people know about his sound, his feud with fellow Mississippian turned Chicagoan Muddy Waters, and that voice that was as powerful and as booming as his six-foot-three frame. But many don't know that he was mentored by the Father of Blues himself.

Born in 1910 in White Station, Mississippi, Howlin' Wolf performed as a solo artist throughout the South before he met Charley Patton in 1930 and convinced him to teach him how to play guitar. In an interview with Arhoolie Records founder Chris Strachwitz in 1967, Howlin' Wolf said Patton would listen to musicians in country houses on the plantation. "Each in one would play for him maybe for Saturday night, Sunday night." That's how Howlin' Wolf got his start: "I would follow them around and try to get them to learn me," he said. "So Charley, he started me out picking the guitar."[5]

Under Patton, Howlin' Wolf learned how to be a showman and a performer; he learned how to mold his raw talent. And after a stint serving in the US Army, he moved to West Memphis, Arkansas—right outside of Memphis, Tennessee—and recorded his first songs: "Moanin' at Midnight" and "How Many More Years." His unique talent caught the attention of immigrant-owned Chicago record company Chess Records, which convinced him to move to Chicago in the early 1950s.

For musicians like Howlin' Wolf, Chicago—including its growing Black population and its reputation for recording all genres of music—represented a potential gold mine. It was the place talent could go to make even bigger names for themselves. It's where he and other famed bluesmen like Muddy Waters, Willie Dixon, Sonny Boy Williamson, and so many more found monetary success, with Charley Patton as a significant guide in the music they made.

6

AN URBAN CHICAGO STYLE

"Anywhere in the world you hear a Chicago bluesman play, it's
a Chicago sound, born and bred."
                    —Ralph Metcalfe Jr. in *Chicago History* magazine

WHEN MUSICIANS LIKE Howlin' Wolf and Muddy Waters moved to Chicago, they became the architects of the city's own style of blues. Chicago blues became a recognizably different subgenre that held on strong to its Mississippi influence. "This migration is what Al Bell from Stax Records always affectionately called 'Mississippi River culture,'" author David Whiteis said.[1] "He's basically saying that we brought our culture all across all the way up [to] the Midwest. He says anywhere there's Mississippi River culture, they like the blues and they like deep soul music."

Ma Rainey, the "Mother of the Blues," recorded her first eight records in Chicago with Paramount Records after being discovered by a Black producer named J. Mayo "Ink" Williams in 1923. Williams, who was originally from Pine Bluff, Arkansas, before moving to Chicago, was the most successful blues producer of his time. As a talent scout, he'd discovered not only Ma Rainey but also Papa Charlie Jackson, a New Orleans–born Black man who also moved to Chicago and became the first person to find commercial success as a self-accompanied singer in the blues.

Mayo Williams left Paramount to create the Chicago Record Company in 1927. And although this venture lasted less than a year, when Williams went back to working for other labels, he set up the Chicago

Music Publishing Company and became publisher for all the music he recorded. As time went on, more and more Black creatives like Williams were able to build their own record companies.

So for blues musicians, Chicago is where the work was. It drew in performers who'd traveled from virtually everywhere. And this drew in the customers too, other working Black folks who'd made their way to Chicago as part of the Great Migration.

Cheryl Corley, a national correspondent for NPR, performs a live show about the connection between blues and the Great Migration called *Chicago Bound: The Great Migration*. In it, Corley narrates the story accompanied by music from singer Lucy Smith. According to Corley, the music usually heard in Chicago at the time was built on the foundation of Mississippi music but became something much more urban. "The Delta blues typically just had vocals and acoustic guitar and a harmonica, and that would lay the groundwork for the urban blues and stuff that you would hear later," Corley told me.[2] "Muddy Waters came to the city and dominated the post–World War II blues scene, and he's considered the father of Chicago blues. . . . It was his rendition of 'Catfish Blues,' which is a traditional song dating back to the 1920s in Mississippi, that became his signature song, 'Rollin' Stone.'"

With such a strong connection, it's almost impossible to separate this movement of Black people to Chicago from the art that was created in the city at that time. Although the music's foundation is its southern roots, its evolution is clearly Chicago.

When Corley thinks of songs that carry that unique sound, "I think [of] Willie Dixon's 'Back Door Man' or 'Wang Dang Doodle' performed by Howlin' Wolf and Koko Taylor with Buddy Guy on the guitar." Her recognition of Koko Taylor emphasizes the fact that it wasn't only men who were pioneering the subgenre of Chicago blues. The names often listed as greats are mostly male, while the influence of Taylor, Memphis Minnie, and other female Chicago blues musicians often goes unnoticed. "Memphis Minnie made a massive contribution to the blues," Corley explained. "She's known for her singing, her songwriting, and she played guitar really well. She wrote hundreds of songs, and 'In My Girlish Days' is just one example. And she became one of the premier blues artists of the 1930s and '40s in a field that was dominated then by men."

By the late 1960s and into the 1970s, audiences were changing. Some younger Black people, now listening to soul and funk, saw the blues as representing the past. But some musicians continued to adapt their sound. Corley pointed to Buddy Guy, who still currently tours and owns a popular club in Chicago, and who played an important place in the transition of blues' sound, serving as a generational bridge. "He's considered the bridge between electric blues pioneers like Muddy Waters and Howlin' Wolf and popular musicians like Eric Clapton and Jimi Hendrix," Corley said. "So all of that came along because blues musicians that were here in Chicago [were] still in the scene."

Today, there is still world-class blues played in Chicago, but that blues scene is a very different one from that of the Great Migration. "There are clubs on the South Side and the West Side, but there are very, very few," blues musician Toronzo Cannon told me in 2019. "Not like it was in the '60s" before the decline.[3] Yet Chicago remains a blues hub, boasting that its annual Chicago Blues Festival is the largest of its many music festivals and the largest free blues festival in the world. And it still produces many of today's biggest names in blues.

In his early fifties at the time of our discussion, Toronzo Cannon is part of today's Chicago blues scene, from a younger generation than the musicians who migrated to Chicago. But even as the industry has changed, Cannon said, there are still Black musicians keeping alive the tradition of Chicago blues—which is seen as "the template for blues all over the world." Though the sound has become more contemporary, he said, with clear soul and R&B influences that appeal to contemporary Black audiences, today's musicians are clearly a product of those who came before them.

Each generation has slightly evolved the music, he said: Muddy Waters influenced musicians like Buddy Guy, and younger musicians like Cannon have further evolved that style, keeping the tradition of blues lyrics that relate to real-life experiences. "It doesn't just stop at B.B. King or Muddy Waters or Buddy Guy," Cannon said. "We're still holding on to the traditions as we know it."

Part III

"YOU AIN'T HEARD NOTHING YET"

ON MY RADIO

Written while listening to "Sweet Thing" by Rufus and Chaka Khan

> "From neighborhood crime watches to Harold Washington's 1983 campaign for mayor, black radio has played a significant role in shaping our communities, attitudes and opinions."
> —Wesley South in the *Chicago Tribune*

FROM 1997 TO 2007, getting the chance to be on WGCI's Bad Boy Radio meant huge bragging rights at school the next day. Hosts Mike Love and the Dizz ran the Birthday Line Monday through Friday, and if you called in and got on the air, it was a time you'd never forget. Ask anybody who ever made it and they'll tell you when they got through. Or if they're like me and never did, they can tell you when they tried (at ages fourteen, fifteen, sixteen, and seventeen in 1999, 2000, 2001, and 2002).

Because I never actually got through to the Birthday Line, I never got to sing to the Bad Boys. But it was a goal! And me and my friends would sing their part in their birthday rhyme for each other every year. For us, it was *the* birthday song—the only one that mattered.

In a 2017 interview by TRiiBE editor in chief Tiffany Walden in the *Chicago Reader*, Mike Love and the Dizz explained just how popular the Birthday Line became.[1] "I was on Oprah Winfrey's show once. In the green room, Oprah came in there and told me how the show's going to go," the Dizz said. "After all of that, she's like, 'I was wondering, can you do the Birthday Line back here for me so I can do it?'

The fact that Oprah Winfrey knew all of the words to the Birthday Line was stunning."

He also said Barack Obama once told him, "You know what? I always wanted to do that Birthday Line."

Chicago is a city of radio innovation—disc jockeys and station managers who have never been afraid to find creative ways to connect with their audiences. Radio legend Richard Steele is that kind of influence. In 1964, Steele went to the New York School of Announcing and Speech and had radio roles at stations in New York City; Roanoke, Virginia; and Boston before moving to Chicago. He said that working in radio at the time, all of the Black people in music and radio industry roles—disc jockeys, musicians, etc.—were close friends when they weren't at work. "Chicago's a little bit unique in that the people here in radio and records were really like family," he said. "We competed in our fields, but off the air or not on a record call, we were all friends."[2]

Here in Chicago, Steele has been a mainstay on stations such as WVON, where he worked twice, and my former home, WBEZ. Steele retired from full-time work in 2014 but is still someone we may catch on-air or at an event for the Chicago chapter of the National Association of Black Journalists.

I wanted to know his thoughts on Black radio and how he's seen it change recently. Steele said that in the past, because the personalities on Black radio were so well known in the community, they were like heroes. This made sense to me. When I was a kid, calling into a radio station meant so much more than just hearing yourself on the radio. It also meant talking to people you admired, whose voices you heard so intimately. When rising music and film star Aaliyah, who I was obsessed with at the time, tragically died in a plane crash in 2001, it was the disc jockeys on WGCI who told me the news through my radio, and it was from them I got every update. I was glad they were the ones who gently broke the news to me and all of the other listeners who came to them every night.

"Back in the day, those people were so well known in the Black community that any of them could be in the Black community and be recognized with love," Steele said about radio disc jockeys. "Today, it's not like that."

Unlike in the past, people have wide options for audio entertainment, outside of turning on one of their favorite local radio stations.

They can stream a podcast or a radio show in another city through an app, they can listen to music on demand, they can check out YouTube playlists—literally everything. And sadly, that has changed our relationship with the local people we hear on the airwaves. "There are people on the radio—like Joe Soto [formerly of WGCI and now at V103] who does a great job and has great ratings, and he's kind of a crossover from the old school—but in terms of the general thinking about people who are on the radio, it isn't like it used to be," Steele explained.

In addition to technical changes in the way we listen to radio, the increase in syndication opportunities for Black radio hosts has meant widespread industry change. "The good news is, for people who have that kind of a deal and it's a syndicated situation, you make plenty money; that's a really good thing," Steele said. "The bad news is when you're syndicated, the people who would have those jobs locally are out of work, so it's a double-edged sword."

So many of today's radio hosts may not have as much renown as their predecessors, but a smaller reach can be just as impactful. Even as the radio landscape changes, their influence is still something I'm grateful for. As Herb Kent, the first Black disc jockey to enter the Radio Hall of Fame, says in his 2009 autobiography *The Cool Gent*, "I'm grateful for the advent of radio and its growth from little wooden boxes hooked up to storage batteries to the Bluetooth radios you wear in your ear today."[3] So let's go back to the very start of things—the first time you could hear a Black voice booming through your radio.

7

THE VOICE OF CHICAGO

"[WVON] was just doing what Black folks thought it should
do. It was playing the music folks and hearing the music that
they wanted to hear."
— Pervis Spann to HistoryMakers in 2002

FOR ALMOST SIX DECADES, Black Chicago has been represented on
WVON, Chicago's first twenty-four-hour radio station for Black audiences. And it was Pervis "the Blues Man" Spann and Wesley South that
set this legacy in motion.

Pervis Spann was a legendary disc jockey who had moved to Chicago
from Gary, Indiana, and before that lived in Battle Creek, Michigan.
He'd moved there from Itta Bena, Mississippi, during the Great Migration. Spann had worked hard to secure a future for his family. "When
we talk about Chicago," his daughter Melody Spann Cooper said to
me, "I don't know too many other places where men go from being
a cabdriver or working at the steel mill and, in a very short period of
time, considering our history in this country, [get] to go from being a
sharecropper to becoming a share*holder*. Only in Chicago."[1]

Although he didn't have a traditional education experience, Spann
had served in the Korean War and used the GI Bill to attend both the
Midway Television Institute and the Midwestern Broadcasting School.[2]
"My dad, with little education, was an amazing man," Spann Cooper
continued. "He was just brilliant in how he thought about things, how
he processed things, and how he went after things. . . . He felt like hard

work, grit, and grind could get him there, and that's what he did. And he took it as far as he could take it."

Spann's future cohost, Wesley South, moved to Chicago with his family from Oklahoma in 1924 when he was ten years old. He served two years in the army before attending Northwestern University's Medill School of Journalism, becoming one of the school's first Black graduates. He then became a professional journalist, working for the *Chicago Defender* and then for Johnson Publishing Company, where he stayed for six years.

South's dive into radio came after he went to work as a columnist for the NAACP. A radio executive at the station that would later become WVON asked him to host his own show, because the station did not have any Black people on-air.

South was already working for the station when, in 1963, brothers Leonard and Phil Chess bought it and changed it to WVON—"the Voice of the Negro." (The Federal Communications Commission dictates that the call signs of radio stations east of the Mississippi River start with *W*.) The Chess brothers are mostly known today as the former owners of Chess Records—the prominent Chicago label known for recording Black blues legends such as Muddy Waters, Etta James, and Howlin' Wolf. In 2008, the story of Chess Records was brought to the big screen in the movie *Cadillac Records*, making the label more of a household name.

Leonard and Phil Chess, who were white Polish immigrants, handled most of the label's production and day-to-day operations, but in the '60s, they started to bring in heavy hitters. Roquel "Billy" Davis was one of them. He previously worked for Berry Gordy and Motown in Detroit but moved to Chicago to take over Chess's A&R (artists and repertoire) and creative departments. This addition gave the brothers the time to turn their sights to other opportunities—like radio.

When they bought WVON, they wanted an outlet to promote the records they were producing. Pervis Spann was among their first hires. He and his future partner Wesley South became part of the team of Black disc jockeys known as the Good Guys, along with Herb Kent, E. Rodney Jones, and Franklin McCarthy. This group of five would be on-air during the station's very first day as WVON, on April 1, 1963. Later, more disc jockeys would be added to the fold, including Don Cornelius, later of *Soul Train* fame.

Not only was the station popular, but it helped bring Black musicians to the forefront, giving them their own platform. "The genius of WVON as it was created by Leonard Chess—he was so smart and wise—was that every single individual at WVON was an out-and-out personality," disc jockey Herb Kent wrote about Chess in 2009. "Each one had their own theme song, their own little signature—a laugh, a sound, or a saying—and every single one was highly entertaining."[3] The Good Guys were seen as community heroes, and their opinions carried weight in Chicago. When they talked, people listened.

And their influence extended past entertainment. This was especially true for South's *Hotline* hour, which was in a talk show format. There South interviewed huge names such as Duke Ellington and Dr. Martin Luther King Jr. He even interviewed both John Kennedy and Jimmy Carter before they became US presidents.

And South and his colleagues were there when, in 1968, the world shook at the murder of Dr. King. Rev. Jesse L. Jackson himself called WVON to report news of the assassination. In Chicago, as in places across the country, riots broke out. WVON's on-air talent appealed for calm. "It is my opinion and the opinion of many—and you were there, Richard, at the time, so you know just how hot things were—but it was VON [that] went on the air twenty-four hours," former WVON general manager Lucky Cordell told Richard Steele on WBEZ after South's death in 2010. "Our disc jockeys—we didn't even have to call them in, they just came into the station to ask the community not to do this: don't do this in the name of Dr. King, he wouldn't like this, he would not go this way." The disc jockeys felt that they played a huge role in calming down the community while also giving them space to vent and grieve.

Of the original five Good Guys, many had long careers in radio. For more than a decade, E. Rodney Jones worked as the station's afternoon disc jockey and became its longtime program director. Herb Kent, "the Cool Gent," would remain on the air at WVON for years. With a radio career that spanned more than seventy years, he was undoubtedly one of the most well-recognized names in Chicago radio until his death in 2016.

Spann and South moved from personalities to owners when, in 1977, the two formed Midway Broadcasting and purchased the station. The men brought very different skills to their partnership. "My dad had money and creativity, Mr. South had connections and savviness," Melody Spann Cooper recalled. She added that although her father and

South weren't friends, they made the business successful and trained Spann Cooper to lead it. "They made it work—not liking each other—but both feeding into me when I would need to make it a generational situation."

In 1986, the station underwent a major programmatic change. The time period was seen as the height of the Black community's political involvement in Chicago, resulting in the election of Harold Washington as Chicago's first Black mayor. And South decided to change the station's format, providing Chicago with its first Black talk radio station.

"So in the confusion and everything, I think the [Black] talk radio thing was born here at WVON," Kent told the *Chicago Tribune*.[4] "We needed a Black talk-radio station, because they got into all kinds of things. Race riots, racism, food stamps, poverty, civil rights—from a Black point of view, which we never had before. Just absolutely phenomenal. Because the white radio stations never gave us that much time. I'm sure they were fair, but it was always a white talk show, not completely Black like this."

In 1999, Spann Cooper became the CEO of Midway Broadcasting, the company started by her father and his partner, taking up the reins of WVON. Working at—and now running—the station has played an integral role in her life. "VON, in particular, has just been my playground," she told me. "And I mean that literally, because I started [working here] when I was fifteen years old, and my dad got me involved."

In 2006, the station moved to its current twenty-four-hour format, making WVON especially meaningful, Spann Cooper said, because most major cities don't have a round-the-clock talk station that specifically caters to Black culture. Even today, it can be difficult to find. "We're able to do it because Chicago amplifies around politics," she said. "It's a segregated town. It's got all of the makings of a never-ending conversation around issues, because we just think differently about it, and we come to that microphone every day being unapologetic about how we approach these issues."

For Black voices in Chicago, WVON has remained a place where we can speak openly and freely. And it has been the place where so many Black leaders have been behind the mic. Like when, in 2002, young state senator Barack Obama filled in for Cliff Kelley while he was on vacation.

"If you listen to the conversations that we had, people let whoever have it—we're free to do that," Spann Cooper said. "It's a free form of ideas and conversations about our place and space in this dynamic city. And so I think that is why we have sustained, why we remain relevant. As long as Black folks are relevant and part of this city, we're going to keep telling the story. And that's what makes us, that's our secret sauce, is our ability to bring it unapologetically."

And this freedom is both an honor and a responsibility Spann Cooper doesn't want the station to ever forget. "I tell the staff that what we do, you can't take it for granted, you've got to honor that ability to address people from that microphone, because it's just been amazing to capture and to story-tell the way that we have with people who've changed the world," she said. "And they've all been there; [it's] just amazing. So I think that's a part of who we are and what we do, [and] if we continue to make it, it'll be more history made as long as we continue to do it and not take it for granted."

8

RISE OF THE BLACK RADIO STAR

"I'm known as the Cool Gent; the King of the Dusties (I invented the term 'dusty records'); the Mayor of Bronzeville in Chicago; the Pied Piper of Teens; and the Black Dick Clark. But you can call me just plain ol' Herbie, Baby."
—Herb Kent in *The Cool Gent:*
The Nine Lives of Radio Legend Herb Kent

HERE IN CHICAGO, Black radio personalities have dominated the field with tremendous careers and names that hold weight in many circles. Even in the earliest days of radio, Black Chicago was there.

Jack L. Cooper was a veteran stage performer and a columnist for the *Chicago Defender*. When the newspaper sent him to Washington, DC, in 1925 to help establish an office there, he was hired as a comedian at local radio station WCAP, becoming the first Black radio announcer in America. This was an interesting and new time for radio. The very first commercial radio broadcast had taken place just five years earlier. In 1922, Ethel Waters became the first Black woman to sing on the radio as part of a marketing campaign for Black Swan Records. Soon the airwaves of the Roaring Twenties were filled with Black music: blues, jazz, swing, ragtime, and *dance band*—a type of jazz music that was used as accompaniment for dances and dance competitions.

Also during this time, the radio industry pushed its way forward with huge strides in technological innovation. Before 1928, radios ran on batteries, but brothers Paul and Joseph Galvin, who created a company that would later become Motorola, created radio sets that instead ran on the alternating current powering most US homes. They then created a radio that was compatible with the electrical system in cars and inexpensive to add to personal vehicles. The first car radio became available in 1930. These inventions made radio programming more accessible to listeners, which helped to create a greater market for Black voices— voices like Jack Cooper.

On the radio in DC, Cooper performed comedy, but he wanted to do more in this new medium to represent the Black voice, so he moved back to Chicago. There, in 1929, he started working on *The All-Negro Hour* on WSBC in Chicago. Cooper was the show's host, producer, and announcer, and he started to incorporate news into its variety show format. By 1937, he was on the air five days a week with multiple shows.

It took decades, but station owners and their sponsors finally started to recognize Black listeners as a business opportunity. In 1947, Richard Durham made history when he wrote *Here Comes Tomorrow*, the first all-Black radio soap opera to broadcast in the US. Durham was no stranger to radio; he'd had a series profiling notable Black Americans titled *Democracy U.S.A.* that aired on Chicago's WBBM between 1946 and 1948, and in 1942 he had also participated in the first NBC–Northwestern University radio institute, a six-week summer program that became renowned for radio training.[1]

Broadcast on WJJD in Chicago, *Here Comes Tomorrow* was about a family named the Redmonds. In one storyline, a Redmond son goes away to fight in the war, but when he comes back to the United States, he faces discrimination everywhere. The scripts showed off Durham's fearless writing skills, while the show also became a launching pad for newer actors and radio personalities. Its featured cast included Jack "the Rapper" Gibson, who talked about how the actors had to sneak in and out of recording sessions to avoid the angry mobs that would gather around the studio, upset because they disagreed with the contents of the scripts. "It was such a controversial show that we were about twenty-five years before our time," he said in an archival interview. "There were times that the script was so strong they used to have to take us out of the studios by freight elevators and put us in taxicabs and go up the alley."[2]

Gibson had begun his radio career at WJJD in 1945 and was becoming a radio star. He was mentored by Al Benson, a beloved Black broadcaster known as "the Old Swingmaster." Unlike Jack L. Cooper, the South Sider used slang in his shows and didn't try to mask his Mississippi accent (he moved to Chicago as a teen in 1923). Gibson recalled that Benson was voted the most popular DJ in Chicago at the time by the *Chicago Tribune*. He "became a superstar," Gibson said. "I'd never seen anything like this, and I wanted to be like him."[3] In 1949, Gibson joined the first radio station to be owned by a Black person, WERD in Atlanta.

Richard Durham's next writing project was a weekly docudrama called *Destination Freedom*, which first aired on June 27, 1948, on Chicago radio station WMAQ. The weekly show was done in collaboration with the *Chicago Defender*, which sponsored the first thirteen weeks. Clarice Durham, his wife, explained why Durham used the series to highlight the Black struggle. "He used the term 'universal people' and he felt that the struggle of Blacks was so similar to the struggles of people all over the world who were exploited, who were oppressed," she said in an archival interview. "And he wanted people to feel pride in themselves, and to see themselves as heroic people and not as helpless victims. And I think that came across. You know, people were very proud of the show and what it was saying."[4]

Subsequent radio legends have built on this strong legacy. Herb Kent is the absolute example. As he explained in his autobiography, Kent was a hit from the start of his career. He started in radio at just sixteen years old in 1944 and maintained extremely high ratings from the 1950s on, keeping his place at number one or two in his time slot as he deejayed for eleven different stations throughout his career.

"I've been on the air long enough to entertain moms and dads, then entertain their kids, and now I'm entertaining *their* kids," he wrote in *The Cool Gent*. "And what I'm proudest of is that through all my years in radio, I have just dominated the ratings. As I've gotten older, I've been referred to as a 'beloved icon,' but let me tell you, brother, these radio stations won't keep you on the air if you aren't pulling in the numbers, no matter how cuddly or well-known you might be."[5]

Kent was extremely clear—and confident—in his talent and value to the industry. He knew that his gift was innate ability, and that how he could choose the best music to play from all genres was a unique skill.

He said he tapped into "Cool School" music: no matter the genre, he knew what made a good song good. But it's also extremely important to note the intentionality of his work, that he knew what he did was for other Black people, that his trailblazing would also make a way for those who came after him.

Kent wrote that as his college professor "at a prestigious university" gave him his final grade for a class—it was, of course, an A—he basically told him that he didn't have a future in the industry: "You have the best voice in the class, Mr. Kent, but you'll never make it in radio because you're a Negro."[6]

Radio is an intimate medium. When listeners hear a person's voice, they connect to them. It can feel as close as a phone conversation with a good friend. So racism and discrimination also play a huge role in what Black people in radio are up against; assumptions and stereotypes have an effect on listenership, which leaks into staffing decisions. What Herb Kent faced is similar to what Black people in radio still face today—whether those biases are explicit or implicit. But it's a great thing for the industry that his professor was very, very wrong.

The rise to radio stardom in Chicago has not been limited to men either. Even in a male-dominated field, Yvonne Daniels's voice stood out. Daniels had started in radio when she was just seventeen and had made her way to Chicago in the mid-1960s, working as a host at WYNR and then cohosting at WCFL. Her father, jazz musician Billy Daniels, had exposed her to so much music that her jazz knowledge surprised the men she worked with, like her cohost radio legend Sid McCoy, who was known for his late-night jazz dispatch. "It surprised Sid at first that we could talk about so many things together on the air, even though I was a lot younger," she told the *Chicago Tribune* in 1973. "I knew most of the people he was talking about, all the jazzmen. Most of them I'd met by accident. I'd stop by to hear them—I love live music—and someone would introduce me and we'd get to talking."[7]

In 1967, she was part of the first all-woman radio team at WSDM. In 1973, she broke another barrier when she became the first woman host at WLS. A decade later in 1982, Daniels brought her talents over to WVON, and then WGCI and WNUA.

Daniels died from breast cancer at the age of fifty-three in 1991, and later that year, a stretch of Dearborn Street was given the honorary name of Yvonne Daniels Way in her memory. Four years later, she was posthumously inducted into the national Radio Hall of Fame. WNUA DJ Danae Alexander, who first worked with Daniels at the all-women station in the early `70s, summed it up perfectly in an interview with the *Chicago Tribune* after Daniels's death: "Before Yvonne, very few women thought about becoming disc jockeys, because disc jockeys were all males," she told the *Tribune* about the industry in Chicago. "Suddenly this new door opened for women, and it was because of Yvonne that it opened."[8]

9

THE CHICAGO SOUND

"'The Chicago Sound' was uplifting. There was no posturing or pretense, which is how it found a pure path to your heart."
— Dave Hoekstra in his *Chicago Sun-Times* blog

IN THE SUMMER OF 1988, entering her junior year of high school, Mary Datcher got her first taste of radio, working at Chicago radio station WGCI as part of a program with the youth organization Junior Achievement. "What we would do is take over two hours of 1390 AM, right after Operation PUSH's program at 11 AM," she told me in an interview. "And after they would go off the air, our Junior Achievement program would go on, which would be called JA AM 1390."[1]

The Junior Achievement initiative was structured to mirror full-time positions held by staff at the radio station. Young people filled all of the popular positions, such as music director and on-air personality. Datcher took a role on the sales team, and not only did she excel at it, she became the number-one salesperson, getting account after account from businesses in her West Side neighborhood of Austin.

"I grew up in the Austin area, my father was a businessman—he had businesses—so I knew the gift of gab, of how to sell, basically working in his business," Datcher said. "And I would go up and down Madison Street, that was my whole thing. And they knew me and knew my dad."

And through this role, Datcher met some of the greatest minds in the business—both those behind the mic and those behind the scenes. "I started befriending the regular staff at WGCI, the real honchos who were making everything work," she said. "Doug Banks was the on-air personality in the morning at the time, Ramonski [Luv] was his sidekick, Irene Mojica was an on-air personality, Tom Joyner was still traveling from Chicago to Dallas as the 'Fly Jock,' Yvonne Daniels—may she rest in peace—she was the night person, such a beautiful deep voice. So this was a period where I was literally working around some great legendary Black folks."

From there, she became an intern and was mentored by music director Barbara Prieto—then a twentysomething Mexican American woman from Gary, Indiana—who Mary says had noticed she had a skill for choosing music for JA AM. "This was a period where they weren't really bothering with rap music," Mary said. "Other than 'Rapper's Delight,' they really wasn't messing with it too much. And JA AM became that introduction to the FM station of what young people were listening to on the hip-hop side."

Datcher, who is the founder of Global Mixx Media Group, also spent years working at record companies Universal and Def Jam, and running operations at George's Music Room—a historic West Side record store that was the number-one stop for national artists passing through Chicago and local artists seeking an opportunity for their music to be sold. There, West Side artists such as Do or Die, Twista, Da Brat, and Psychodrama were able to first sell out their music.

Datcher knows how Chicago radio stations cultivated strong relationships with record labels. "Radio Day would be a day that was set aside for most radio stations to have record company representation there to sit down with that program or music director to pitch their music, and each label had a company rep," she explained. "If that label did not have a company in-house rep, they have what we call indie— basically independent consultants who would be a hired gun to work that record on their behalf. Most of the time, indies were working for small mom-and-pop labels who maybe couldn't afford a full staff. Or they were also what we call 'hit men' for major companies that did not want to get their hands dirty."

She says that in the late '80s and early '90s, Chicago was a powerhouse for label reps. "Chicago, being the second market in the country, had probably the most labeled reps in the country outside of New York," she said. "All the imprints that you may have seen under the major labels, at the time, had their own in-house infrastructure, full-blown divisions. That's how many reps there were at the time." And many of these reps, like Mary, were Black.

This had not always been the case, Mary explained. "Now, rewind maybe ten to fifteen years earlier, you barely had any Black representation for these major companies," she said. The way was paved by early Black label reps from Chicago—like Granville White, the first Black regional rep for CBS Records, which is now Sony Music.

But there was another reason why this shift occurred, and Chicago played a huge part: the city's Black radio stations demanded representation. "Very rarely did you see white record reps walk into a Black radio station in Chicago," Mary said. "Because they felt like this: if you want our Black radio stations to continue to break your music, make this money for your white operated companies, then you need to have Black representation come into our Black radio stations. This was Chicago."

Directors like E. Rodney Jones at WVON made these types of demands and stuck by them. "So in the early-to-mid '70s it was a new wave of Black regional reps for labels being hired." This change showed how Black radio stations could support Black artists and was one of the reasons why Jones in particular was seen as such an influential force in the music industry. "We called him the godfather," Marshall Thompson of the Chi-Lites told the *Tribune*. "Rodney was the one who started our career and put us in the position to still be on tour [40 years later]."[2]

In addition to being a crucial point of promotion for the major labels, Chicago was also home to its own thriving recording industry. "We had Record Row, from Twelfth and Michigan all the way to Twenty-Sixth and Michigan," Mary said. It was "lined with independent record companies—that not only were Black owned, but they had Black artists. And that was the heart of where a lot of that music came from." Sadly, many of these labels' contributions are not given their due in popular conversations.

Vee-Jay Records was the most successful Black-run record company before the rise of Motown in Detroit. Founded in the 1950s in nearby Gary, Indiana, Vee-Jay stood for the initials of cofounders Vivian Carter Bracken and Jimmy Bracken. The first record the Brackens ever recorded was "Baby, It's You" by the Spaniels. The song reached number ten on *Billboard*'s rhythm and blues chart in 1953. In 1954, the Brackens moved Vee-Jay to Chicago, where it took its place on Record Row.

In 1964, Vee-Jay released *Introducing . . . the Beatles*, the first Beatles album in the United States. Two years before, Vee-Jay had released a successful British single in the US to much acclaim and worked with the Beatles, then an unknown group, as part of a larger deal. Unfortunately, it was this contractual coup that caused problems for the company. As a small independent label, it couldn't move all of the units necessary to keep up with such high demand for records like *Introducing . . . the Beatles* alongside its other obligations. Vee-Jay went bankrupt just a couple years after achieving massive success.[3]

Before that, Vee-Jay also worked with record producer Carl Davis, one of the influential machines behind Chicago music—as did several other local labels. "Carl was the Babyface of Chicago in the late '60s to the '70s," Mary said. "He was the producer behind the Dells, the Chi-Lites, the Emotions, you name it—that '70s sound that came out of Chicago was Carl Davis. How many people even bring him up under the age of fifty? They don't."

But Carl Davis's name should be widely known outside of music history circles. He worked at places such as Columbia subsidiary Okeh before forming his own labels, Dakar and Chi-Sound Records, where Kenneth "Babyface" Edmonds got his start. And Davis was indeed the producer behind many of the biggest songs and artists of his time.

The Dells, who rose to fame in the 1960s with a string of hits, were one of the groups the movie *The Five Heartbeats* was loosely based on. The group recorded all of the songs the Heartbeats sang in the 1991 film, and their songs "A Heart Is a House for Love" and "Nights like This" were top-twenty hits on the *Billboard* Hot R&B Singles chart in the United States.

The Dells actually discovered the Opals, the group that the musical *Dreamgirls* was based on. And then Davis helped the Opals discover the sound, look, and other minute details of their band. "I heard something totally fresh in the Opals," Davis recalled in 2006. "There were other girl groups, but the Opals had a cute sound. We got Curtis [Mayfield] to write songs for them. He was my assistant producer."[4]

Fifty-plus years later, Chicago artists are still making waves. In 2017, for example, Chance the Rapper's album *Coloring Book* became the first streaming-only album to be nominated for and win a Grammy when it took home the prize for Best Rap Album. Chance also received Best New Artist and Best Rap Performance that year for his song "No Problem."

But when we think about Chicago's influence—that Chicago sound—even here in Chicago, many of us don't know our own impact. "We don't know how influential and impactful we have been on a global scope until somebody outside the marketplace has either incorporated [Chicago work] into their own creative piece or they have stolen it, " Datcher said.

Part IV

"AND YOU SAY CHI CITY?"

DANCING DOWN

Written while listening to "Angels" by Chance the Rapper

> "I had to dance. . . . Being on stage was, for me, making love. It was an expression of my love of humanity and things of beauty."
>
> —Dancer Katherine Dunham in an
> interview with *Essence* magazine in 1976

AFTER A FEW DAYS OF NONSTOP CRYING, my first month as a freshman at Florida A&M University in 2003 was looking up. I'd met a few friends from home—FAMU's Chicago Club was and still is a mighty force—and I'd joined a dance team. Not just any dance team, though. Yes, there were teams that were already on campus. And yeah, they were having tryouts, trying to grab at the new influx of talent who were eager and ready and willing to start long nights of practice, buy expensive uniforms, and give up all their free time—all for the love of dance.

But me, I went for a new team, yet one that felt very familiar. I'd already known about House Arrest 2, because all the big Chicago dance teams with legacies dating back to the '90s had the word *house* in their names, including House-O-Matics and, of course, House Arrest. (I'd later learn that House Arrest was founded in 1990 by teens who would always be "on punishment" when they got in trouble—trouble they'd said felt like being on house arrest; seriously the most teenage thing to name a team after.) And these teams I'd known from long days spent at "dance downs"—competitions held throughout the South and West Sides—in my own teenage years. They weren't just good; they were legendary.

Here in Florida, though, that reputation hadn't yet spread. No one had even seen footworking, our Chicago style of dance. So, it was just me and my new friend Maisha, also new to the team, excitedly yelling and staring at the TV in the Orange Room café as we waited on our mozzarella sticks. On that screen was Kanye West's "Through the Wire" video, showing all of these places I knew all too well: the places where I shopped, the Harold's Chicken where I got my six-wing with mild sauce, and right there, at the Halsted Mall, boys footworking in House Arrest 2 jerseys.

The thing that I remember most about what made our heads initially turn toward that TV was that the voice coming from it was very, very Chicago. Living in Florida, that wasn't something you heard too often at the time. There was no Facebook yet, so of course, no Twitter, no Instagram, and no Snapchat either. Black culture was still very fragmented, and sharing music electronically was still very new. But here was Chicago—Black Chicago—right here in Tallahassee, not a fifteen-hour drive away.

Watching the video meant a lot to two homesick girls living nine hundred miles away from the only city they really knew. A celebration of all that it meant to be Black in Chicago, it showed our own cultural staples and it signified this widening explosion of Black Chicago culture that we were right on the cusp of, that I'd soon be able to enjoy.

Today, Chicago's influence reverberates on a global scale. One day recently, I was scrolling on social media and saw a video of young people in Japan footworking—Chicago footworking. I immediately let out a chuckle, not because I didn't love seeing the dance form spread across seas but because I *did*. I remembered the first time my dance team performed onstage at FAMU in 2003. As soon as we started to footwork, the audience soured: *Booooo! What is this? Get off the stage.*

We laughed about it, but it was awkward, and for eighteen-year-old Arionne, who was trying to find her place on this campus as a freshman, it was disheartening. Without a TikTok to connect with people who didn't live near you or a YouTube to see dancing from other parts of the country, let alone the world, our dancing seemed weird to this body of students who came from all over. And even the large population of

Chicago students could not surmount the fact that much of the audience simply did not know what the hell we were doing.

But the next time we performed, the audience was more curious: *Oh, this is really a thing they do? Hmmmm.* Next time, we got cheers: *Hey hey hey!* And for the rest of my time there, people would stop me on campus and say, "Hey, aren't you that girl that's always dancing onstage?" A switch had been flipped. They didn't just put up with our footworking, they loved it, they craved it. Organizations gave us special invitations to perform at their shows and to come to their parties; this included Florida State University down the street. Chicago culture—*Black* Chicago culture—had found its way to Tallahassee.

Two decades later, I'm on all of these new social media channels that didn't exist when I was eighteen, watching people who are not hundreds but thousands of miles away doing the same dance genre we had to fight for. It's a wild feeling. I never, as a kid, put together the story of how dancing to house music changed throughout the years and how footworking became a Chicago staple turned worldwide phenomenon. But I can now see why it would catch on and spread like wildfire.

But the start of all of this dancing is the music from which it grew: house music. Being a bit of a youngster—I was born in 1985—the first house sound I personally remember being played was Steve "Silk" Hurley's "Jack Your Body," which came out in 1987. I remember it being played at every cookout, wedding, and family reunion, maybe even every school dance, although by the time we got into the 1990s, it was everywhere. DJ Chip's "Bank Ski," "Where U From?," and "Hey, Hey, Hey" were the songs of my childhood. This is the type of music my CD player and then iPod were filled with: tracks with DJ voices strong over the beat. Sometimes those tracks were made especially for a dance team like mine, with the team's name and the DJ's name intertwined over and over ("*House Arrest 2, House Arrest 2, House Arrest 2, RP Boo*").

House music, in its essence, is a music that makes you feel free. It's why it has the power to take over an entire summer weekend every year during the Chosen Few Picnic, a house music festival that has drawn thousands and thousands of Chicagoans annually for three decades. "If you watch the news, you might not believe that some thirty or forty thousand people can be in a park on the South Side for twelve hours drinking and eating," Chosen Few Picnic cofounder Alan King told me in 2019. "And there's no violence, no security incidents, nothing in frankly our twenty-nine-year history."[1]

House is a unifier. It brings people together. And we can track it back to exactly how, where, and when it started—at a place called the Warehouse.

10

THE SCENE THAT HOUSE BUILT

"I think those type of parties we were having at the Warehouse, I know they were something completely new to them, and they didn't know exactly what to expect. So it took them a few minutes to grow into it, but once they latched onto it, it spread like wildfire through the city."

—Frankie Knuckles in 1995

NOW THAT IT'S AN INTERNATIONAL PHENOMENON, people forget that house music is Chicago. It's a genre that was created at the parties and clubs in this city before it expanded to something that the entire world wants to dance to.

But it does have roots in New York City. In the 1970s, the type of music that would turn into house music started as a form of disco. But a shift happened when DJ Frankie Knuckles, who had been working under DJ Larry Levan, tried something new. "Frankie Knuckles was kind of like his apprentice and so Frankie Knuckles wanted his own shine," DeJuan Frazier said in an interview.[1] Frazier is a founder of House Arrest Dance Team and its later iteration, House Arrest 2. "But [Frankie Knuckles] wasn't going to get that in New York, and he wanted to play the type of music that Larry Levan was playing. So somebody came along, the founder [of the nightclub] the Warehouse, and was like, 'Hey, I got a club in Chicago. I want you to come in and be the resident DJ.'"

The Warehouse was Black and Brown and queer, and located in Chicago's downtown. It was started by Robert Williams, who had enjoyed New York City's popular queer clubs. He wanted to re-create that same vibe in Chicago and opened US Studio, which eventually moved to 206 South Jefferson Street and reopened as the Warehouse.

So Frankie Knuckles decided to make his way to Chicago to work with Williams. He got a state-of-the-art sound system and took up his residency at the Warehouse. But the music he played was different from the music played by Larry Levan in New York. That difference is what birthed the Chicago house music genre.

"What made it house music is he started to add his own sounds on top of the records that were already out," Frazier said. "DJs were on top of different baselines; they would only play certain parts, just completely revolutionizing the sound. And they started to call it 'house music,' because it started off at the Warehouse."

Like with other genres, if it's something that people want to hear, they're going to ask for it. And when they do, an industry pops up from that demand. "People will go to different clubs and be like, 'Hey, I want to hear the music they play at the Warehouse. I want to hear that house music,'" Frazier said. "And so initially, that's where the name, the sound, and all that stuff came from."

By the mid-1980s, DJs throughout the city were doing what Frankie Knuckles was doing: taking songs that were already out and adding to them. But that meant everyone was playing similar music. The music that he was playing at the Warehouse was now being played at parties and clubs all around the city, primarily for Black and Latino audiences.

"They decided, because . . . everybody's playing the same thing and the only thing that was different were the sounds, they said, 'Hey, let's make our own stuff,'" Frazier said. "And so it would be the same kind of baseline, but then they would play all the instruments, their own keyboards, if there were words on top of it, they would say it, and they would literally make it in their house, in the basement, in the garage, in the closet—that's what it was."

From this change came "On & On" by Jesse Saunders. Saunders, who is from Chicago, is credited with making what is considered the very first original house song in 1984. "It wasn't a remake of something, it wasn't somebody else famous, it wasn't a disco record—none of that," Frazier noted. "He made it, and that song took off." At the time, "taking off" meant a song was being played everywhere—you could hear it being bumped loudly at house parties, at clubs, in cars. It also meant it'd be included when you bought a mixtape at the mall or recorded your favorite songs from the radio.

With the popularity of Saunders's song, other DJs felt they could do the same. And in 1986, Marshall Jefferson came out with the House Music Anthem. Officially titled "Move Your Body," it was the first house song to use piano, making Jefferson one of house music's founding fathers.

Said music executive Mary Datcher, "I was a part of that new generation of record and radio folks that loved house music, because I couldn't get away from it." When she interned at WGCI, she was witness to how house music was taking over. She started spending time with the Hot Mix 5, which might be the first DJ crew in the city to achieve commercial success. "They were the front line of the mix show when it came to spinning a lot of music on commercial radio," she said. "There were other DJs that kicked off the house music scene or radio, but it was mainly on college radio."[2]

The Hot Mix 5 was originally on a different station before moving to WGCI. But on WGCI, one of Chicago's most prominent Black stations, is where the group became famous. It consisted of a total of eight DJs who came and went to and from the crew. Working in an expanding industry, they had to quickly become businesspeople. Datcher said DJs were making so much money that they had to learn how to handle it: they had to become their own accountants, managers, and publicists seemingly overnight. "Each DJ might do a separate party, three parties in one night, and they're making a thousand dollars each party," she explained. "So here you have these DJs that are growing to be businesspeople, and they're getting national [and] international acclaim."

House's international appeal came quickly. In the mid-1980s, the House Music Tour of Europe helped launch the genre's worldwide spread. In 1987, Hurley's "Jack Your Body" became the first house song to hit number one in the UK.

"That's when I started understanding the international side of how house music was influencing overseas," Datcher said. "You're talking about DJs who were maybe two or three years older than me . . . and they're making damn near $8,000 to $10,000 a week: DJing, producing music, and licensing and selling off these tracks to other people overseas."

But as it often goes with young people in creative fields, the young Black and Brown people who were making this genre were being taken advantage of. Even if they were making what seemed to be good money, they were owed more—especially in the way of rights and royalties. Predatory companies "knew they didn't have the business sense of protecting themselves—protecting their copyrights, protecting their publishing," Datcher said. "And so, in the next few years, it becomes all these predatory stories of people really taking advantage of young Black talent. Some of the best music of our soundtrack of our lives, when you hear about it, on the back end, they didn't get paid for their royalties, they didn't own the rights of the publishing, or the licensing."

For Frazier, this time period was when he really started to grow into that music person all of his friends know him to be today. And it really started where many Black Chicago kids had their first musical experiences: the roller rink. Although Chicago is a huge skating city, on Saturday nights at places such the Rink and the Route (formally known as Route 66), no one would *actually* be skating. Instead, the main rink would turn into a dance floor. It was a club-like atmosphere for Black teenagers to gather and dance, and that trend continued well into the late '90s and early aughts.

"Every Saturday, I was there, just on the wall, just listening to the music, watching everybody else dance, and this is when the dance style starts to formulate," Frazier said. He started coming in with blank tapes and asking the DJ to record his set for him. "He would record it and give it to me for free," Frazier continued. "So I would have house music and now everybody knows me in the neighborhood: Juan has house music on tapes!" So he started making mixtapes for kids in his neighborhood, the same exact thing he'd be doing for his friends.

"When house music came along, now everybody's dancing to it, but it's no set dance style per se," Frazier said. "So the first thing that people were doing off of house music was stepping—and not like, 'Step in the Name of Love,' it was like fraternity step." This is why a lot of dance teams that started in the late 1980s had fraternity-type names, like U Phi U. "And instead of 'juking' [as it's called now], they called it 'jacking,' and one of the first organized groups was TWJ—Together We Jack—and they did fraternity stepping off of music," Frazier said.

Other teams had the word *house* in their names, because they danced to house music. One of the oldest and most respected of these teams was

House-O-Matic, which also started in the late '80s, right after U Phi U. "I love hearing the story from Ronnie [Sloan, House-O-Matic's founder], because they used to always dance off of house music, but they weren't doing footwork, because footwork wasn't around just yet," Frazier said. "So when they would do talent shows, they would do like New Edition, and then put on house music at the end and do like a fraternity set. So House-O-Matic, the name, started off as a joke, because it's the play with 'house music' and being 'on automatic' so it's like soon as the house music comes on, they're going to house automatically. And it was a joke, but they liked the name."

After U Phi U and House-O-Matics became the first two dance teams out, the dance style started to change. The teams started to mix in dance moves with the stepping they were doing. It still wasn't footwork, Frazier explained, but the dancing started to move in that direction. "Now, U Phi U and House-O-Matic, they're getting all this pull in the city, everybody knows them from the parades, they're performing at [the historic New Regal Theater on the South Side], they're doing everything: everybody [else watching] wants to start their own group."

And so because of these groups' popularity, the new groups were trying to incorporate "Phi" and "house" into their own team names: Beta Phi House, Theta Phi House, House Squad, Fire House, One House, and of course Frazier's team: House Arrest.

For decades, footworking continued to be something that was known mostly in Chicago. Then, in the 2010s, the popularity of YouTube and camera phones created a new global push for the dance as a new and growing art form. "It was a game changer," Frazier said. "So then you had a crew that come together like the FootworKINGz that took full advantage of this new technology. And that was King Charles, Prince Jron, Boodilla—Curtis footworked with them—and they're the ones who really took it on a global scale. In fact, they started a crew called Creation Global. Once people started seeing them on YouTube, they started flying them out to Japan, to L.A., to Brazil."

Current footwork dancers, in addition to leading master classes and starting team chapters around the world, have also expanded the idea of what kinds of music dancers can footwork to. "What I liked that they did, was they danced off of house music and tracks, but they also dance off of regular music too," Frazier said. "And by them doing that, people were like, 'Yo, what kind of dance style is this?'

Because even if they didn't get the dance, they liked the song, so they would watch it."

As more people watch footworking online, it becomes a gateway into learning more about house music. "And then once they start diving down that rabbit hole, then it's like, 'Oh snap, there's some music that goes with it,'" Frazier said. "So now, these guys took off so now you've seen them in commercials, at the Super Bowl, and *Dancing with the Stars*, Madonna—and I think that is awesome. I love it. They always shout out Chicago."

11

"IT'S A DRILL"

"I think that the drill scene provided and created a platform that was independent—it was by the artists, for the artists. It kind of ripped through the industry. It created something that didn't need the industry."

—GOATHAUS Studio co-owner
Mark Buol to *Complex* magazine

EVERY FORM OF HIP-HOP MUSIC is shaped by who and what started it. When it comes to drill, it's a subgenre of rap that has international appeal. Even the United Kingdom has its own version of drill. But that subgenre, and the drill that is talked about in clubs and music circles throughout the world, is all heavily influenced by Chicago-style drill, because it all started in Chicago over a decade ago.

Chicago drill was born out of the frustration of Black teens and young adults living in neighborhoods of the city where gun violence was rampant. They used this form of music to express those feelings: the only way to protect yourself, the music's lyrics often said, is to shoot first.

When drill reached London, the production and lyrics of the region's youth created a slightly new sound, a sound that garnered popular acclaim. But what wasn't new was the heart of drill music: the idea of it being the voice for the young and unheard remained. Young Black people in the UK today are using drill to explain what is happening in their own communities: a rise in stabbings, violence with a different tool of harm. "If Chicago drill is a gun, ours is a knife," a South London teen told *Fact* magazine.[1]

Yet, as the BBC pointed out in a 2021 look at the continuous evolution of the subgenre worldwide, drill today is not always about violence. Late Brooklyn rapper Pop Smoke, who was working with London producer 808Melo when he rose to popularity in 2019, made music that was seen as party music, fun and even funny at times, and he wasn't pigeonholed as a dangerous or violent rapper.[2]

By 2020, drill could be found not just in the United States and in the UK but in countries around the globe, everywhere from Australia to Brazil. All this growth was not what kids from Chicago expected in the early 2010s when they started to blast music from local rappers like Chief Keef. Keef is not the rapper who invented drill, but he is one of the subgenre's most recognizable names, and has been since he came on the scene as a teenager.

Dometi Pongo is a journalist, executive producer, and former host at MTV News, where he covered hip-hop, art, and culture. He told me that when he was growing up in Chicago, Keef's music always felt real and relatable. "Being in Chicago and being so close to the content, what Chief Keef talked about felt so much like my reality that it didn't feel new to me," Pongo said in an interview. "And it wasn't until I traveled that I realized how new Chief Keef's aesthetic was for the rest of the world."[3]

But although the music might sound slightly different based on its location, it still holds the original sounds of Keef's work: both the actual composition of the music and the attitude and perspective. "It's rooted in that Chief Keef aesthetic—meaning that heavy bravado, the 'kicking it with my friends with the pistols all in the camera,' the low-budget videos where 'we're trying to prove to you that what you're seeing in the video right now is our every day, we just happened to turn the camera on and give you a peek into it,'" Pongo said. "He was the first person, in terms of national acclaim, to really give shine to that."

Chief Keef is drill's "golden child," Pongo explained. But the impact of rapper Bump J made him the subgenre's "forefather" even before the term *drill* was ever applied to it. Bump J was incarcerated from 2008 until 2017 as drill music exploded from the streets of Chicago, but he remained a significant influence on rappers such as drill "godfather" King Louie.

Louie, who started to popularize the subgenre especially here in Chicago, credits late rapper Pac Man with first coining the term *drill*. Pac Man was affiliated with the then popular group L.E.P. Bogus Boys. His 2010 track "It's a Drill" is recognized as the first time it was used.

"It was just a term back then," King Louie told DJ Vlad in 2021 while explaining how he saw the subgenre grow from Pac Man to what it is today. He added that what is now seen as drill music by the masses sounds different from what is heard on that particular Pac Man track or even when listening to Louie's older music, like his 2013 mixtape *Drilluminati*. "None of the beats on *Drilluminati*, none of the production, is really like what it is today or what the masses think drill is," he said in the interview. "Drilluminati is a way of life. It ain't gotta be just those types of beats."[4]

It was Chief Keef who took the street sound of drill international when his music hit mainstream radio stations. As he rose to industry fame, labels held a bidding war over who would sign him. In the end, Keef signed with Interscope.

What drew the music world—and then, specifically, the music industry—to Chief Keef was his authenticity. When you listen to Keef's music, it's clear he was rapping about a life he knew, one that he lived. But that same authenticity put the industry and those associated with it in a bind. Even though the music was hip-hop, a genre built on originality and self-expression, the public started to question whether the violence in Keef's music (and that of other similar artists) was too much—if it was too dangerous, if the teenage rappers themselves were too dangerous.

It's a cyclical argument that has happened with every new subgenre since rap shifted from its party music origins in the 1970s to an art form that allowed mostly Black and Brown people to speak out against the political and societal conditions in their communities.[5] With drill, these lyrics are pointedly focused on gun violence and the conditions that perpetuate the feeling of needing to shoot or be shot. And when the subgenre's popularity spread to people outside of those communities, these questions became a public conversation.

"It was real self-expression," Pongo told me, "and I think that's the conundrum of hip-hop in a bubble: It's like, is hip-hop exacerbating the problems in our community or is it trying to display the problems that are in our community? Is it a mirror? What came first, the chicken or the egg?

"It put a lot of music commentators, like, 'Yo, I don't want to lambaste this kid for rapping about the reality that he sees every day, because we know he's not some kid who's just talking about this. This is literally his everyday existence.'" But if this reality rightfully belongs to artists like Keef and they have the right to self-expression, the question then becomes: What happens when those who do not live it try to glorify—and copy—it? Keef "inspired a lot of posers who want to tap into that same sound but don't come from that reality," Pongo said.

People were confused about supporting his music, with some arguing it encouraged violence. "How do we unpack the fact that his influence is so large that people from the burbs, who cling to the hip-hop aesthetic, feel like in order to be authentic, [they] need to mirror or mimic what Keef is doing because [they] see it working for him?" Pongo said about reporting on Keef's music in the early 2010s. "So it's a weird thing whereby how do I celebrate that this kid has found a way out while trying not to congratulate him or champion the most negative parts of his existence?"

In 2012, Chief Keef's song "I Don't Like" become a true sensation when Kanye and Jadakiss added verses to the song's remix. For years to come, this version of the song would dominate the airwaves and party scene, especially when the party was in Chicago. And from Atlanta to Los Angeles to New York, DJs would play the song along with a crowd call to see if there were any Chicagoans in the building. It was *the* song played to get the crowd extra loud.

"The song was bubbling organically, and then Kanye jumps on the remix with Jadakiss, and it gave it new life," Pongo explained. But who was helping who with this new version of Keef's song is up for debate. Keef, who had not yet attained mass mainstream appeal, now had a verse from one of the most listened-to rappers in the world. And Kanye, who had never been known as a hard-core rapper, was on the hottest street record. "From Chief Keef's perspective, what it did at the time was kind of give Kanye street validity at a time [when Chicago's hip-hop sound] was either Common or Bump J, Chance or Chief Keef. Because we have so many diverse sounds—we've got the poetry thing and then we've got the gutter, street thing—and both of them are thorough."

Regardless, this mix of Keef, Kanye, and Jadakiss worked. "People were trying to figure out what our sound was," Pongo said. "And I feel like Kanye jumping on that was giving it mainstream appeal that it needed and kind of like a stamp of approval from the backpacker himself, and then also a fusion of these worlds."

As Keef grew in fame, he and his friends gathered some powerful adversaries, like then Chicago mayor Rahm Emanuel. In 2015, all Keef wanted to do was make an appearance as a hologram at a benefit concert to raise money for the families of two victims of violence on Chicago's South Side: his friend twenty-two-year-old Marvin Carr, and thirteen-month-old Dillan Harris, who was killed by a car fleeing the shooting. But the mayor was on a mission to shut him down.

Keef, then nineteen, had explained that he had changed as a person and was no longer promoting violence. The event would be labeled a "Stop the Killing" event and would instead encourage the people to put their guns down. Generally, if a person of influence wants to help raise money for grieving families who need it, that is seen as a good and generous thing to do. But Emanuel claimed the planned concert was dangerous and vowed to shut it down. Venue after venue backed out of hosting the event. Keef then posted online that the concert would be in a secret location, the promotional video boldly saying, "Banned by the mayor of Chicago: Chief Keef, from a secret Chicago location."[6] Keef's team said at the time that cops were searching for Keef's hologram projector in an attempt to seize it.

The performance was eventually held at Craze Fest in nearby Hammond, Indiana (just over the Illinois-Indiana border), but Hammond police shut it down. "No one ever gave me a reason why they didn't want the hologram to appear," Craze Fest promoter Malcolm Jones told the New York Times. "They didn't have a real reason. They believed that it would start trouble, but the first thing Chief Keef said via hologram was: 'Chicago, we need to stop the violence. Let our kids live.'"[7]

Today, lot more younger rappers are breaking the mold of what it means to be in a certain subgenre of hip-hop. Pongo uses rapper G Herbo as an example. Herbo, who used to go by the moniker Lil Herb, was just sixteen years old when rapper turned mogul Mikkey Halsted heard his music on YouTube and became his manager. Mikkcy, known for being a talented lyricist, had been signed to Cash Money Records in 2000. His management of Herbo is a clear display of connecting two generations that may be different in sound but in not skill or desire to put on for their city.

"I don't know if Herbo considers his music drill or not, but I consider it drill, because Chicago gangster music with a hard beat, I call it drill music," Pongo explained. "And the difference between Herb and a lot of Chicago rappers is Herb has that vibe that he's going to give you that street music but he also has bars. He's a rapper's rapper, and I think that's what attracts somebody like Mikkey Halsted, who was, of course, respected by the streets but who is also more what I call 'backpacking but you might have a Glock in it.' I feel like that was the bridging of the generations."

And this bridge is one that's creating a brand-new kind of influence. "There was a time when Chicago was called the 'City of No Love'—you couldn't get into a circle if you didn't know a certain person, or there would be an older guard that if you didn't know these people or if you weren't a part of this community, you were not going to get your music covered," Pongo said. "But now, we have a culture of artists who have been through that, giving access to a younger generation. G Herbo and Mikkey is like a good illustration of that."

Part V

BLACK LIFE IN PRINT

BLACK EXCELLENCE, BABY

Written while listening to "Les Fleurs" by Minnie Riperton

> "It has been *Ebony*'s privilege to record, dramatize, and interpret this progress, from obscure court decisions to spectacular armed conflict; from the triumphs of a Jackie Robinson to the cathartic cries of a Marian Anderson or Gwendolyn Brooks."
>
> —*Ebony* editors in the November 1965 issue

PACKED ALONGSIDE RAGGED COPIES OF my very first bylines in the *Defender* are several copies of every *Jet* magazine that included a freelance article of mine—after I or my mother had grabbed all the copies from a supermarket checkout line. A byline on *Jet*'s website already meant the world to me, but a print byline in *Jet* felt sacred—a little piece of history that I didn't ever want to lose. And it was a small lifestyle article too, just one of a few I'd get to do after meeting a *Jet* editor at an event.

Being at the event itself felt glamorous. I had on a little cheap dress I thought would make me look more mature—*polished and professional* was what I wanted it to say, even though my bank account did not say the same—and I immediately put on the little Fashion Fair sample of "Jet Red" lip gloss they gave us in the gift bags. That day felt like a break, like I was in the kind of room I'd always hoped to be in: editorial and Black.

Even if Chicago is no longer the physical home of *Ebony* and *Jet*, I feel like the essential foundation laid by Johnson Publishing Company is still here, because this is the place where Black voices have thrived. Looking back, we can see that John and Eunice Johnson gave us a lot. In 1942, we got *Negro Digest* (later *Black World*). In 1945, we got *Ebony*. In 1951, we got *Jet*. The city has always been a place where Black voices are amplified, but JPC's creation of glossy print magazines elevated the Black perspective and gave us gorgeous Black faces to match.

Today, that perspective is still essential as more Black journalists are making the decision to forgo job opportunities at mainstream publications to create their own Black-led media organizations. The gaping void in representation that the Johnsons saw may be smaller, but it is still there.

Today, Black journalists aren't legally shut out of newsrooms, but that doesn't mean it never feels that way. We are often underrepresented in the mainstream, our voices edited out of stories—if the stories we want to report even make it past the pitching stage. As Black journalists, our perspective is often seen as a hindrance to the obtuse idea of objectivity, with non-Black editors telling us we aren't able to cover certain stories fairly—that is, until we are called on to be the unofficial (and unpaid) consultants to other journalists on Black life: *Is this a term you'd say? Is this hair a dreadlock or dreads or locks? What does this tweet mean?*

We are good enough to be translators, sure, but in those same rooms, we often aren't trusted to guide coverage and aren't seen as good enough to be decision-makers. In many newsrooms, we are there for promises of diversity, and yet that diversity is just for show, to be able to check off a box on the next news survey that comes around to show their "commitment" to inclusion.

So it's no wonder that Black news consumers are more likely to feel misunderstood by traditional media organizations because of our race or another demographic trait, according to a 2020 Pew Research survey.[1] This statistical takeaway is consistent with my anecdotal one: media as a whole remains very white, and the overall coverage reflects that.

It is, then, so important to recognize that Black media is still an essential part of telling our story. Our perspective is essential. And when, as Black journalists, we get frustrated and lost and ready to quit, we can look at those who came before us and remind ourselves that our voices matter.

So that is what we will continue do in the coming chapters—dig deep into the archives and look back at more original documenters of the culture.

12

IF I WERE A NEGRO

"The reason I succeeded was that I didn't know that it was impossible to succeed. For me, then, ignorance was a blessing. Since I didn't know that it was impossible to do what I wanted to do, I did it."

—John H. Johnson in his autobiography
Succeeding Against the Odds

FOUNDED IN 1922, *Reader's Digest* was for years and years the bestselling consumer magazine in the United States, keeping that title until *Better Homes and Gardens* bested it in 2009. However, it has never been a publication with an editorial mission to be for and by Black people. Of course, Black writers like Alex Haley, of *Roots* fame, have worked on its staff. But overall, flipping through its pages—and those of other popular magazines—Black people don't always feel represented. And they definitely did not see any representation in the magazines of the 1940s.

There was a clear need for something different when, in 1942, twenty-four-year-old John H. Johnson used a $500 loan (more than $9,000 today) to launch *Negro Digest*, his own version of a family magazine, with a Black focus. Johnson had a clear vision: to show Black lives on the covers of a magazine the same way mainstream magazines showed white lives. But no matter how clear that vision was, nobody believed in it. "When I finally decided to try and put it out, nobody else thought it was a good idea but me," Johnson laughingly recalled in an interview with the HistoryMakers in 2004. "And I didn't have any money. So the question was, what was the best way to get started?"[1]

Johnson said that aside from the NAACP's *Crisis* magazine and the National Urban League's *Opportunity* magazine, there weren't any successful Black magazines still in existence in 1942. But potential funders didn't think a new one could be profitable, so Johnson made a very risky move: he put up his mother's furniture to get that $500 loan. At first, most of the content came from republishing existing articles. *Negro Digest* launched in November of that year.

It was a struggle. Most distributors also didn't think the magazine would sell, so Johnson, who was working at Supreme Liberty Life Insurance Co. at the time, used the insurance company's mailing list to solicit subscribers, using some of the loan for postage. Subscriptions went for two dollars (about thirty-seven dollars today), and he got about three thousand responses. He also did a very Chicago thing: he asked friends to go around to newsstands asking, "Hey, do you carry *Negro Digest*?"

One of the things the magazine became known for was its popular columns. One column, If I Were a Negro, asked well-known white people how they'd solve the problems of Black people. In October 1943, just a year after the release of the magazine's first issue, the column featured an extremely prominent guest writer: First Lady Eleanor Roosevelt.

With the country in the midst of World War II, her column pushed for Black support of the war, although Black people were still fighting their own battles to be recognized as full citizens at home. "If I were a Negro today, I think I would have moments of great bitterness. It would be hard for me to sustain my faith in democracy and to build up a sense of goodwill toward men of other races," she wrote. "I would still feel that I ought to participate to the full in this war. When the United Nations win, certain things will be accepted as a result of principles which have been enunciated by the leaders of the United Nations, which never before have been part of the beliefs and practices of the greater part of the world."[2]

In September 1940, a year before the US entered the war, the country had enacted its first peacetime draft. Black men were required to register—they were expected to risk their lives for their country while still bound by Jim Crow segregation laws. Even while in the military, Black men were relegated to labor and service units, faced harassment by white soldiers, and had separate facilities—blood banks, hospitals, barracks, and the like—that were anything but equal to those of their white counterparts.[3]

There's no indication the First Lady's plea actually pushed more Black people to participate in the war, but it did help boost *Negro Digest* readership—a boost the Portland State University Library says happened overnight.[4] Within a year, the magazine boasted a circulation of fifty thousand.

Johnson later attributed the publication's growth to the fact that it became a place for Black expression and inspiration. "It was a ray of hope," Johnson told NPR in the early aughts.[5] "It gave them the feeling that there were Black people in other cities and in other countries like themselves who were doing well and it inspired them to do better."

Negro Digest ended publication in 1951, probably because the launch of JPC's other publications (*Ebony* in 1945 and *Jet* in 1951) caused a decrease in readership. But JPC relaunched *Negro Digest* a decade later. At that time, Black people's interests had shifted to the idea of Black Power and Pan-Africanism, and so the magazine's content needed to shift with it. That meant including more Black literature, history, and culture. It started to become more of a literary magazine, eventually changing its name to *Black World* in 1970 to reflect this new direction. This new version of the publication became "The Magazine of the Black Consciousness Movement."

The new *Negro Digest*'s masthead still listed Johnson as editor, but it added two other names in significant roles: Hoyt W. Fuller as managing editor and Doris E. Saunders as associate editor. The two coauthored the magazine's Perspectives column and had strong fingerprints not just on *Negro Digest* but on the legacy and direction of Johnson Publishing Company as a whole.

Fuller led the magazine's shift in focus and took over leadership of the Perspectives column. As he became more engaged in the connection between politics and literature, the magazine became a place that welcomed and boosted the work of writers who were part of the Black Arts Movement—a Black nationalist movement that started after the assassination of Malcolm X in 1965.

Before returning to JPC to lead *Negro Digest* in the early 1960s, Fuller had left an editorial post at *Ebony* magazine in 1957, frustrated that the publication did not do enough to support the struggle for Black freedom. In the interim, Fuller traveled, spending much time in Africa, living in Algeria and the Republic of Guinea, and he infused his global views into *Negro Digest*. He also pushed for the magazine's name change to *Black World*, as Black people across the country pushed to replace the word *Negro* with *Black*. In 1969 he even helped organize a protest to push John Johnson to change the name, then quietly sat at his desk at the JPC office as chanting protesters gathered with signs outside.

In the book *Building the Black Arts Movement*, author Jonathan Fenderson argues that Fuller's contribution is even larger than what is often attributed to him. "Rarely out front or on stage in the lime-light, Fuller occupied the background—a position that afforded him tremendous power and influence in the movement yet relatively marginal public visibility, fame, or notoriety," Fenderson wrote. "In a creative campaign built around artists, Fuller did not necessarily fit the bill; still, he remained one of the Black Arts movement's most influential and unique luminaries."[6]

Associate editor Doris E. Saunders was also a quiet but critical force who helped shape Johnson Publishing Company's legacy. Before the magazine's relaunch, Saunders had a very important and distinct role, not just at *Negro Digest* but at Johnson Publishing Company as a whole. A Chicago native, Saunders started at JPC as the company's librarian. In 1949, a twentysomething Saunders had written to Johnson and suggested that he create a special library in the new building he'd purchased for JPC. This library could be a way to document Black life for JPC editorial and advertising. She worked as JPC's librarian for years before being promoted to run the company's Books Division around 1961.

Thanks largely to Saunders, today the Johnson Publishing Company archives are one of the most important collections of its kind. When JPC put up its photo archive for auction in 2019, it sold for $30 million. A portion of that acquisition found its home on the South Side, at the Stony Island Arts Bank, a cultural space run by the Rebuild Foundation, which provides free arts programming.

That part of the archives lives on the bank's second floor and includes Johnson Publishing Company publications starting from the 1940s and additional books, photographs, and other objects from the JPC library. Approximately eleven thousand volumes line the library's walls. The collection is a gift from John and Eunice Johnson's daughter, Linda Johnson Rice, who donated it in 2018 when she was the CEO of Ebony Media Operations, the successor to JPC. "The Bank is a testament to John Johnson," Rebuild founder Theaster Gates told the *Tribune* when the collection was announced. "The Bank's existence is the fourth-generation insistence that Black can make Black better."[7]

It really is that extension into and influence on the work of today's artists, writers, photographers, and creatives that serves as the most visible legacy of Johnson Publishing. Throughout 2022, the Rebuild Foundation and Anthony Gallery showcased work at the Stony Island Arts Bank from both emerging and established artists whose work spotlights the importance of Black space and Black art.

Adeshola Makinde's exhibit, *Is where it's at!*, is a perfect example. When Makinde thinks about the work in his exhibition, one piece rises to the top of his favorites list: a larger-than-life canvas image of the legendary Louis Armstrong—Makinde's largest scale piece he's done to date. "To me, [Armstrong] represented unrelenting optimism, amidst what I could imagine was pretty, pretty unbearable things that he had to deal with going to certain clubs he went to, at the height of which he was doing his thing," he said. "So, I wanted to show that in the show." The title of the piece is *What a _____ world!*, a play off Armstrong's famous song "What a Wonderful World." The piece is "kind of asking that question as to: 'Is it really?' That piece means a lot to me," Makinde said.[8]

For Makinde, this opportunity to show his work in the Arts Bank—a place he says is "inextricably linked to Black excellence"—is an honor. "When people are viewing the show, I want them to feel proud of what they're seeing, especially Black people viewing the work," he said.

Makinde created many of the works in *Is where it's at!* over multiple years since 2019. They include many archival prints on canvas and mixed media collages that pay homage to *Ebony* and *Jet* magazines and the legacy of Johnson Publishing Company as a recorder of Black life—and also Black joy. "Once I was able to figure out the feeling and the mood that I was trying to portray in the show, a lot of the source material that I was finding really was easy to find, honestly," Makinde said. "[For] a lot of the newer collage work in the show, I went towards more '70s-era *Ebony* because it felt like a more joyful, green time, in the way that the imagery was shown."

With the abundance of material that Johnson Publishing magazines provide, Makinde is still sorting through everything he's found so far. "It's just endless, in terms of the amount of source material," he said. "There's still so much stuff on my table that's just scattered about that

I'm still going to use . . . and to give a new light to that—a part of my art practice is trying to do that."

As visitors to the Stony Island Arts Bank view the strong images of Black pride—especially the collages with sayings such as "Dare to be more" and "We don't owe nobody nothin'"—Makinde wants the pieces to feel familiar but also be thought provoking and a way to start conversations. "I just want people to take in the work, make their own conclusions as to what things might mean to them," Makinde said. "But the point of this show is to just show what Black people have offered to the world, especially in terms of culture and everything in between."

13

THE JPC LAUNCHING PAD

"Then EBONY arrived in 1945 . . . to inform us and assure us
that our lives were so important, they could never be edited out
of the history of our people."
　—Maya Angelou in "Then Ebony Arrived," November 1995

GROWING UP IN CHICAGO, Charles Whitaker pretty much always knew
he'd work at *Ebony*. In 1974, he toured the just two-year-old Johnson
Publishing Company building on Michigan Avenue while just a high
schooler at South Shore on the city's South Side. From that moment on,
that feeling was cemented. So when he went to work there in 1985 as an
associate editor, it was surreal.

"At the time when I started I was in a cubicle, and there were all
these school kids coming through, and I'm like . . . I remember being
a schoolkid, seeing these writers at their desks, thinking, 'Oh, I want to
be one of them someday,' and now I was one of those writers and these
kids are looking at me."[1]

Whitaker is the first Black dean at Northwestern's Medill School of
Journalism, where he's been teaching writing and editing courses since
1992. He's the coauthor of a magazine-writing textbook and coeditor of
a textbook about twentieth-century magazines called *Curating Culture*. A
native Chicagoan, Whitaker worked as a newspaper reporter in Miami
and Louisville before diving into magazine journalism and joining the
Ebony staff.

"It was an amazingly proud, full-circle moment to be one of those people sitting in those cubicles and sort of understanding what that meant and what that represented for these young people who are coming through and touring this place," Whitaker told me.

The decor in the JPC offices at the time can only be described as both gold and groovy. A lobby with a rounded red couch and gold-accented walls and fixtures. Totally different carpets and wallpaper for each room and each floor. Bright colors like yellows and purples punctuated the golds, browns, and tans. And patterns! Patterns everywhere. "The floor for *Jet* magazine was all leopard print: wall-to-wall leopard print carpet," Linda Johnson Rice told Curbed in 2020. "It was a weekly news magazine. It was racy—it was all the news that had happened to African Americans within a week across the country."[2]

The very bold, beautiful designs of the offices and homes in 1970s TV shows had absolutely nothing on the glamour of Johnson Publishing Company. The images of the gold bathroom sink are particularly striking. "This gilded sink is one of my favorite pieces, too," the famed Lee Bey, photographer and author of *Southern Exposure: The Overlooked Architecture of Chicago's South Side*, told WBEZ in 2017. "In an otherwise very modern building, you have this sink that looks like it was stolen from Pompeii, right? It's gilded and looks like a shell, and it has these classical knobs and faucets. . . . It looks like money, doesn't it? It's probably one of the only classical, design wise, elements in the building."[3]

Even the inception and creation of this space exemplifies Black excellence. The eleven-story building was designed by a Black architect, John Moutoussamy, a World War II veteran, Illinois Institute of Technology graduate, and student of the famed Mies van der Rohe. Moutoussamy was the first Black person to become partner in the large Chicago architectural firm Dubin, Dubin, Black & Moutoussamy.

Moutoussamy's career took off when, in 1969, he designed the apartment complex Lawless Gardens, which received an award from the Chicago chapter of the American Institute of Architects. Although his work on the Johnson Publishing building may be his most renowned, his well-known modernist work continued after its completion in 1971. He designed the Woodlawn Neighborhood Health Center in 1972, three City Colleges of Chicago—including Harry S Truman College in 1976—and the Alpha Kappa Alpha headquarters in 1983.

When it came to the Johnson Publishing building, Johnson said at the building's dedication in 1972 that its architecture reflected the company's "openness to truth, openness to light, openness to all the currents swirling in all the black communities of this land."[4] The building was intentionally grandiose and modern, built in the traditional International Style, but with a twist. Johnson told Moutoussamy "that he did not want one of those 'shirt front' glass and steel buildings."[5] Everything about the spacious 110,000-square-foot building yelled its importance, with its front facing Michigan Avenue and Grant Park and a rooftop sign with words EBONY and JET on either side of the Johnson Publishing Company logo. Its large, recessed windows made for maximum light and maximum shadows.

Johnson rightfully wanted people to know that this was the first and only structure in downtown Chicago built by a Black person. "This new building reflects our faith in the strength and vitality of that long line of Black men and women who have contributed so much to this country and this community," Johnson said in *Jet* at the time.[6] "[It] is a poem in glass and marble which symbolizes our unshakeable faith that the struggles of our forefathers were not in vain and that we shall indeed overcome."

The Johnsons themselves were the epitome of strength and vitality. When the couple founded their new publication in 1945, it was Eunice Johnson who picked the name *Ebony*. It was just three years after the launch of *Negro Digest*, and they wanted to pattern this new publication after *Life*, the nation's most influential picture magazine. *Ebony* was to be a bright, beautiful display of Black life that felt closer to the gorgeous glossies, with large photos and imageries.

As Brent Staples pointed out in the *New York Times*, "As a close student of *Life*, Mr. Johnson would no doubt have seen the dehumanizing images of African-Americans that appeared in the infamous 1937 issue of the magazine whose cover caption read 'Watermelons to Market.' The cover photograph showed an unnamed black man—shirtless and well muscled—sitting with his back to the camera atop a wagonload of melons."[7] And Johnson was correct in his thinking that Black people were as ready for their own glossy with affirming images instead of degrading ones. *Ebony* sold out its initial press run, moving all twenty-five thousand copies of that November 1945 issue.

For decades to come, *Ebony* would continue to display what it meant to achieve success in settings where that entailed breaking barriers.

"*Ebony* was first and foremost, in John Johnson's mind, a blueprint for success," Charles Whitaker told me. "The classic *Ebony* story was 'X black person overcomes all of these adversities and now is at the top of their game'—whatever that game may be, the top of their career, they have scaled the mountain, despite all of the slings and arrows that they had to endure along the way."

Whitaker was first an editor at *Ebony* from 1985 to 1992. He then returned in 1999 and stayed at the publication until 2001. And even during his tenure, in the '80s and '90s, he says, there were just so many firsts to write about. "There was a joke amongst us junior editors, when I was there, where we dubbed *Ebony* the 'Chronicle of African American Firsts': You write about the first Black whatever, the first Black fill-in-the-blank.... There were still Black people who were cracking glass ceilings, but I came to appreciate how important that is, how important it is to sort of single out those people who are having these monumental accomplishments but also saying to young people, 'Yes, you may be enduring this, but look at what this person endured and how much they were able to achieve.'"

Unlike the many Black newspapers that were prevalent at the time, like the *Defender*, Johnson intended for *Ebony* to, as he had written in its first issue, "mirror the happier side of Negro life—the positive, everyday achievements from Harlem to Hollywood."[8] In that vein, covering the many firsts was a way the magazine could be more celebratory. And yet, Johnson added, "when we talk about race as the No. 1 problem of America, we'll talk turkey." Profiling Black achievement still meant recognizing the significant work that went into reaching those never-before-seen heights.

When Whitaker wrote these features, he tried to show how these firsts were collective wins, highlighting the importance of community and those who supported their rise. "I personally tried to write those stories in a way that really showed what it took, that it wasn't necessarily that these people were magical and mythical and so much better than everyone else—even though they had to demonstrate that they were better than everyone else—but there also was a village of people behind them who saw something special in them and also helped them up that mountain. So these weren't singular individual achievements necessarily; these were community achievements.

"That's an important message that I don't think we hear enough of today: Yes, people are going to rise, and we'll have these great accomplishments," Whitaker continued. "But behind them, it's not just their parents, there's usually a whole raft of people who are behind them, making this possible. It takes a village, as they say, right? And so I tried to sort of write as much about the village as I did about the person, and that was really important."

Not only was *Ebony* highlighting these community successes, it was also the very realization of it. Neither John nor Eunice Johnson grew up wealthy, yet together they created this dream of a place in which Black people could thrive. Working at *Ebony*, whether as a journalist, in its advertising department, or in many other roles, was a crowning achievement. A Black person at *Ebony* would not only be doing meaningful work for Black culture but also working with the best in the business. For Whitaker, an *Ebony* job meant that "Charles Sanders, whose story had first inspired me to work for *Ebony*, was my boss now," he said. "So now I'm working for Charles Sanders, whose story had been so influential in my life."

On top of being a talented musician, Sanders was an experienced reporter who came to *Ebony* from a Black newspaper, the *Cleveland Call & Post*. In his early days as an associate editor at *Ebony*, Sanders had traveled to Sweden to cover Dr. Martin Luther King receiving the Nobel Peace Prize in 1963. And in 1965 he went to Paris to open *Ebony*'s first overseas bureau, also writing a column for *Jet* called Paris Scratchpad. When he returned to Chicago, he became *Ebony*'s managing editor.

"Charles Sanders was very good at editing within your voice and making really subtle changes that improved your text so much," Whitaker said. "He would mark it up and you get the copy back, and you were like, 'Oh yeah, that is so much better.' But you didn't feel that he had taken ownership of a piece away from you."

Whitaker also worked with Lerone Bennett, who was a major influence on *Ebony* as a place of historical education. Bennett had joined Johnson Publishing as an associate editor at *Jet* in 1951 before moving over to *Ebony* in 1953.[9] At *Ebony*, he became known for his essays on race, culture, and politics that placed these issues in their historical contexts. He was the first journalist to discuss Thomas Jefferson and Sally Hemings, the enslaved Black woman he had children with, in his 1954 piece "Thomas Jefferson's Negro Grandchildren." He also launched the Ebony Hall of Fame, which ran annually for a decade, using reader ballots and announcing new additions to the Hall of Fame in February during what was then Negro History Week.

"Bennett exerted an immediate influence over the magazine's histori-cal content, employing an understanding of Black history as a 'living history' that would come to underpin much of his later work," histo-rian E. James West wrote about Bennett in his book *Ebony Magazine and Lerone Bennett Jr.*[10] Given Bennett's significant contributions to the publication, he rose to the position of executive editor in 1958. A staple at *Ebony*, he stayed at the magazine for a total of fifty-two years. "I learned a lot from Lerone just by reading his work, because he was such a graceful and elegant writer as well," Whitaker said. "So I modeled a lot of my writing on Lerone's writing."

Whitaker then took on the role of helping develop younger jour-nalists at *Ebony*. It's what might have sparked his love for journalism education. "As I climbed the ranks of *Ebony* and became a senior edi-tor . . . I'd sort of taken on the role of mentoring younger writers and providing more formal guidance about writing and reporting, because there really was not a lot of that because we worked so much. *Ebony* did not believe in freelancers, and so every writer and editor wrote three or four stories per issue. So it's a fast pace, even for a monthly magazine."

And as fast as things moved for the magazine's staff, Johnson Pub-lishing Company wanted to move even faster. Just years after develop-ing *Ebony* as a lifestyle magazine, it wanted to do something that was everywhere, at all times—it wanted a news weekly.

14

WHAT'S HAPPENING IN BLACK AMERICA

"Our mission is to tell it not only like it is but also like it was and like it must be. There are many voices in Black America and we are captive of none. The voices are sometimes contradictory because they are the voices of laborers, professionals, militants, moderates, revolutionaries and street people. JET speaks to, for, about all of them, for all of them make up Black America."
—John Johnson in the publisher's note for the twenty-fifth-anniversary issue of *Jet*, published November 11, 1976

THE JOHNSON PUBLISHING COMPANY introduced *Jet* magazine six years after *Ebony*. The staff at the two magazines worked to carve out different roles as information vehicles. While *Ebony* was a look at Black lifestyle in print, *Jet* was billed as "The Weekly Negro News Magazine."

"*Jet*'s role was to show all that was happening in the Black community," Charles Whitaker said. "The unofficial tagline for *Jet* was 'If you didn't see it in *Jet*, it didn't happen in Black America.' So it was a digest of everything."[1]

Because of its creation at the beginning of the 1950s, a decade that was particularly tumultuous for Black America, *Jet* and its staff of highly skilled journalists—including reporters, photographers, editors, and more—were properly placed to capture and report key events. The president at the time was Harry S. Truman, who after succeeding the late Franklin Roosevelt in 1945 was in the middle of his first (and only) elected term. Truman had been voted back into office with the support of Black voters and the NAACP, so Black leaders were vocal in discussing what they wanted from him.

Black labor leader A. Phillip Randolph was the organizer of the first successful Black union, the Brotherhood of Sleeping Car Porters, which was created to support the Black porters who worked on the Pullman railroad cars. As he said at a Senate Armed Services Committee hearing, "I personally will advise Negroes to refuse to fight as slaves for a democracy they cannot possess and cannot enjoy."[2] Under pressure from Randolph and other Black leaders, Truman had signed Executive Order 9981 on July 26, 1948. It abolished segregation in the armed forces and established the President's Committee on Equality of Treatment and Opportunity in the Armed Services to recommend revisions in military regulations to achieve desegregation.[3]

The official launch of the civil rights movement, by some accounts, was the meticulously planned bus boycott that began on December 1, 1955, when longtime NAACP member Rosa Parks refused to give up her seat to a white man on a public bus in Montgomery, Alabama. Other accounts mark the official start as the year before, when in the *Brown v. Board of Education* case, the US Supreme Court ruled that public school segregation on the basis of race was unconstitutional. Two years later, on September 3, 1957, the high schoolers known as the Little Rock Nine desegregated Central High School in Arkansas. Days later, on September 9, President Dwight D. Eisenhower signed the first major civil rights legislation since Reconstruction, the Civil Rights Act of 1957, which put in place protections for voter rights.

Because every issue of *Jet* had a feature titled This Week in Negro History, the publication was able to chronicle these events as they occurred. And because it was a Black publication, its recollections of events had the nuance absent from white media publications.

"They had librarians and writers kind of reading everything, to make sure that everything that's happening in Black America was documented somewhere, because so much of it was overlooked or it was only visible in the [local] newspaper that was rooted in that community," Whitaker explained. "So *Jet*'s role was to fan the nation and the world to make sure that everything that was important to Black people—and not just

Black America—was documented, so that there would be a record of this that all of Black Americans, [and] to a certain extent all Black people throughout the diaspora, could see."

It was series of news events, starting with a voting rally, that brought thirty-six-year-old *Jet* reporter Simeon Booker down south. Held in Mound Bayou, Mississippi, in April 1955—almost a year after the *Brown v. Board of Education* decision—the rally became the first time Booker would visit the South to cover civil rights. Weeks later, Rev. George Washington Lee, who was one of the speakers at the rally, was murdered, and Booker returned to investigate it.

Before coming to *Jet*, Booker had been the first full-time Black reporter for the *Washington Post*. But in 1952, John Johnson, who had a knack for snagging top Black talent, hired Booker to build Johnson Publishing's bureau in Washington, DC, where Booker would work for more than fifty years. Booker, a journalist with keen reporting chops, would be a dogged and fearless reporter in his coverage of what was happening in the South.

Another murder in August 1955 rocked the nation and brought Booker to Chicago. When a white mob killed fourteen-year-old Chicagoan Emmett Till while he was visiting family in Money, Mississippi, Booker and *Jet* photographer David Jackson formed a trusted relationship with his mother, Mamie Till-Mobley. In addition to later covering the open funeral on the South Side, Booker and Jackson met Till-Mobley at the train station to retrieve Emmett's remains, and they were both present when she saw his body for the first time at A. A. Rayner Funeral Home.

And so it was *Jet* that published photos of the first moments when Till-Mobley was reunited with her son's body. Jackson's photos are close up and graphically clear. In his coverage, Booker wrote, "Her face wet with tears, she leaned over the body, just removed from a rubber bag in a Chicago funeral home, and cried out, 'Darling, you have not died in vain. Your life has been sacrificed for something.'"[4] And as the rest of the world appeared to move on from Emmett's death, *Jet* did not, continuing to cover updates on the case for months.

This is what many people see as the start of the civil rights movement, and it was Booker and Jackson who helped propel that launch. It's indicative of the power that Black publications have—a role in the media ecosystem that can never be replaced, even if white mainstream publications dramatically improved their coverage of Black communities.

Although *Ebony* and *Jet* were very different publications, what they had in common, of course, was that they both brought an authenticity that made them trusted media sources. "The other key to *Ebony* and *Jet* was writing in an authentic, interpretive voice," Whitaker said. "All events are filtered through the lens of the writer, and all of the choices that we make about what we choose to highlight and what we choose to omit about an event that we have covered, those are subjective choices. . . . That authentic interpretation coming from a Black perspective really matters, and it colors the way that the event is depicted in a way that lands very differently than it often does, even with the most well-intentioned colleague who is not of the Black community. There is nuance that is sometimes lost."

Nuance is something that stands out as original and irreplaceable about Black media. This was a key talking point during my interview with Danielle Robinson Bell, assistant professor of integrated marketing communications at the Northwestern University's Medill School of Journalism. "That's the power of nuance, right? It's just not only in the visuals, but the copy spoke to the target audience in a way that resonated with them and reflected their lived experiences, and there are nuances to that that get missed."[5]

Danielle, an expert in how brands and organizations connect with audiences, went deep into how, both in marketing and journalism, it's that nuance that makes the difference. That's what makes it work. "At the end of the day, you can't research and insight your way into someone's authentic lived experience and have it be reflected in media in a way that resonates with the audience themselves," she said. "It's just not enough."

John H. Johnson passed away in 2005 and Eunice Johnson in 2010, but not before their legacy was cemented as the royal family of Black magazine publishing. By the early aughts, *Ebony*'s circulation had reached about 1.8 million and *Jet* an estimated 900,000.[6] Although the now digital-only magazines have traded hands among other owners, the direction of the brand lies with new Ebony Media owner Eden Bridgeman Sklenar, who says she's building on the brands' history while preparing them to launch into the future.

"[We need to be] that home or safe space that the voiceless can turn to and be heard," she told *Ebony* in March 2021. "[Publishing] the images of Emmett Till took 'boldness,' which is one of the pillars we're standing upon on this rebirth. [Bringing what was happening in America] to a place where you couldn't not talk about it—where you had to face what was really happening. So we want to be a medium for those conversations to happen, but also a place for the healing to happen."[7]

15

CELEBRATION OF BLACK CUISINE

"So many people looked to Ebony for recipes that they were familiar with, or had been part of our culture. And I think that's why people loved that column so much. Maybe they didn't get the recipe for their grandmother's pancakes or sweet potato pie. But we could create it for them, and we would bring all of that stuff to life."

—Charlotte Lyons, who became *Ebony*'s
food editor in 1985, to the *New York Times*

WHILE AT A BLACK HISTORY MONTH event focused on the connection between art and food, Cliff Rome, a Chicago chef and restauranteur, said something extremely profound: When you think about Black history, Black culture, and Black community, Black cuisine played some part in it. "Food is such a connector," he told the crowd. "[If] you think about anything you go to do, it's food—food is always at the base of it."[1]

There isn't one kind of Black American cuisine. Even traditional soul food recipes differ depending on the region of the United States they're made in. But the celebration of Black cuisine, collectively, and what it means to Black people is what makes it special. That celebration often stemmed from Chicago—specifically, downtown at the Johnson Publishing Company building.

Ebony editor Charles Whitaker spoke on how the food served at

Johnson Publishing Company played a part in making the company the
"it" place to visit. Anyone who was anyone made their way there. "The
thing about Johnson Publishing Company that I didn't fully appreciate
until I started working there was what a draw it was for the Black elites,
for celebrities, for politicians of all sorts," Whitaker told me. "And so in
my second week there, James Baldwin stops by and there's a company-
wide luncheon for James Baldwin. And so we're sitting having lunch—
with James Baldwin."[2]

The *Ebony* cafeteria was one of the places at the JPC building where
everything went down. The women who cooked there made amazing
soul food dinners and lunches every single day, and so it also became
the spot where famous people would stop on by for lunch. "I wasn't
expecting famous, legendary, iconic people just to be dropping in and
having lunch," Whitaker continued. "And then Sammy Davis Jr. drops
by, and so he's there with Frank Sinatra and Liza Minnelli—because they
were on tour together—and they come by and have lunch."

Every day was special, but when illustrious figures in the Black community were coming for lunch, the ladies in the cafeteria pulled out all
the stops. "You have these sumptuous, magnificent meals with these
famous people just kind of shooting the breeze with John Johnson and
[*Ebony* editor] Lerone Bennett and Bob Johnson, who was the editor
of *Jet*," Whitaker said.

Outside of the lavish lunches for famous guests at JPC, *Ebony* had
robust food editorial work that displayed the breadth and importance
of Black cuisine. Archived issues of *Ebony* show just how much the
publication celebrated Black food on its pages.

Much of this work was led by home service director Freda DeKnight.
DeKnight was *Ebony*'s first-ever food editor. Culinary historian Dr. Jessica B. Harris, author of the book turned Netflix special *High on the
Hog: A Culinary Journey from Africa to America*, called DeKnight "the
national, if not international, face of African-American food."[3] With
Ebony's readership reaching countries around the world, that's a pretty
accurate description of this trailblazer's work.

DeKnight's own book, *The Ebony Cookbook: A Date with a Dish*—
now republished as *A Date with a Dish: Classic African-American Recipes*—is a collection of her columns. She explained within that there had
long been a need for a nonregional cookbook with diverse recipes from
Black people all across the United States. "It is a fallacy, long disproved,

that Negro cooks, chefs, caterers and homemakers can adapt themselves only to the standard Southern dishes, such as fried chicken, greens, corn pone and hot breads," she wrote. "Like other Americans living in various sections of the country, they have naturally shown a desire to become versatile in the preparation of any dish, whether it is Spanish, Italian, French, Balinese, or East Indian in origin."

Yet her book, DeKnight said, is also a celebration of the origins of Black cuisine in the country and an ode to all those cooks who found innovative ways to create their meals. "Years ago, some of our greatest culinary artists were unable to read or write but their ingenuity, mother wit and good common sense made them masters in their profession without the aid of measuring equipment or science," she wrote. "Needless to say, the old methods they used were tried and true, and no matter how advanced the art of cooking is today, therein lies the basic success of the 'old school' cookery."[4]

DeKnight passed away in 1963 at just fifty-four years old, and decades later, new food editors Charla Draper and then Charlotte Lyons would carry forward her vision. Enter the Ebony Test Kitchen—a state-of-the-art space designed to create, cook, and test new recipes. Often described as psychedelic, the kitchen walls had swirls of multiple shades of orange, sage green, and deep purple in a marbled pattern that was undeniably original. Light green cabinets and countertops and a bright orange refrigerator finish off the very '70s look.

Although the kitchen was originally designed when the Johnson Publishing Company building was first completed, Draper told me she was the very first *Ebony* editor to cook in there after her hiring in 1982. "My goal when I went into the test kitchen position was to say, 'I'm going to get this test kitchen up and running, and it's going to be equivalent to any kitchen in a general market facility,'" she said, having come to *Ebony* from Kraft Kitchens, where she was supervisor of grocery products.[5]

When she got to *Ebony*, she wanted to push it forward by making changes that resonated with the *Ebony* reader. "For example," Draper said, "I initiated a column called Reader Favorite Recipe. And with that section, I would ask people to send in their favorite recipe for cobbler, or sweet potato pie, or spareribs. I would give them the food subject or topic, and we got hundreds of recipes."

Draper would narrow those hundreds of entries to about ten to twenty, then prepare them in the Ebony Test Kitchen. From there, she'd narrow the group down to finalists, and the Johnson Publishing Company employees would come taste them and vote on their favorite.

"The recipe would appear in the magazine, and the reader would get a shout-out with their name and the city and state they were from, and then the reader would also get a twenty-five-dollar honorarium," she said. "And that resonated with people. That gave them an opportunity to be more involved with what was in the food section. It let me know they were paying attention. That was one of the things that was very rewarding."

As she worked in her role, Draper noticed something else: that *Ebony* could be making much more money from its food section. "One of the things that I was able to do during my tenure was help the magazine gain more food advertising," she said. "Traditionally, African Americans spend more money on food prepared in the home than the general market consumer. However, *Ebony* wasn't getting the advertising that represented the amount of money we were spending on food in the home."

Draper, who came to *Ebony* not only with industry experience but with a master's degree in marketing communications from Roosevelt University, knew how to update the food sections. The Date with a Dish column appealed to advertisers. "By updating the food section and creating some elements that kept the readers engaged and made the section more attractive to both *Ebony* readers and potential advertisers, I was able to help increase food advertising."

Charlotte Lyons, who had come from Betty Crocker, took over from Draper in 1985, and in the process gave celebrities like Janet Jackson, Gregory Hines, and Mike Tyson tastes from the famous kitchen. She served as food editor for twenty-five years before the kitchen was closed in 2010 when the Johnson Publishing Company building was sold. Fearing that the kitchen could be lost, in 2018 Landmarks Illinois bought the test kitchen and removed it from the building.

In 2022 this important piece of history was in the news again, because the kitchen became part of an exhibit at the Museum of Food and Drink in Brooklyn titled *African/American: Making the Nation's Table*. Jessica B. Harris is its lead curator.

"Food pages at *Ebony*, quite simply, celebrated what we now call the African diaspora," Harris said in a video about the test kitchen. "It expanded the kitchens of African Americans."[6]

Part VI

BLACK LUXURY, BABY

FIRST TASTE OF BEAUTY

Written while listening to "Have You Seen Her" by the Chi-Lites

> "When they found out how much money I was going to spend, word got around."
>
> —Eunice Johnson

THERE IS A CERTAIN ART to dressing as a Black woman. Sometimes it's big: winter furs, bright colors, shiny things. And sometimes it's subtle: a new pair of shoes, a well-made bag, a carefully applied dab of your signature lipstick color.

"My mom loves Fashion Fair," my friend Danielle said at one of our breakfast adventures. "When you bought something from Fashion Fair—and you still do to this day—she would go to the Fashion Fair counter, and after making a purchase, she would get samples."

These baby-sized lipsticks were perfect for a tiny Danielle, who was playing with beauty and learning to experiment. "She would get these little samples of lipstick," she continued. "And if you can imagine the hands of like a three-year-old little girl, it would be perfect size for my hands. It would be like a little vial, I couldn't even like turn it, it would just be that little thing of that shade. And oh my God! I loved it. I would put them in my little purse, and [my mom] would let me put it on."

I can imagine a little girl putting on her makeup and gliding around the house because it made her feel beautiful, fun, and grown up—like her mom. "It was just such a fond memory of not just my mother, but I knew it was Fashion Fair," Danielle added. "I knew it was this brand that she knew and loved. I'm forty-four so we're talking about forty-some-odd years ago. To this very day, my mother still talks about Fashion Fair."

The reason why I can envision a little Danielle is because I can vividly remember a little Arionne doing the same thing with my mama. It made me think about my own connection to makeup. "Fashion Fair was iconic in the Black community," my mama remembered. "Every fashionable Black woman that I know had one or two products, even if they didn't have the whole line."

My Addie, my daddy's mom, taught my mama an important fashion rule she would later teach me, one that could make you feel luxurious even if you didn't pay a ton of money: always pay attention to your head and your feet, even if you feel like a mess in between. So we spent a lot of time and effort on our face, hair, and shoes. It didn't necessarily mean spending a ton of money. But it did mean that pulling those things together could make most outfits look amazing. It's probably why even today I feel most comfortable in a strong, brightly colored lipstick and a pair of Nikes—anything in between is just a bonus. And by watching my mama, I learned even more lessons that she didn't even have to say: it's OK to add a high heel in the middle of winter; match as much or as little as you want; your skirt can be whatever length you want it to be; have signature colors.

As far as makeup, she said it was the touch of just a little bit of Fashion Fair lipstick that helped complete her glamorous looks. "I used to love a red, sometimes a pink," she told me, "but especially a red."

I must get that from her. Today I can get "Catfight," a vivid red, or "Magenta Mist," a bright purplish pink, from my local Sephora, because Fashion Fair is back—and it's owned by two Black women.

Desiree Rogers, who is also the CEO of the makeup and skincare line Black Opal, bought the company along with her partner Cheryl Mayberry McKissack in 2019. Both women are former *Ebony* executives who had influential roles at Johnson Publishing Company, with extremely long résumés. Rogers had huge roles at other companies, such as being director of the Illinois Lottery, the president of Peoples Gas and North Shore Gas, and president of social networking at Allstate Financial. Then she took on White House roles as the special assistant to the president and the social secretary under President Barack Obama.

She did all of that before joining Johnson Publishing as its president in 2010.[1] McKissack's résumé is equally impressive. In addition to several years at top companies such as IBM and US Robotics, she was the COO and president of digital at Johnson Publishing Company and then CEO of Ebony Media Operations.

They are two women who are more than equipped to carry on the legacy of the iconic Eunice Johnson. While she and her husband, John Johnson, built a Black media empire, Eunice identified and successfully filled a void in fashion and beauty while raising millions for charity with the Ebony Fashion Fair. It started as a tour to two hundred cities across the United States, Canada, and the Caribbean, and featured fashion from the finest of design houses, often handpicked by Johnson herself. When she realized the difficulty in finding makeup to match the tour's models, in true Black woman form, she made her own.

Even the legendary Naomi Campbell has memories of wearing the brand as a girl with her mother. "I learned from looking at what my mother used to do," she told *Vogue* in a 2020 video of her ten-minute makeup routine.[2] "So I used to sneak into my mother's makeup bag, which she had Fashion Fair and Flori Roberts, which were the only brands you could find those days for dark skin."

So let's highlight some of the industry-changing fashion and beauty that started right here in Chicago—what it looked like then and what it looks like now.

16

MAKING FASHION FAIR
FOR EBONY SKIN

"Mrs. Johnson took her job, and her personal shopping, quite seriously. Her spending budget for the European fashion shows was huge, and she was interested in only the best, most opulent examples of high fashion. With her daughter, Linda, by her side, she broke barricades, shopping at the important Italian houses of Valentino and Emilio Pucci. When she first went to Paris in 1958, doors reluctantly opened to these well-dressed, turned-out, beautiful brown-skinned Americans with a thick checkbook."

—André Leon Talley in *The Chiffon Trenches*

WHEN JOY BIVINS WAS WORKING ON an exhibition about Ebony Fashion Fair, she knew it would also be "about introducing people to the fabulous Eunice Johnson."[1] Bivins, who is now director of the Schomburg Center for Research in Black Culture in Harlem, was the director of curatorial affairs at the Chicago History Museum when she was working on *Inspiring Beauty: 50 Years of Ebony Fashion Fair*.

"I was interested really in the social history and the impact of this Johnson Publishing Company in general," she told me in an interview. "And so it was a great kind of way to think about how you can use these really beautiful things, which could have just been its own exhibition, to really tell a story about Black folks in Chicago and the ways in which the Ebony Fashion Fair traveled the country and then had an international presence."

The Ebony Fashion Fair had been the baby—and later success story—of Eunice Johnson of the Johnson Publishing Company. Fashion icon André Leon Talley described her as "a true visionary, impeccable in style, and a self-educated American who loved beauty, art, and most of all, fashion."[2]

(After Talley was forced to resign from his post as Paris editor at *Women's Wear Daily* in 1980, it was Eunice Johnson who called him. She flew him out to Chicago and hired him on the spot as *Ebony*'s New York–based fashion editor—paying Talley the exact same salary he had at *WWD*. For him, this meant a great deal. "My family did not read *WWD* at all, nor would they even have known where to purchase that publication," he wrote in his autobiography, *The Chiffon Trenches*.[3] "But they all subscribed to and read the monthly *Ebony*, as well as *Jet*. . . . Finally, I had a job that would make my entire church family and all my aunts and cousins proud.")

Ebony Fashion Fair as a concept had started as part of the magazine and was curated by home service director Freda DeKnight—the same editor who had led *Ebony*'s food section and created the Date with a Dish column. DeKnight would travel to fashion capitals of the world, such as Paris and Milan, to acquire clothing for *Ebony*'s pages. It is customary in the fashion industry for clothes to be borrowed or simply given to magazines—fashion editors should not have to purchase them—but many designers did not see any value in putting their clothes on Black models.

The fashion show itself had a modest start in 1958 as a small fundraiser. Two years earlier, Jessie Covington Dent—a New Orleans pianist, teacher, and community leader—had asked Johnson Publishing Company to sponsor a fashion show fundraiser for the Women's Auxiliary of Flint-Goodridge Hospital in her hometown. And after its success, Eunice Johnson decided to take the show on the road, raising money for other charities.[4]

For the fifty years it ran, it raised over $55 million for charities. But first the Fashion Fair had to surmount a series of hurdles, such as traveling through the still-segregated South and convincing major fashion houses to change how they thought about Black people in fashion—tall feats for anyone.

But Johnson was no stranger to adversity. Born in Selma, Alabama, in 1916, she received an undergraduate sociology degree from Talladega College in 1938 before moving to Chicago and receiving a master's degree in social work from Loyola University. It was here where she met John Johnson, and they married in 1941. Even after she was well known and her business thriving, Eunice Johnson still had to face racial discrimination. "It was difficult for her, the only black woman on the front row of houses, navigating and decimating the often-nuanced discrimination," Talley wrote. "While she quietly built up her reputation, she supported the industry and established a standard for her shows."[5]

Johnson was determined to use her influence to expand fashion's view of Black women, both in the industry and as consumers. If you scroll through editorials and watch videos from New York Fashion Week today, the decades-long push for diversity in the fashion industry can be seen as models of all colors and many more sizes are taking their rightful place in the pages of elite magazine and on runways wearing the world's top fashion houses.

Eunice Johnson is to thank as a pioneer of such efforts. In 2001, she told the *New York Times* that in the 1960s, it was Ebony Fashion Fair that had convinced Italian designer Valentino Garavani to use Black models in his shows. "I was in Paris, and I told him: 'If you can't find any Black models, we'll get some for you,'" she said. "'And if you can't use them, we're not going to buy from you anymore.' That was before he was famous."[6]

The Ebony Fashion Fair exhibition Bivins curated in 2013 was about this kind of influence, but also about *Ebony*'s desire to bring luxurious fashion looks that appeal to Black women's aesthetics. Virginia Heaven, the consulting costume curator, worked with Bivins to review thirty-five hundred ensembles to choose sixty-seven to display, all organized around three themes: vision, innovation, and power.[7]

"What we wanted to do is look at the ways in which the Fashion Fair was part of that project to show the best of a Black culture, to really represent Black beauty through the acquisition and then the exhibit of these objects—these beautiful, beautiful costumes, if you will," Bivins said. "But also the ways in which they were chosen with an eye towards what Black women in particular would respond well to."

As the Fashion Fair continued to grow, so did the level of clothing that was displayed. "The fabrics became more luxurious and glamorous:

lots of fur, lots of leather, lots of sequins; these complete looks, the ways in which the models display that the garments were also part of it," Bivins said.

No matter where Black people were, the Ebony Fashion Fair would bring this luxury to them, even if they didn't live in a fashion or commercial capital. Looks from designers such as Christian Dior, Givenchy, Yves Saint Laurent, and Alexander McQueen would be coming to towns and cities in all parts of the country.

"One of the places that I learned that the Fashion Fair was really big in is like Rochester, New York," Bivins said. "There's New York City, where you can see the height of fashion, but then there would be the smaller venues or smaller geographic locations where you would get the same show that I would get in Chicago or in L.A. or where have you. . . . There were just places where you're not necessarily going to have access to these kinds of garments in the department store. But you could see them on the stage at Fashion Fair."

Black folks are no stranger to fashion shows as fundraisers, whether it's in a grand ballroom or a church fellowship hall. And the Ebony Fashion Fair gave attendees something great in return: when they purchased the ticket for the Fashion Fair, they received either a year subscription to *Ebony* or a six-month subscription to *Jet*. "People of all kinds of organizations do fashion shows for fundraising purposes," Bivins said. "But the show not only had obviously this wonderful fashion component to it—all the best designers and top fashion designers—but it was also a platform for Black organizations to raise money for scholarships and whatever their philanthropic goals were."

Bivins pointed out that both *Ebony* and the Ebony Fashion Fair were influencing audiences, and those same audiences were also influencing what was on the stage. Eunice Johnson, who cared deeply about her audience, wanted to know what they liked and what would please them. "The thing is, it's an interplay," Bivins said. "It's not just the publication influencing Black culture but also Black culture influencing what was in the publication as well. So it's a back-and-forth, and in that way, it's a celebration of a certain aesthetic, certain aesthetic tendencies, certain ways, at least in the past, that Black people—Black women in particular—showed up in public."

How those audience members showed up to the Fashion Fair proved that fashion is just as much reality as it is fantasy: dressed in furs, sequins, freshly pressed suits, whatever was their best. Even if they don't have the money or resources to buy the newest clothes, a pillar of Black women's fashion has always been what many in the community call being "well put together."

"Fashion is in many ways fantasy, but there are realities to it: Most people are not buying couture or alta moda or what have you, but the ways in which one puts oneself together was very much kind of part and parcel of the show," Bivins explained.

That balance is something that drove Eunice Johnson in her work year after year. "The vision of style, grace, and elegance that were on the pages of *Ebony* were all the vision of my mother, Eunice Johnson," Linda Johnson Rice said during a 2021 interview. "She wanted to take you on a journey with her. She wanted to bring Paris to you."[8]

As the Ebony Fashion Fair grew in popularity, not only did it show how the fashion industry mistreated Black people, but it also exposed other flaws—like broader issues in beauty. There were few cosmetic brands that had shades for Black models. Models had to mix their makeup to find the right match, so with so few options, there was a clear opening in the market.

The Johnsons launched the cosmetic line Fashion Fair in 1973. It was advertised in *Ebony* and *Jet*, and customers could initially purchase the makeup only by mail order. That in itself was an accomplishment, but the Johnsons also wanted Black women to be able to walk into a department store and buy makeup that matched them, the same way non-Black women could. John Johnson then went and negotiated counter space at Marshall Field's in downtown Chicago to corner that market as well. The brand grew exponentially—from one department store in Chicago to twenty-five hundred department stores on three different continents.

"Even if you didn't go to the Fashion Fair shows, you were familiar with the brand, because for some women this is their kind of entry into higher-end cosmetics, because you bought them at [department stores such as] Carson Pirie Scott or at Marshall Field's," Bivins said. "This was a way of, again, that imprint of Johnson Publishing Company not just being about producing magazines but really producing an empire where the brand is everywhere."

And the makeup? It looked impeccable—on its customers and the Ebony Fashion Fair models. Edith Poyer was a product development director for Fashion Fair, working for the company for twenty-five years. She said that the colors were unique and perfect for medium to darker skin tones. "They would be flawless," she told WGN. "I can't find a better way to describe it. And that is what the women who came to the counter, and stood in line, waiting sometimes they were 10 deep waiting. We were considered a powerhouse in our day."[9]

With Revlon, Avon, and Max Factor trying to follow closely behind Fashion Fair with lines of their own, Fashion Fair stayed in the lead for decades, before falling into bankruptcy and folding in 2018. But with its relaunch in 2022, co-owner Desiree Rogers is reimagining the brand with its legacy in mind, asking the question "What would Mrs. Johnson do?"

"She was such a trailblazer, such a trendsetter," Rogers told Lindsay Peoples Wagner, editor in chief at The Cut.[10] "What does Fashion Fair look like in 2021? . . . It's not about copying. It's about reclaiming that position that we once had in 1973, being that trailblazer, being a little bit different."

17

THE LIMITLESS ART
OF FASHION

"Abloh forced a shift in who is allowed to be taken seriously by
the industry at large. He was a young Black man breaking all
the rules, and influencing a generation through his instinctual
talent."
  —Fashion journalist Scarlett Newman in her *Teen Vogue* piece
            "What Virgil Abloh Left Behind," January 2022

ARCHITECT, DJ, ARTIST, FASHION DESIGNER—it's not a stretch to say that
Virgil Abloh was anything he wanted to be. Abloh was once the creative
director for his friend Kanye West, but the designer was more than his
celebrity ties. The Chicago-area native (he grew up in nearby Rockford,
Illinois) worked from an architecture student at Illinois Institute of Technology to the artistic director of menswear at Louis Vuitton—the first
Black person to hold such a position at the iconic French fashion house.

"Virgil Abloh that was someone that I looked to, being an immigrant
kid, [and] his parents were from West Africa as well," artist Adeshola
Makinde told me in an interview about Abloh, a first-generation Ghana-
ian American. "That was someone that was like a North Star in terms of
what was possible, and so definitely in terms of [being from] Chicago."[1]

In 2019, Chicago's Museum of Contemporary Art opened an exhibit,
Virgil Abloh: Figures of Speech, celebrating his love of architecture; his
luxury streetwear label, Off-White; and his other fashion-forward work

in the visual arts. One of the exhibition's displays was actually his IIT master's thesis: a design for a downtown Chicago skyscraper that leaned toward Lake Michigan "like a tree bending toward sunlight."[2] These Chicago ties were a clear through line of the exhibit. A large-scale replica of the CD case of the *Yeezus* album that he designed for Kanye seemed to physically center the exhibition, which also showed racks of clothes, his architectural designs for Chicago, and influences from his DJ career.

And maybe it's because of this thinking—that anything and everything can be art—that Abloh was also the king of the remix. He believed that changing even just 3 percent of something creates something totally new. That was visible in a display of seventy-five shoes, each pair changed slightly (color, laces, structure) to create new pairs. "Streetwear in my mind is linked to ['ready-made' art pioneer Marcel] Duchamp," he told the *New Yorker* in 2019. "It's sampling. I take James Brown, I chop it up, I make a new song. I'm taking IKEA and I'm presenting it in my own way. . . . It's Warhol—Marilyn Monroe or Campbell's soup cans."[3]

Carrie Shepherd, then a journalist for WBEZ, interviewed Abloh for the opening of the exhibit. He explained pretty clearly his reasoning for how seemingly different industries—which all were a part of him—are connected. "We're not talking about fashion just in the silo of fashion," he told her. "We're talking about fashion in the silo of an institution of art."[4] And fashion is art. Abloh showed that through his work and his design partnerships with everyone from retail brands like Nike and IKEA, even everyday brands like McDonald's and Evian.

In 2021, Abloh died from cancer at the age of forty-one, and months later, fashion journalist Scarlett Newman penned an in-depth feature on Abloh's life, "What Virgil Abloh Left Behind: Black Creatives Remember the Designer's Impact on Fashion," for *Teen Vogue*. "It's as if now the fashion industry exists in two realms: Before Virgil, it was an industry slow to shift the needle and firmly rooted in tradition," she wrote. "It was often disinclined to loosen its reins, and make way for the new guard to lay its own foundation. But after Virgil emerged on the scene, a shift happened. A shift in ideas, in who made the rules, and in how we define luxury."

In an interview, Newman told me how Abloh's legacy involved exploding the box that Black designers are put in, especially when he was named to his post at Louis Vuitton in 2018. "He's the first one to come from streetwear to hold a title like that in an industry, where previously, streetwear has been looked down upon—it's heavily associated with Black folks, so we're still in a time where fashion is reckoning its relationships and its proximity to the Black community."[5]

When Abloh started his brand Off-White in 2012 and premiered his first line at Paris Fashion Week in 2013, he showed how streetwear could be—and should be—considered luxury. Even then, going from streetwear to a design house like Louis Vuitton seemed like a far leap, but it was a leap Abloh had no problem making, even as others in the industry doubted him. "People were dismissing him, dismissing Off-White, dismissing what he had the capability to do," Newman explained. "And then, [he went on to] start his own line, Off-White, generate a conversation around that—kind of changing the idea of what streetwear means in the grand landscape of fashion."

Ignoring the doubters, Abloh showed his first collection for Louis Vuitton at Paris Fashion Week in 2018, wowing the industry with a collection he named "Colour Theory," a rainbow of colors that bounced off the runway in the gorgeous Palais Royal gardens.

"To go on and become creative director, lead design at Louis Vuitton Men, probably heralded as one of the greatest design houses in the world, it is just really wild to me even saying it out loud," Newman said.

Abloh was armed with engineering and architecture degrees and a wealth of experience, but he had no formal fashion training. He would tell everyone his mother taught him how to sew, and those who knew him spoke about the clothing they would make together, even back in his younger days. "When you're at the top of these ateliers, you're expected to have come from Central Saint Martins or any of the top design schools, really put in your hours, and you're supposed to have cut your teeth at these institutions—things that he did not do," Newman said. "He had a completely alternate route to high fashion, and the white fashion community took an issue with that. It really took a few collections at Louis Vuitton for people to really understand that Virgil was a talent and wasn't just this kid making graphics for Kanye West.

"To be able to go from that to Louis Vuitton, it just goes to show you that hard work, good work, consistency, originality—these are things that clearly the fashion industry values, and it is possible for us Black folks to achieve great heights within high fashion." With his fearlessness and resulting success, Abloh was—and still is even after his passing—a huge inspiration. He proved that the limits, placed on Black people in fashion by an industry that did not value what people like him contributed, did not exist.

"I don't think you have to know Virgil Abloh's personal struggles to be able to see how tough a journey it was to reach that height at Louis Vuitton," Newman said. If you think about like how he came up, he has all of these degrees, he has this incredible portfolio of design work . . . and the reception to Off-White from journalists, from fashion industry insiders is very dismissive."

For decades, streetwear, created and primarily boosted by Black people in urban centers, was dismissed as not being true fashion by the white gatekeepers who were given the power to determine what was fashion and what was not. "You could just read the press around it at the time: The people in fashion at the top, they don't have a concept of what streetwear really is to its core, because ultimately those are all white people," Newman said. "Streetwear is made up by Black folks. White folks in the fashion industry don't care about Black folks. I mean, I'm a Black person working in the industry, and I'm seeing the effects of that." But today streetwear is viewed in a new and better lens than it was in 2012, Newman says, and that's in part because of Abloh.

Abloh's legacy is twofold: it's both what he created and who he inspired. While there has yet to be anyone who has stepped directly into his shoes—which are extremely large Nikes to fill—he opened a door that's now available for more Black people to walk through, and for those who are outside of the traditional world of high fashion. As fashion journalist Robin Givhan explained in her tribute to Abloh's life for the *Washington Post*, that was his intention. "As he moved through the backstages of Milan and Paris, he blazed a trail and made it plain that he wanted other young Black designers to use the path he cleared."[6]

Part VII

HAIR THAT MAKES A STATEMENT

THE SHINE OF A CROWN

Written while listening to "I Am Changing" by Jennifer Hudson

> "My hair don't get long . . . it get bigger. I'm Black, baby! It get big!"
>
> —Selyna Brillare on Instagram, talking about the gravity-defying hair of Black people

BESIDES MY YAWN, the *click-click-click* of the gas stove would be the first thing I'd hear as I hopped on the kitchen chair my grandma had so artfully positioned in front of it. It would always be at the crack of dawn, or often a bit earlier, when our little Englewood block of Sixty-Eighth and Parnell would still be quiet. No one yet on their way to work, nobody on the bus stop at the corner, no schoolkids giggling as they cut their way through sideways and alleys to get quickly to Parker, the elementary school where I went, or to Robeson, the high school right next to it.

It felt like we were the only ones up as the hot comb sizzled straightness into greased-up pieces of my hair. That was step number one—leaving no edge behind, no piece of frizz missed. I sat very still, not wanting to move and accidentally get burned. ("You'll be just fine if you don't move," Grandma would remind me.) And, of course, wanting to look my very best for Picture Day.

After all, elementary school Picture Day is when you can shine. You wear your best hairstyle and your best dress, and for a little Black girl like me, it meant getting as fresh as possible. Like Easter Sunday fresh, matching ruffle socks and Mary Janes fresh. And like my mama had always taught me, having pride in your appearance can be a way to show the pride you have in yourself. It's what her mama—my grandma who was sick with the pressing comb—instilled in her, and what her mama instilled in her.

When I was growing up, hair care was a huge part of how we were raised. And that's partly because of what it means for us. The presentation of Black people in the world is not a form of vanity. Our hair, clothes, and everything else have been used throughout history to dehumanize us, to create a separation between us and others, and to deny us opportunities. This goes back to slavery, when our appearance was tied to how we were treated and the type of work we were given: for example, working in the enslaver's house meant we had to look a certain way. Even after the legal abolition of slavery, having what was seen as a presentable appearance meant Black people had a better chance at employment.

It's been centuries since, and hair discrimination still occurs. Even today, assumptions are made about Black people of all ages and sexes based on how we wear our hair, especially with locs and other natural hairstyles. For Black girls in particular, studies show, hair discrimination can happen as early as five years old, and as adults, Black women are one and a half times more likely to be sent home from the workplace because of their hair. It's why a team of Black women leaders thought of the CROWN Act ("Creating a Respectful and Open World for Natural Hair"), a proposed law that prohibits race-based hair discrimination. It has been enacted in some form in twenty-three of our fifty states as of July 2023.[1]

So hair care has always been a huge deal in Black households. My aunt was working at Soft Sheen when I was born, and we benefited a lot from her work there. My mama says it made her a pretty popular teacher when my aunt arranged for new products to be donated to the small Catholic school where she taught second grade. Because Soft Sheen, and its growth, is an example of just how essential Black hair care is to Black culture.

In 1979, Soft Sheen Products changed the game of Black hair care when it developed its Care Free Curl line. The company, started out of Edward and Bettiann Gardner's South Side basement, took off when it provided a more innovative way to relax and condition Black hair. And, in the '80s, it was the leader in a new phenomenon—the "Jheri curl." You know: Michael Jackson, Rick James, and like half the cast of the movie *Coming to America*.

Influence? 'Nough said.

Black hair can mean a lot and has had different meanings throughout history: a way to climb social circles and show status; a means of self-expression; a political statement, even. For generations and generations of Black women entrepreneurs, it's also been a way to economically empower communities as women take advantage of the change in cultural trends.

In recent years, I traded in straight tresses for my naturally curly ones, and the hot comb and grease for new curly creams and serums. Like many women in the last ten to fifteen years, I wanted to embrace how my hair looks naturally and work to find solutions to keep it healthy. But the meaning of it all has still been the same: a way to look my best so that I can feel my best, an appreciation of one of the first things you see when you look at me, a direct line drawn from my crown to my academic or professional performance.

On a rainy February morning in 2019, I sat in the office of Monique Rodriguez, founder and CEO of the hair care company Mielle, to interview her for a Black History Month project I never quite finished. I'd ambitiously set out to interview and write about twenty-eight different Black business owners over the course of twenty-eight days. Before the project fell completely off, I did make it to the Mielle headquarters and warehouse to interview Rodriguez about her business. I wanted to know how she'd become one of the most sought-after examples of Black women winning in the beauty industry. At the time, in addition to its top-selling hair care products, Mielle had also launched a skin care line.

Monique Rodriguez is undoubtedly one of Chicago's biggest hair care entrepreneurs right now. Her products are on the shelves of national retailers like Target, Walmart, Walgreens, and CVS—the stores that every burgeoning beauty enterprise dreams of getting placement in. Rodriguez herself is a walking testament not only to hard work as a businesswoman but also to the very products she sells. As a former RN with lush locks that drape down her back, she drew on her love for science to develop products to nurse her own hair back to health. That led to the creation of Mielle in 2014.

"I started talking about hair care and just really sharing my jour-ney, because I used to wear my hair straight all the time and [was] just transitioning from always being straight to wearing my hair naturally curly," Rodriguez said, her locks pinned up in a high bun.[2]

When she decided to become a beauty entrepreneur, Monique said, she had no intention of selling products. Her goal was to open a salon, but using social media to show her own hair became a fruitful marketing tool. Then something else unintended happened. "My intention was not to start [a] product line until I started making different products and posting the recipes online," Rodriguez said. "The feedback was just so overwhelming, because people started asking, 'Can I just buy it? I don't want to make my products, I want to put whatever you put in your hair, because your hair is beautiful.'"

Those people? Those people are me, intensely watching every video to see how it's done while lacking the desire to painstakingly mix and create, wanting the extra-special results but not the extra-special work. Like many other Mielle customers, what I want is to just buy it from the geniuses like Monique Rodriguez who've already figured out the right formula—who already have the key—and for that, we're all will-ing to pay.

And that willingness is something Rodriguez understands. "My focus is to just continue to build and continue to learn and expand my distri-bution," she said. "I want Mielle to be the next P&G, the next household beauty brand like every product that you have [in] your bathroom. I want it to be a Mielle product."

Products—why we need them and what we use them for—is where we start our look into Black hair care and the Black entrepreneurs who built their multimillion-dollar businesses.

18

FROM RESPECTABILITY TO BLACK AND PROUD

"Chicago, in my opinion, is the capital of Negro America. The people here are accomplishing things. The atmosphere is one of commercial striving, endeavor and promise."
— Annie Turnbo Malone

BEFORE THERE WERE large Black hair care companies like Mielle, there was Poro. And before there was Monique Rodriguez, there was Annie Turnbo Malone.

The buzz around Malone most recently amplified after the release of Netflix's *Self Made*—a scripted miniseries based on the life of famed millionaire Madam C. J. Walker. Walker's contribution to the Black beauty industry and to Black economics as a whole has never really been hidden. She's a fixture in Black history, someone often researched for Black History Month projects, someone featured on murals. But Annie Malone's influence has been much less known, even here in the city where her connection to Black Chicago and the state of Illinois goes back to the 1800s.

In the miniseries, Malone is fictionalized as "Addie Monroe." Played by Carmen Ejogo, Monroe is the mean and evil adversary of Walker, played by Octavia Spencer. Although Monroe and Walker were indeed business rivals, the series fails to capture Malone's success. There is argument about who became a millionaire first; both Walker *and* Malone were millionaires with fruitful businesses that included both beauty lines and education.

What is accurately hinted at, however, is Malone being an early inventor of a hair care product formulated for Black hair that had a focus on health and hygiene. Her Wonderful Hair Grower was a product that helped change how Black women took care of their hair, and even the fictionalized version of the Walker-Malone relationship shows Malone as the originator of this formula, which Walker later adapted.

Born in 1869 in Metropolis, Illinois, to two formerly enslaved parents, Annie Malone was not from a family of means. Like Walker, she was orphaned as a child when both her parents died. She too was raised by siblings. She too became a self-made businesswoman.

But Malone was in the industry first. She was good at chemistry, and after years of experimentation, she put those skills to use to create her Wonderful Hair Grower in 1900 to remedy hair loss and breakage. That year, she and her sister moved to Lovejoy, Illinois, a community located on the Mississippi River that's credited as the first Black town to be incorporated (formally called Brooklyn, Illinois).

There, Malone started selling her hair grower door-to-door. The popular product was, according to Kathy Peiss's *Hope in a Jar: The Making of America's Beauty Culture*, made of sage and egg rinses. Its success carried Malone and her sister to St. Louis in 1902, where preparations were underway for the Louisiana Purchase Exposition, also known as the St. Louis World's Fair.[1] Malone had already developed a whole line of products when she met Walker there. Walker became a salesperson for Malone's Poro Company before creating her own product, which she also called Wonderful Hair Grower.

Hair, during this time period, meant more to Black people than just self-expression. Having what was seen as well-groomed or well-maintained hair could open doors for jobs and opportunities held by white gatekeepers. Similar to today's struggles—as shown in recent lawsuits about hair discrimination—a Black person's appearance could often be directly correlated with getting hired and making enough money to feed themselves and their families.

"The market, therefore, was ripe for an Annie Malone or Madam C. J. Walker to introduce a line of health and beauty products made by Black people for Black people," Ayana D. Byrd and Lori L. Tharps wrote in *Hair Story: Untangling the Roots of Black Hair in America*.[2] "Both of these women knew firsthand the unique hair problems Blacks faced in this era, like chronic hair loss and scalp diseases, and tailored their products to address them."

In addition to creating formulas, Malone helped to popularize straightening tools like the hot comb. According to the National Museum of African American History and Culture, her "Marcel Comb" may have been one of the first pressing comb prototypes.[3] Associated Negro Press founder Claude Barnett stated that although it's unclear who invented the hot comb—which likely had several inventors under several names—he believed Malone was the "first to successfully commercialize the idea" for Black women in the US.[4]

Malone trademarked the name "Poro" in 1906 as her business continued to grow. The name itself means "laws of ancestors" in Mende, a language spoken by the largest single cultural group in Sierra Leone.[5] This push to trademark may have been due to competition from new entrepreneurs like Walker.

In 1917, Malone created Poro College to educate her "Poro agents" on how to sell and use her products.[6] Tens of thousands of people worked for Poro. In *The Rise & Fall of the Associated Negro Press: Claude Barnett's Pan-African News and the Jim Crow Paradox*, historian Dr. Gerald Horne wrote that Poro advertised that by 1922, it had "enthusiastic agents in every state in the United States and in Africa, Cuba, the Bahamas, Central America, Nova Scotia and Canada."[7]

In 1930 Malone's beauty college moved from St. Louis to Chicago, where it took up an entire block between Forty-Fourth and Forty-Fifth on Park Way—now King Drive, where the most recent *Chicago Defender* newspaper office sat. That location became known as the "Poro block."

An Associated Negro Press article in the *Afro American* newspaper quoted Malone about her decision to move to Chicago. "We have felt for some time that Chicago was the logical place for our main plant," she said in a statement. "In the first place our volume of business among the 200,000 colored residents of Chicago is larger than at any other single point. Again, we are closer to the sources of supply with consequent savings from a manufacturing and shipping standpoint. Too, Chicago, in my opinion, is the capital of Negro America. The people here are accomplishing things. The atmosphere is one of commercial striving, endeavor and promise."[8]

Malone's 1927 divorce from and subsequent fight with her third husband, Aaron Malone, is regarded as the start of Poro's demise, worsened by the start of the Great Depression two years later.[9] But the company continued to operate until Malone's death in Chicago in 1957.

As with Walker, Malone's success meant more than just that of an individual. In addition to employing and uplifting thousands, both women were philanthropists and staunch supporters of community advancement. "When you bought a jar of Wonderful Hair Grower," authors Byrd and Tharps said, "in essence, you were investing in the future of the Negro race."[10] Hundreds and hundreds of Black women worked for Malone and Walker to support their families, by selling Black-owned products that went into Black homes. The businesswomen then famously—and very intentionally—donated much of their earnings back to Black communities.

This model is one regularly attempted throughout the decades, especially in the beauty industry: from selling door-to-door cosmetics with companies such as Avon and Mary Kay to today's "girl boss" multilevel marketing businesses. The idea that women can take care of their families while also working for themselves is a draw for many women, but especially for Black women, to whom the traditional job market has never been kind.

Hair norms changed in the 1960s, as they often do. Yet this transition in Black hair care was the largest one yet. Previously, straight hair was seen as being closer to whiteness, and being closer to whiteness meant survival and opportunity. But during the civil rights movement, when "Negro" became "Black" and Blackness became something to be celebrated, this ideological shift was reflected in how people wore their hair.

Ayana Contreras, author of *Energy Never Dies: Afro-Optimism and Creativity in Chicago*, said that when thinking about how "Black is beautiful" was viewed at the time, it's important to also take into consideration what the Black Power movement meant then. "The interesting thing is when we talk about Black Power now, we're mostly talking about identity politics," Contreras told me in an interview.[11] "And what we're missing is how much of the original primary definition of Black Power was rooted in, I guess you would say, Black capitalism. But that was what it was about: it was about Black people building economic power in addition to thinking about what it would look like if Black was assumed to be beautiful."

As the trend of tying Black beauty with Black Power grew, so did the market offerings. Based in Chicago, Johnson Products was created by door-to-door salesman George Johnson and his wife, Joan Johnson. They created the company in 1954, and it first gained popularity with a straightening product called Ultra Wave in 1957.

As the '60s began and people wanted to show off big, beautiful afros, Johnson Products created products that could help make afros look their best, the Afro Sheen line. Afro Sheen became Johnson Products' most popular line. Before the company's decline in the late 1970s as large companies entered the Black hair care game, Johnson Products' sales grew to $40 million, and it became the first Black-owned business to trade on the American Stock Exchange.

"So in tandem," Contreras explained, "what you had going on was business incubating, people working together, but then you also had this thread of aesthetic choices that were made to really highlight Blackness [rather than] suppress or oppress or minimize Blackness. And part of that was the afro, because there was a point where, not that long before the afro was en vogue, it was really, really taboo to walk out of the house with your hair unstraightened—extremely taboo."

But it's important to note, Contreras said, that this change is indicative of more than just beauty standards: it shows how those standards are intertwined with political, economic, and societal changes. Before this period, she explained, few Black people wore their hair natural on television—aside from a few trailblazers such as actor Cicely Tyson and jazz singer Abbey Lincoln—because it was seen as "really super controversial for a man, let alone for a woman" to do so.

"I do think that that turnaround happened very quickly," Contreras said. "But it also happens in hand with the push for political representation, for economic power through Blackness."

19

AT THE ROOT OF CHANGE

"We were not into profits per se like, you know, some
companies wanted all the money to be profit. But we didn't
know. Plus when we did know, we still continued to use the
best in our products. I think that's why they were so successful."
—Bettiann Gardner on using the highest grade
of ingredients in Soft Sheen products

INTERVIEWED AND HIRED by Edward Gardner himself, Mary Brooks joined
Soft Sheen Products in 1981 as a sales coordinator, an in-house liaison
for sales representatives across the country. Back then, she says, it was a
"family affair"—but one that was booming with opportunity and growth
just two years after the launch of a product that would define the '80s.

"There was just the one building on Eighty-Seventh Street—1000
East Eighty-Seventh Street—and everybody was in that building," she
told me in an interview.[1] "So there was marketing and sales and customer service and the executive offices and the plant and the shipping
and the quality control. I mean, everything was in that one building."

Soft Sheen had just launched a product that would change its trajec-
tory forever. The shiny, curly, wet Jheri curl was more than just a fad. It
was the setup for Soft Sheen's exponential financial growth. The company's 1979 launch of Care Free Curl capitalized on this wave, dominating
the product market and expanding Soft Sheen into a multimillion-dollar
business. "When I started there, the curl phenomenon had just taken
off, and boy, did it explode," Brooks said.

As reported by *Crain's Chicago Business* in 1995, the company hit $50 million in revenue in 1982, up from $1.5 million in the late '70s. And just ten years later, revenue was up to $91 million.[2] In 1983, Michael Jackson's curl in the music video for "Thriller" cemented the trend. "Soft Sheen Care Free Curl became synonymous with all curl products," Brooks said. "It didn't matter what you had used to get the curl—you had a Care Free Curl. That's how you know the brand just took over with the market, and so we couldn't even keep up with demand." Soft Sheen was boosted into the ranks of companies whose brands became synonymous with general product names: Kleenex, Xerox, Post-its, Band-Aids.

Care Free Curl also helped to push Soft Sheen into head-to-head competition with major competitors such as Johnson Products and Luster Products. Luster was another major Black hair care company from Chicago, founded by Fred Luster Sr., a barber who created the company in 1957 to make products for his clients. Luster created his own relaxer and had been relaxing his own clients' hair before selling the relaxer itself. Luster's products, like its famous Pink Oil Moisturizer, was always a mainstay in Black houses.

Edward and Bettiann Gardner had continued this Chicago tradition of being a hub of Black hair care when they founded Soft Sheen in their Chicago basement in 1964. Like beauty industry entrepreneurs of the past, Edward Gardner knew how to sell. For years he had worked at Chicago Public Schools as a high school teacher and assistant principal, but on the side, the couple bought and sold beauty supplies, traveling to Black hair salons and learning the specific needs of Black hair. "Mr. Gardner had almost been like a Fuller Brush man," Brooks continued, referring to the term coined in 1922 for men who went to homes selling all types of brushes for the Fuller Brush Company, from cleaning to grooming.

When the Gardners created Soft Sheen, their door-to-door sales method continued with its first product: a hair and scalp conditioner. And everyone in the family had a role to play in the business. Like the Johnson and Luster families, the Gardners were ready to contribute to Chicago's blossoming hair care industry. "There's something special about Chicago as far as the Black dynamic," Brooks continued. "Soft Sheen was a leader but not the only company. . . . Chicago—for Black businesses, Black entrepreneurs—was like a mecca back in the '80s. Everybody was doing something."

Chicago was the perfect ground for these Black entrepreneurs. And even with competition, the Black hair care industry was filled with camaraderie. Sales teams like those Brooks was in traveled across the country to the same places and trade shows. Even coming from different companies, they were connected. "For the most part, everybody in sales is like a hustler—they're out to get it," she said. "And so no matter what company you work for, we all had that same kind of mindset, because there was really good money in Black hair care."

But there was something different about the Care Free Curl products that Soft Sheen had developed: it kept Black hair moisturized, which allowed it to thrive and retain length as it grew. In the Black community, "hair has always been top of mind," Brooks said. "So in the '80s, when you start to see people, you know, entertainers that you kind of looked up to with the curl, you wanted the curl, and the fact that it made Black hair [soft]. See, people think Black hair does not grow and that was never the truth."

These new products helped combat a common misconception about Black hair. Throughout the decades, Black-owned hair care companies have continued to combat the mistruth that Black hair does not grow, that it's not easy to manage, that its difference somehow makes it inadequate. These companies had to combat society's singular, white-centered beauty standards. In the 1960s, during the popularity of Johnson's Afro Sheen, came the first wave of the "Black is beautiful" messaging that emphasized the afro and the gravity-defying nature of Black hair. From there, Black performers began embracing a different kind of style in the last half of 1970s—a style that needed its own special products to keep the hair soft. "When you got this Care Free Curl and you had to moisturize constantly, the hair didn't break," Brooks explained. "So it got longer hair. . . . Of course, you had a lot of ladies that hated laundry day because there was oil stains on pillowcases and furniture and seat covers and everything," she joked. "But it was a fad that lasted a long time."

Soft Sheen made millions on Care Free Curl alone. It was the bread and butter that supported the introduction of Optimum Relaxer, Sportin' Waves Pomade, and more bestsellers. Because of this success, employees like Mary Brooks were able to grow along with the company. She moved up the ranks at Soft Sheen to strategic planning manager and strategic vice president, before moving to South Africa in 1994 to work as a consultant and then general manager of a Soft Sheen subsidiary there. "I don't think that kind of growth could have happened in any other environment," she explained. She stayed with the company while she was based in Johannesburg until 1998.

As the Gardners made more money, so did their employees. As with Johnson and Luster Products, Soft Sheen employees were happily tied to the success of their company. "All of them—Mr. Johnson, Mr. Gardner, Mr. Luster—they were all Black businessmen that the people looked up to, and the thing is, they provided a lot of jobs that fed a lot of Black families in Chicago," Brooks said.

As influential businesspeople that communities looked up to, people like Edward Gardner also had voices that carried a lot of weight. And that weight was instrumental. When Harold Washington ran to become Chicago's first Black mayor in 1982, Brooks said, all of Soft Sheen was there to help. "Soft Sheen was one of the biggest supporters of Harold Washington's campaign for mayor," she said. "If we were employees, we [were encouraged] to volunteer to work on the polls."

Washington's run as mayor was against then Cook County state's attorney Richard M. Daley, whose late father, Richard J. Daley, was the city's longest-serving mayor at the time, having served six terms from 1955 to 1976. The younger Daley would later take his father's title by serving as mayor for twenty-two years, but that tenure didn't start in 1982. Awaking the "sleeping giant" of Black people in the city with the support of major city players like Edward Gardner and getting fifty thousand new Black voters to register, Washington won the election. It was a grassroots, from-the-ground-up, people-united kind of movement that got the city its first Black mayor, and the benefit of that achievement paid off far beyond the city limits.

Seen as one of the greatest Black leaders of his time, Washington died from a heart attack seven months after his reelection in 1987, but before his death, he profoundly impacted city politics in a way that can still be felt today. He instituted a Freedom of Information Act order so that people could see government records, made sure there were more underrepresented groups in city government and contracts, fought for Black and Latino representation in ward redistricting, and improved renters' rights. He led the charge for the state's Dr. Martin Luther King Jr. holiday bill, and he made Chicago the first "sanctuary city" when he barred city departments from working with federal immigration enforcement.

In fact, it was the work and presence of Harold Washington that inspired the country's first Black president. "When Harold got elected in 1983, I had just gotten out of college," Barack Obama told WBEZ in February 2018.[3] "And so, I was in New York. I was trying to figure out how I could make a difference in the world. Full of idealism, inspired by the civil rights movement, but there was no movement around at the time. And so, Harold's election was big news."

Harold Washington was able to defeat one of the city's most powerful political families with the power of the people—more than 99 percent of the Black vote and 82 percent of the Latino vote. Affectionately called by his first name, Harold proved anything could be possible. "There was a sense, not just that one of America's largest cities had elected an African-American mayor, but to me more importantly and more interestingly, that it had been a grassroots movement that had swept him into office," Obama continued.

The Gardners viewed such contributions to society as essential and wanted to continue their philanthropic efforts. Passing the leadership baton to their children—their son, Gary, became president of the company in 1985—allowed the Gardners to focus more on social engagement, and that extended to their love for the arts. The original Regal Theater, which was at Forty-Seventh and King Drive in Bronzeville, had a soft place in Bettiann Gardner's heart. So when the couple bought an old theater at the intersection of Seventy-Ninth Street and Stony Island Avenue, they aptly renamed it the *New* Regal Theater.

"We felt that plays should be on the South Side, because we attended a lot of plays and we'd have to travel north up and down one street and, you know, really hard-to-find places," she told HistoryMakers in August 2002. "So we felt that something should be on the South Side for entertainment and entertainers."[4]

It was reported that Edward Gardner had given his wife the theater as a birthday gift—a story that she said was not quite true. "It was something I wanted, and so he went to see it and everything," she said. "And I agreed, but he could not give it to me, because it's owned by the New Regal Theater Foundation, which is a not-for-profit 501(c)(3). So I think that was just a saying that was cute. But it was not accurate."

The New Regal itself was a historic treasure. Also called the Avalon Regal Theater, it extended the legacy of its Bronzeville predecessor. The Gardners used grant money to renovate the theater and open it in 1987, painting a large mural titled *Bright Moments, Memories of the Future* on the building's side to honor performers such as Josephine Baker, Billie Holiday, and Nat King Cole who used to perform at the first Regal. For the next sixteen years, the New Regal was Chicago's premier stop for Black performers. Although the Gardners closed the theater in 2003 due to low attendance and high operational costs, it is now under new ownership and, in recent years, more community members have rallied around fundraising to bring back this cultural institution.

Part VIII

BLACK REPRESENTATION ON THE BIG AND SMALL SCREENS

BLACK AND WHITE
AND TECHNICOLOR

Written while listening to "TV Is the Thing (This Year)" by Dinah Washington

> "I saw the general-market world, the white world. I felt that it was my mission to see to it that black talent had an opportunity to get national television exposure. We wanted to make each show evolve into a shocking moment."
> —Don Cornelius on 1970s television

WATCHING *SOUTH SIDE*, a comedy show that streams on Max, I can't help but laugh. Not just any type of laugh but a fall-out-the-chair, grab-the-remote-and-rewind kind of laugh.

This is because it's so unlike many other shows that supposedly take place on Chicago's South Side (like *Shameless*), which don't even feel like they belong in Chicago, let alone on my side of town. *South Side*, however, which was created by Diallo Riddle and Bashir Salahuddin, filled its writers' room with Chicago writers—and we can tell. The authentic representation gets better with every rewatch, but what I appreciate the most (on top of the belly laughs) is that when I'm watching this show, I feel seen.

Represented.

There's always been a need for representation of Black people on-screen—in film and then later on TV. As long as there has been a film industry, there have been Black people working in it, working to reverse the unfair and harmful depictions that white mainstream filmmakers created. But many people don't know about the wave of Black filmmaking that happened in Chicago.

"The reality is that Black cinema has existed since the early days of silent cinema," Sergio Mims, a film critic and cofounder of the Black Harvest Film Festival, told me. "There have always been these independent Black filmmakers who work outside the studio system, because the studio system—even if it was the studio system in the silent era—they're not going to let Black filmmakers make movies. It was impossible to break into that system. [Mainstream movie companies] weren't going to let them present more realistic images of Black people."[1]

At the dawn of the twentieth century, there was a huge hole in the representation of Black people in films, but there was also a gaping hole in the market. With Chicago's Black population expanding, the city's Black Belt had a thriving theater scene, with its own vaudeville troupes and many, many theaters. The growing crowds of Black residents were hungry for entertainment. Plus, Chicago itself was an epicenter of film-making at the time. Now when we think of the film industry, we mostly think of Hollywood. But that was not the case then.

"I think what people don't realize is just how central Chicago was to the early film industry," said Allyson Nadia Field, a University of Chicago professor and author of *Uplift Cinema: The Emergence of African American Film and the Possibility of Black Modernity*.[2] "A lot was happening right here. Filmmakers, like William Selig, who was based in the South Loop at the time and then moved to studios up north, [and] Essanay Studios [in Uptown]. These were major manufacturers of films. And this was one of the hubs—New York and Chicago—before folks moved west and really founded Hollywood in Los Angeles, because of climate and a lot of other factors. Chicago is one of the main places in the turn of the century and into the teens."

So Chicago provided the perfect opportunity for a Black filmmaker to come in and make history. William Foster took advantage of that opening, making the first Black film by a Black filmmaker with an all-Black cast called *The Railroad Porter*.

In the '50s, as TV rose in popularity, the same opportunity presented itself as with film. Nat King Cole, who grew up in Chicago, was one of the first Black people to host a network television series when *The Nat King Cole Show* went to air in 1956. But because racist sponsors would not sponsor the show, it didn't last. It ended just a year later. That's why it was even more monumental when Don Cornelius created *Soul Train* here in Chicago in 1970, and Chicago-based Johnson Products became the show's sponsor—showing beautiful afros during commercials and pushing the idea that Black is indeed beautiful.

"In a way," secretary of the Smithsonian Lonnie G. Bunch II said about the Johnsons' marketing, "the Johnsons captured the tenor of the time and used that desire to express one's blackness as a key to their marketing strategy. Whenever I think about the commercials, I smile and recall a time when we were all discovering our blackness."[3]

With this long history of showing Black life both in film and on TV, Chicago's massive role in getting Black people on-screen goes back over a century. This city, its South Side, is where it was all birthed.

20

SILENCE AND
THE SILVER SCREEN

"In a moving picture, the Negro would offset so many insults to the race—could tell their side of the birth of this great nation—could show what a great man Frederick Douglass was, the work of Tousant LaOverture, Don Pedro and the battle of San Juan Hill, the things that will never be told only by the Negroes themselves."

—William Foster under his pen name "Juli Jones" in the *Chicago Defender* in 1915

IN THE ERA OF SILENT FILM— the very first version of motion pictures—Black people were shown on-screen as unintelligent and animalistic, dehumanized in every way possible. The example often mentioned is *The Birth of a Nation*. The 1915 silent film by white film director D. W. Griffith takes place during the Civil War and Reconstruction, and it's still widely considered the most racist movie ever made. In it, white people in blackface portray Black Americans as dangerous, and the story implies that the Ku Klux Klan is the only heroic force to stop them. The film was so extremely popular that it became the first feature film to be screened at the White House. And no matter how racist and offensive it is, it is still lauded by some as being "innovative" and the "most artistically advanced film of its day."[1]

But even before Griffith, movies such as *Ten Pickaninnies* in 1904 and *The Wooing and Wedding of a Coon* in 1905 portrayed Black people the same way. In fact, filmmakers like Griffith "just took that from literature that was already available on the stage and vaudeville," Dr. Mark A. Reid, University of Florida professor and author of *Redefining Black Film*, told me in an interview.[2] "And it was very much southern writers who were doing this. But even in Europe, there were these types of images. And so they were borrowing from an international depiction of Black people, and especially the ones who have arrived at a certain class."

Blackface, which had been common in minstrel shows and other forms of entertainment for white people, continued into vaudeville, a kind of theater variety show act. Vaudeville was infamous for its blackface acts, and those acts in turn were a key influence on early filmmakers. The portrayal of Black people in silent film "comes out of always creating Black males as passive, Black females as angry matriarchs; there's no sense of love between a Black male and a Black female," Reid said. "It's not only that, it's also the image that Black people have this desire for white flesh."

William Foster was the trailblazing Black filmmaker who combated this stereotype on film. His company, Foster Photoplay Company, is considered to be the first Black-owned film production company in the US that employed all-Black crews. While not much is known about Foster's early life, *Uplift Cinema* author Dr. Allyson Nadia Field, who is writing a book on Foster, says he was born in Tennessee around 1860 and was likely born enslaved or to enslaved parents. Foster made his way to New York and worked in horse racing before coming to Chicago around age forty.

"He rose to become one of the key figures in the Black cultural scene of the late nineteenth and early twentieth centuries; he's really at the heart of Chicago Stroll," Field told me in an interview.[3] In the 1910s and '20s, the Stroll was the strip of State Street between Twenty-Sixth and Thirty-Ninth Streets seen as the heart of Black culture. It was the spot for both day and night life for Black folks, and it was filled with cafés, theaters, clubs, and other places to gather. "The name 'the Stroll' was actually coined by Foster, at least according to his friend the famed vaudeville and film actor Flournoy Miller," Field said.

When he arrived in Chicago, Foster immediately found himself at the center of this cultural scene. He owned a publishing house for sheet music—the William Foster Music Company. At the same time, he gained valuable entertainment experience as the manager of acts such as comedic duo Bert Williams and George Walker and as the business manager at the Pekin Theatre. Located on Twenty-Seventh and State Street, the Pekin was Chicago's first Black-owned theater and is thought to be the country's first Black-owned theater to have a stock company, a troupe of actors that perform there regularly. And Foster also worked as a journalist: using the pen name "Juli Jones," he wrote for the *Chicago Defender* covering sports and the *Indianapolis Freeman* covering Chicago nightlife.

Foster was interested in continuing to invest in Black culture and Black talent when he made his first film with Foster Photoplay in 1913. Seizing the opportunity to create a film for the same Black audiences he saw attending Black vaudeville shows night after night, he made *The Railroad Porter*. The film, which featured the performers from the Pekin Theatre stock company, is a short comedy about a Pullman porter whose wife is being wooed by a café waiter. This film is credited as being the world's first film with an entirely Black cast and director.

"[*The Railroad Porter's*] sort of this slapstick comedy, but it's interesting, because it really showcased the new professions and modern life that were open to Black people at the time," Field explained. "The hero's the Pullman porter." When the film was screened for audiences at the Pekin and other theaters in Chicago, not only did live music accompany it, as was standard for silent films, but one of the stars of the movie, Lottie Grady, also sang live between reels.

Thinking back to this time—and the likely early life of Foster himself—suggests that the energy in the theaters that showed the film must have been contagious. Black people who had seen firsthand or been the direct descendants of chattel slavery, Black people who had been abused and dehumanized, Black people who were still fighting for their own representation were seeing themselves on-screen as business owners, as workers, as people enjoying their lives. An experience like that could happen here in Chicago because here was where this Black middle-class life was possible. Here is where Black people, just like the fictional character in the film and like Foster himself, were building and creating this new world in the Black Belt. They were, in real life, the heroes of their own stories. "[Foster is] someone who's really engaged with the significance of what moving pictures can mean for a community that had been so misrepresented and underrepresented," Field said. "So he's really someone who understood the power of movies to both denigrate but also to uplift."

In addition to making an average middle-class Black man the hero, the film featured figures prominent in the South Side cultural scene that Chicago audiences would have recognized. "The café waiter—who's this fashionably dressed guy who woos the porter's wife—he's played by Edgar Lillison, who was in fact the proprietor of the popular Elite Cafe," Field said. "So there were all these kinds of in-jokes for Black audiences at the time, who would be watching these films and recognizing these figures that they see every night." Recognizing the faces of folks seen every day walking the Stroll likely made both the film more personal and the slapstick more authentically funny.

The reviews of Foster's screenings show the warm reception they received. The *Chicago Defender* said singer Lottie Grady, who played the porter's wife, was "a howling success" as the Foster Photoplay Company's leading lady. The paper also praised Foster himself, saying, "Mr. Foster is to be congratulated and every encouragement given [to] him. It is always gratifying to see a member of our race embark into a new field of endeavor."[4]

Through his subsequent films, like *The Butler* and *The Barber*, Foster continued to highlight this kind of middle-class hero, but Professor Reid says Foster also never shied away from showing the full depth of Black life and included characters who weren't just squeaky clean. Because he was Black, Foster knew how to give life to these characters and portray them as dynamic as they were in real life. "Sometimes the more exciting part of the Black community is the community outside of the law," Reid said. "There were very famous Black gangsters in Chicago, that even though they were gangsters and they dealt in crime, they helped the Black community, just like gangsters in Harlem helped the Black community."

And there were other Black filmmakers like Foster. As Dr. Jacqueline Najuma Stewart lists in her book *Migrating to the Movies: Cinema and Black Urban Modernity*, many of the earliest Black-owned film companies were headquartered along and around the Stroll near the Foster Photoplay Company, which was headquartered at the Grand Theater Building on 3110 South State Street, and later at 3312 South Wabash. There was "the Unique Film Company (3519 S. State), the Peter P. Jones Photoplay Company (3704 S. Prairie and later 3849 S. State), and the

Royal Gardens Motion Picture Company (459 E. Thirty-first Street), founded by Virgil L. Williams at his popular Royal Gardens nightclub with actor Samuel T. Jacks."[5]

As part of this burgeoning scene, Foster publicly encouraged the inclusion of more Black people in film. After *The Birth of a Nation* premiered in 1915, he wrote an article for the *Defender* titled "Moving Pictures Offer the Greatest Opportunity to the American Negro in History of the Race from Every Point of View."[6] Not only did he argue that more Black folks in movies would mean improved representation, he also pointed out the industry's potential profitability. Seeing music as a model, he believed Black people could come together and popularize Black films across the world. He wrote, "The world is very anxious to know more of the set-aside race that has kept America in a political and social argument for the past two hundred and fifty years."

As demand grew for the kinds of films people like Foster made, more and more companies—including those owned by white people—wanted to get in on those ticket sales by also making "race films" for Black audiences. Another enterprising Black man named Luther J. Pollard led the Ebony Film Corporation. But unlike Foster Photoplay, a company that became so revered by Black people, Ebony was a predominantly white-managed company, and their comedies often also appealed to white audiences. That led to much debate among Black people about who and what white people were laughing at, but Pollard believed that comedies could be a way into commentary about representation. He used all-Black casts and thought his films showed that Black people could be creative and funny. His films, which were marketed and catered to a mainstream audience, were profitable.

Nevertheless, although Pollard was respected, many thought his presence was a front for just another white-helmed company to appear to be Black-led. Ebony Film Company remained controversial; it did not help the company's reputation that it also continued to distribute films it made before bringing on Pollard, films created under its previous name: Historical Feature Film Company. The portrayals in many of those earlier productions were insulting parodies of what white people thought of Black Americans.

In May 1917 the *Defender* ran a story with the large heading EBONY FILM CANCELLED after the Phoenix Theatre refused to show one of those films, a movie called *A Natural Born Shooter*. This movie, and others from Ebony, were not like movies such as *The Railroad Porter* where there are jokes but the Black characters are treated with dignity. People said the movie aimed to humiliate Black people, because the jokes, which were also for a white audience, exploited the old stereotypes for laughs. The article called the film "junk" and "rotten stuff," and stated that the *Defender* was staunchly against it—and maybe against Ebony itself.[7]

"The very name 'Ebony' is nauseating; it means 'black,' and when a set of men exploit such rot they deserve no support from any direction," the author of the article wrote. "There is no justification for the spectacle presented in some of these so-called comedies, and if it is in the power of the Defender to put an end to such exhibitions, our readers can rest assured that it will be done."

Regardless of the argument of whether Black people could successfully lead the creative direction of white-owned film companies, Reid said that one thing was often very different in Black-owned companies: the hiring. When Black people owned the production of a film, they didn't just hire a Black cast—they also hired Black technicians and talent behind the camera. "They act as mentors to these technicians and tradespersons," Reid said. "It's really about labor, Black labor within the film industry. And labor is not just the talent, you see, the stars that you fall in love with."

Just like today, though, the moviemaking business was expensive, and it's likely that Foster struggled to keep his business afloat. He started to rent and sell off his equipment, and at some point returned to his journalism work. In 1929 he moved to Hollywood, where he became a director for a European-owned company called Pathé Studios, which was based in France. By this point, "talkies"—films with sound—had been invented and the industry was in a period of change. With his films in hand, Foster hoped to use the experience working for Pathé to learn how to make talkies and create another company. Unfortunately, he died in 1940 before he had the chance.

21

TALKIES

"One of the greatest tasks of my life has been to convince a
certain class of my racial acquaintances that a colored man can
be anything."

—Oscar Micheaux in *The Conquest:
The Story of a Negro Pioneer*

WILLIAM FOSTER'S FILMS have been lost to time—it's unknown if any
copies still exist, and if they do, what condition they are in. The same
is true of the work by most of his silent era contemporaries. Although
the exact number of films created during the silent era is unknown, it's
estimated that only about 25 percent of all feature-length silent films
made in the US have survived.[1] For race films, some estimate around 80
percent have been lost, and it's likely that number could be even higher.[2]
It's unclear how these numbers translate to films of other lengths, such as
the shorts that Foster made. "So far, we haven't found any of [Foster's]
films," *Uplift Cinema* author Allyson Nadia Field told me. "Most silent
era films are lost for a variety of reasons having to do with materiality,
but also the value that folks placed on them at the time."[3]

In the case of silent films by Black people, this devaluing means that
almost an entire genre of work is lost. It's why it's so special when a
short clip is discovered, when a piece of writing is unearthed, or when
we are able to see the work of a Black creator of the time because,
somehow, they prevailed. "[Black silent film] was not preserved, and so,
no, we don't know a lot about William Foster or the other filmmakers,"

Sergio Mims, a film critic and cofounder of the Black Harvest Film Festival, told me in a 2021 interview. "Fortunately, we do know a lot about Oscar Micheaux."[4]

During the silent era, the contributions of Black cinema were remarkable, but it wasn't until talkies came along in the 1920s that Black filmmakers were able to really find longevity in the industry. Moviemaking was—and still is—an expensive business. It took some time for Black film companies to learn how to make their popular films profitable, and how to create a business model that would allow them to make the money they needed to survive.

Going into this period of technological transition, Black filmmakers had a strong foundation. Because of filmmakers like Foster and others across the country, there was a market for the race films created by and for Black people. Although there was some disagreement about what types of films would "uplift" Black people, Black audiences were eager to watch more movies that represented them.

Oscar Micheaux was one of the most famous directors to capitalize on this demand for race films. Starting his career in the silent era, he was the only Black filmmaker who lasted long enough to make films with sound—and find success with them. Micheaux was born in 1884 in Metropolis, Illinois, to formerly enslaved parents, moved to Chicago at seventeen, and worked in the city's stockyards and steel mills. He was also a Pullman porter, and like many Black men in this role, he used the job to save money, get to know the country, and make connections while overhearing the business dealings of the wealthy.

Micheaux left Chicago in 1904 and moved to South Dakota, where he became a homesteader on a reservation, farming the land and taking care of livestock. There he married a woman named Orlean McCracken, the daughter of a Chicago pastor. But married life wasn't bliss for these two. Micheaux wrote about his struggles with both his homestead ambitions and his marriage in his book *The Conquest: The Story of a Negro Pioneer*. Published in 1913, the novel draws on his experiences to create the story of the fictional Oscar Devereaux, who must deal with drought and marriage issues.[5]

In the coming years, Micheaux's marriage continued to deteriorate. While he was away on business, his wife left him, joining her family in Chicago. Her father also sold Micheaux's property, keeping the earnings for himself. The couple divorced in 1917,[6] and Micheaux again poured his life into a novel, writing the story of Jean Baptiste, a homesteader who had a bitter marriage with a preacher's daughter.[7] This book, *The Homesteader*, was the launching point for Micheaux's film career and the door to a celebrated legacy.

Brothers Noble and George Perry Johnson had created the Lincoln Motion Picture Company, a Black-owned film production company in Omaha, Nebraska, in 1916, and they were searching for films to produce when they came upon Micheaux's latest novel. They approached him to buy the rights to turn the book into a film, but the very entrepreneurial Micheaux decided to make the movie himself.

In 1918, Micheaux founded the Micheaux Film & Book Company and began to make silent films. After he used the abandoned Selig studio on Chicago's North Side for filming, *The Homesteader* became Micheaux's first film in 1919, six years after Foster's *The Railroad Porter*. Although Foster made the first film produced and directed by a Black filmmaker with a Black cast, Micheaux's film was the first one long enough to be considered a feature.

Micheaux's other early movies were all made in the Chicago area, including one that would become known for its intensity and statement against racist violence. After *The Birth of a Nation* in 1915, many Black filmmakers wanted their chance to rebut and invalidate the stereotypes within it with their own films. But unlike some of those attempts, Micheaux's response, *Within Our Gates*, was met with commercial success. It was popular and, possibly because of this fact, it survived—becoming the oldest known surviving film made by a Black director.[8] "*Within Our Gates* . . . is arguably one of his best movies," Mims said. "It's an anti-lynching film, and it's very, very powerful. Now, it's very melodramatic. It's very much [a] movie of its period, and there is a very dramatic and very disturbing lynching sequence."

The film features Chicago actress Evelyn Jarvis and covers topics such as lynching, the Great Migration, and the "New Negro"—Black people's refusal to submit to Jim Crow practices. This type of complex commentary marked a maturity in Black cinema. "With the release of Micheaux's *Within Our Gates*, with its multilayered discourses on Black migration and patriotism, African American identity, and cinematic representation, we see an assertive post-*Birth*, postwar, post-riots Black filmmaking practice," Dr. Jacqueline Najuma Stewart wrote in *Migrating to the Movies*. "By extension, this film announced the emergence of an

African American film culture no longer in its 'infancy' but exhibiting the acute self-consciousness of adolescence."[9]

Foster's movies were all short comedies, but Micheaux was known for producing dramas and action films that were much more serious. These types of films spoke to the discourse around what a race film should and should not be. At the time, as Black creatives aimed to fight against the depictions of Black people as unintelligent, many people thought it was important to make race films that showed Black people in a serious light.

Heading into the 1930s, Micheaux had experienced over a decade of success in moviemaking. He was known for being frugal in budgeting his films. He often used nonprofessional actors to save money, and his films were not lit or edited well. "His films were always very, very low budget—he did the best he could with what he had," Mims explained. "Many people complain about the technical shortcomings in his films. He could only make a film where he could pay to hire crew, and he distributed the films himself. He went around even delivering prints. He was a one-man band."

Micheaux did declare bankruptcy in 1928, forcing him to rely on white financial backers for his business.[10] But once talkies had grown in popularity, Micheaux was still standing, and in 1931, he released his first talkie, *The Exile*. Based on his first book, *The Conquest*, it was the first full-length sound feature with a Black cast.

In total, Micheaux wrote, produced, directed, and distributed over forty films between 1919 and his death in 1951, consistently challenging the preexisting images of Black people on film. Almost a century after his first film, the US Postal Service honored this legacy with an Oscar Micheaux stamp and a two-day star-studded ceremony with director Spike Lee and actors Ruby Dee and John Amos in attendance. Micheaux's work is also making its way back to the big screen: seventy years after his death, Micheaux's 1935 thriller *Murder in Harlem* showed at the illustrious Cannes Film Festival with a new documentary about his life, *Oscar Micheaux: The Superhero of Black Cinema*.

22

SINGING COWBOYS

"Little children of dark skin—not just Negroes, but Puerto Ricans, Mexicans, everybody of color—had no heroes in the movies. I was so glad to give them something to identify with."
—Herb Jeffries to the *Los Angeles Times* in 1998

SURPRISINGLY—OR MAYBE NOT—many Black stories about the American West included Chicago in their storylines as a means of comparing city life to life in the West. Oscar Micheaux's early silent films like *The Homesteader* and even his first talkie, *The Exile*, are westerns in which Chicago has a great presence, showing the city as a growing metropolis and then juxtaposing it with places like South Dakota.

In fact, Baptiste, the main character in *The Homesteader*, is a nod to "Father of Chicago" Jean Baptiste Point DuSable, Chicago's first non-Indigenous settler. In the film, Baptiste wants to keep his connection to Chicago. Although he loves being a homesteader in South Dakota, he sees Chicago as uniquely embodying the heart of Black city life. "He had lived in the windy city before going West, and was very familiar with that section of the city on the south side that is the center of the Negro life of that great metropolis," Micheaux wrote in the novel on which the film was based.[1]

Later in his career, Micheaux began to replace Chicago with Harlem when creating his films' dual settings, possibly to explore its cultural scene in his art. But at first, as a filmmaker, he wrote about the places he knew, and like many others who'd made their way to Chicago for one opportunity or another, this place was one he knew really well.

And how it often goes, subsequent Black filmmakers continued to innovate on the foundation of their predecessors. This was the case in 1937 when a twentysomething Herb Jeffries created the first all-Black western musical. The film, *Harlem on the Prairie* (a.k.a. *Bad Man of Harlem*), featured the handsome Jeffries as the hero and was also the first all-Black western musical. The *Defender* reported on the film's announcement, "This is the first time a western has ever been made with Race actors, and may offer such a novelty that some of the white deluxe houses may interest themselves in running it as a novelty offering."[2]

Jeffries, by this time, had been living in Chicago for a few years. Born in Detroit in 1913, he used to perform as a teenager in a local speakeasy—a fact that helped him catch the eye of influential jazz trumpeter and singer Louis Armstrong, who encouraged him to move to Chicago. The *Defender* credited Jeffries's rise to fame in the city to his singing with famous jazz pianists: Earl "Fatha" Hines and his orchestra at the old Grand Terrace café in 1933 and with Erskine Tate and his band at the Sunset Cafe in 1934.[3] Jeffries also toured with Hines through the South. This tour is when Jeffries decided he wanted to be a Black cowboy. After seeing young Black boys file into Black theaters to watch white Hollywood stars on the screen, he wanted to create his own movies for this audience.[4]

Jeffries found financing for the film and wrote all the songs himself. He stars as Jeff Kincaid, a younger cowboy who protects reformed criminal Doc Clayburn, played by the famous Spencer Williams (once managed by William Foster). Flournoy Miller, the friend of Foster's who claimed Foster coined the name "the Stroll" for the hub of Black culture on State Street, was also in the movie.

The *New York Age*, a prominent Black newspaper of the time, reported that *Harlem on the Prairie* set the record for the highest-grossing all-Black picture and that two years later it still held that title.[5] Jeffries's blockbuster hit was soon followed by *Two-Gun Man from Harlem* and *The Bronze Buckaroo* in 1938, and *Harlem Rides the Range* in 1939. Jeffries, who was born the same year that Foster's *The Railroad Porter* premiered and who'd also made Chicago his home like Foster and Micheaux, was now a star—a star who, like his filmmaking predecessors, created something that had never been done before.

By the late 1930s, there were 430 all-Black theaters across the country, and as Michael K. Johnson explains in *Hoo-Doo Cowboys and Bronze Buckaroos*, Jeffries's westerns and films like them "provide a vision that counters the way most Hollywood Westerns marginalize or ignore the role Blacks played in settling the West."[6]

At this point, it was almost two decades after Micheaux released *The Homesteader*, and audiences were different. Black moviegoers wanted to see more than just dramas. Audiences now included both adults and children, and when they went to the movies, they wanted to be entertained. They wanted music and action.[7] So Jeffries, a music entertainer already, created his own version of the westerns they'd see coming out of white mainstream studios in Hollywood, combining his music with action and humor.

After his initial series of films, Jeffries continued singing and performing for most of his life, everything from jazz to country. In the '40s, while performing with Duke Ellington's orchestra, he sang lead vocals on a recording of "Flamingo" that sold over fifty million copies, according to the Hollywood Walk of Fame.[8]

Jeffries's film work, however, was not beyond critique. Black westerns like Jeffries's are sometimes said to draw their comedy from white-created, minstrelsy-type caricatures of Black people. In his films in particular, Jeffries, who was light skinned and mixed, used makeup to darken his complexion. Seemingly, based on later interviews, this was mostly at the advisement of white producers and financial backers who told him he was too light.

His practice of skin darkening continued for years, including when he performed later with Ellington. White actor John Garfield, a financial backer of Ellington's 1941 musical revue *Jump for Joy*, asked Jeffries to wear dark makeup because his "color doesn't go with the rest of the people in this show."[9] Jeffries was performing alongside Dorothy Dandridge, and the show was created to illustrate Black pride and to spark discussions about social and racial justice. A lyric from the titular song was "Fare thee well, land of cotton / Cotton lisle is out of style." So this darkening act was particularly egregious and immediately drew the attention of Ellington.

"I look down in the pit, and Duke, he can't believe what he seeing—I thought my zipper was open," Jeffries joked in a 2009 interview with musician Tad Calcara.[10] "So I'm dancing around, I'm looking: 'What

the hell is he looking at me like that for?' . . . I get back during inter-
mission and I'm in my dressing room. He comes popping in there. I'll
never forget. He says, 'Who the hell do you think you are? Al Jolson?'"

Al Jolson was a white entertainer so famous for his minstrel act
that he was grossly called the "king of blackface." Jeffries said Ellington
immediately told Garfield to put an end to the darkened makeup. "It
wasn't five minutes [before] Garfield came in and said, 'Mr. Jeffries,
just do what you were doing before—forget about the makeup,'" Jeffries laughed.

As influential as Jeffries's contribution to western film—and to country music, for that matter—is to history, it's often omitted from books
and collections. He received his Hollywood Walk of Fame star and was
inducted into the Oklahoma-based Hall of Great Western Performers
in 2004. But it was not until after this legendary singing cowboy, "the
Bronze Buckaroo," passed away at one hundred years old in 2014 that
many people saw the full picture of his contributions.

"He has these gorgeous tones, and he really knows how to phrase a
ballad," jazz critic Gary Giddins told the *New York Times*. "The mystery
is why that didn't lead to a bigger career."[11]

23

DANCING, AFROS, AND A WHOLE LOTTA SOUL

"You can bet your last money, it's all gonna be a stone gas,
honey! I'm Don Cornelius, and as always in parting, we wish
you love, peace, and soul!"
—Don Cornelius, signing off of *Soul Train*

DON CORNELIUS, then a former radio disc jockey, had only been in TV for three years when he launched what would become one of the most influential TV shows in history.

A South Side native, Cornelius held multiple jobs before entering into media, including serving in the US Marine Corps and selling tires, cars, and insurance. After completing a three-month broadcasting course in 1966, he found a home at Chicago's premier Black radio station, WVON. A year later, Cornelius became a sports anchor for *A Black's Views of the News* on local TV station WCIU. Some claim the program was the first nightly Black news show in the United States.[1]

With funding of just $400, Cornelius created the *Soul Train* pilot in 1970, using the show he'd done at high schools as a DJ as the blueprint. "*Soul Train* was developed as a radio show on television," Cornelius told the *New York Times* in 1995. "It was the radio show that I always wanted and never had. I selected the music, and still do, by simply seeing what had chart success."[2]

With this approach, *Soul Train* became an instant hit, playing off the idea of the popular show *American Bandstand* from Dick Clark. Clark would later, in 1973, attempt to create his own show for Black audiences called *Soul Unlimited*, but Black leaders pressured ABC, where it was airing, to cancel the show. They did not want Clark's show to hurt the success of *Soul Train* and told ABC they refused to support it. But it was a syndication deal for *Soul Train* in 1971 that truly spread the series to the masses. Instead of a local daily show it became a nationwide weekly one, making its way to eighteen other markets beyond Chicago in just that first year.[3]

Soul Train was never just a weekly show. It was also a movement. Even decades after it last aired in 2006, *Soul Train* lines are still happening at Black weddings, birthday parties, and lively family reunions across the country. Wherever there are Black folks gathering, there's *Soul*.

"I think the beautiful thing about *Soul Train* was that it was giving households across America this view of Blackness that was glowing and shining and really beautiful and on our own terms," Ayana Contreras, the author of *Energy Never Dies*, told me. "That's probably the most important part."[4]

It's not an exaggeration to say that *Soul Train*, as a single show, dramatically increased the number of Black people on TV in a given week. "*Jet* magazine historically would list all the different times Black people would be on TV throughout the week in the back," Contreras explained. "When *Soul Train* started airing, that was very minimal. Very minimal. Maybe you might have Diahann Carroll, you might have Bill Cosby, you might have a couple of other people guest starring on something, and that might be about it. And so to actually see real young people and real artists that people heard on radio and not for the 'white gaze,' that was really powerful."

Before *Soul Train*, many Black TV performances were not only small in number but also specifically created for white mainstream audiences. "The only other time you might see Black people performing specifically would be on shows like *[The] Ed Sullivan [Show]*—and, of course, *Ed Sullivan* was programming for the least common denominator, meaning white middle-class nuclear families," Contreras said. "And so they wanted a very specific thing. When they did book Black acts, they were definitely crossover and definitely pop oriented."

In addition to its place as a leader in Black entertainment, *Soul Train* was part of another legendary initiative: showing that Black was beautiful. When Johnson Products became a *Soul Train* sponsor in 1971, the hair care leader was the first Black company to sponsor a nationally syndicated television program, and it helped make that syndication possible. Its bold ads encouraged Black people to embrace their natural beauty.[5] Black Chicago firm Vince Cullers Advertising created a campaign for Johnson's Afro Sheen they named "Wantu Wazuri," which means "beautiful people" in Swahili. During the commercial breaks, the ads would run as sixty-second spots.

"They came up with this catch line which was 'Beautiful people use Afro Sheen,' which of course was relating to 'Black is beautiful'—an important catchphrase of the moment," Contreras explained. "It was also very powerful because before that, hair care products that you saw on television were primarily advertising ways to take the Blackness *out* of your hair, or products that were definitely not for us. So I think that's another thing: seeing us on our own terms, in our own way, in our natural state was something that was revolutionary and really beautiful, and that relationship [of] Johnson Products with *Soul Train* lasted throughout the '70s."

Looking back at "Black is beautiful" advertising, we can see that it reflects the work of the many Black advertising agencies that started in Chicago. Vince Cullers, who started his agency in 1956 after leaving a role at *Ebony*, is credited with being the first Black person to own a full-service advertising agency.

Cullers may have been the first, but he was not the last—not by a long shot. And the most well-known Black advertiser who came after him is Tom Burrell. In 1971, Burrell and his cofounder, Emmett McBain, founded Burrell McBain. The company would later be renamed Burrell Advertising in 1974, after McBain left the company.

It's no coincidence that Cullers, Burrell, and so many other Black advertising agencies were headquartered in Chicago. "When you think about this country and Black life—talk about living while Black in this country and where that experience takes place, where it's concentrated— where would you tap into, right?" Danielle Robinson Bell, assistant professor of marketing communications at Northwestern, explained in an interview.[6] "You can't do that without mentioning Chicago."

Bell spent many years in the advertising industry and worked at Burrell herself as a young creative. There she picked up many gems of knowledge that still guide her thinking today. One of those gems Burrell shares often: "Black people are not dark-skinned white people." That means that just changing white advertising to include Black people without considering Black culture simply cannot work. "It wasn't just about 'We need to see ourselves' as in 'We need to see someone in the ad who looks like me,'" Bell said. "That was a part of it, but the deeper part of it was 'We need to see someone who looks like me who is in a scenario, who is being messaged to, who was being depicted in a way that reflects my lived experience—not just what I look like.'"

Bell's favorite example of this is Philip Morris and its mascot the Marlboro Man, a white man in a cowboy hat whose slogan was "Come to where the flavor is. Come to Marlboro Country." To appeal to Black consumers, Philip Morris first tried a Black version of the Marlboro Man but kept the same characteristics: same slogan, same hat, sitting on a horse.

When Burrell and McBain got their hands on the advertising campaign in 1971, they flipped it. "Black man, with a cigarette, but it was almost like somebody was walking down 125th Street and snapped a picture, and that was the ad—that's just how real 'slice of life' the ad looked," Bell said. "And the tagline was 'Where the flavor is.' That's it. That's the power of nuance." This ad felt more authentic, as though it was actually made for Black people and culture, because it was.

Research is essential to marketing, but it cannot replace lived experience, Bell explained. Advertisers need the expertise of Black people in order to market to them in a way that is credible. "At the end of the day, you can't research and insight your way into someone's authentic lived experience and have it be reflected in media in a way that resonates with the audience themselves," Bell said.

To this day, Bell teaches her class what she learned from Burrell: If you have a creative presentation that is geared toward Black people, you'd better be prepared to answer the question "What's Black about it?" "And if you could not [answer that question for Burrell], you'd better go find it."

Part IX

THE OPRAH EFFECT

A FULL CUP

Written while listening to "Fantasie Nègre" by Florence Price

> "When it comes down to it, life can be measured in exchanges
> of energy. Positive or negative: What is the energy you choose
> to bring to the world?"
>
> —Oprah Winfrey in *The Path Made Clear*

WHEN I WAS ABOUT TWENTY-FIVE, I remember being upset and crying about some decision I was making. Maybe it was spending money on myself instead of on something I deemed more responsible. Maybe it was choosing to go on a vacation with my friends. Maybe it was something as simple as deciding one day that I could not deal with the pressure of motherhood and calling off from work to stay in bed and sleep after taking my son to school. Whatever the reason—it's not important now—I remember my friend Lydia offering me this very important piece of advice during our annual vision board party: *It's not being selfish, and even if it is, we all need to put ourselves first.*

As young, single moms in our twenties, we were pretty career driven but sometimes needed that reminder, the very important idea that you cannot pour from an empty cup. I have a disabled son who requires special care—care that my salary at the time would not really allow me to outsource. Lydia has two bubbly twins—smart and funny, but still, she has double the trouble! But I recognize that as natural as it's always been for me and my friends to bring up the idea of self-care, it has not always been such a welcome concept. In fact, we are just one generation removed from our mothers who were—and sometimes still are—struggling against society's idea that women should be selfless humans who put everyone (their spouses, their kids, their jobs) above their own well-being.

In 1992, when a guest of *The Oprah Winfrey Show* told women in the audience they should put themselves first on their list of priorities, the audience booed. Author and life coach Cheryl Richardson was the first Oprah guest to ever bring up this concept of self-care, and it was not something women at the time were used to embracing. It was as if, Oprah now says, they were telling women to abandon their families and run away. (Even though, honestly, sometimes a physical vacation away from duties is helpful too!)

But twenty years later, in 2012, the live audience in *Oprah's Lifeclass* applauded and whooped when relationship expert Iyanla Vanzant—who most of us learned about because of *The Oprah Winfrey Show*—explained how putting yourself first is the only way you can be of service to others. "No, it's self-*full* to be first," she said, "to be as good as possible to you, to take care of you, to keep you whole and healthy. That doesn't mean that you disregard everything and everyone, but you want to come with your cup full. *My cup runneth over.* What comes out of the cup is for y'all, what's in the cup is mine. But I've got to keep my cup full."[1]

Today, I do recognize that we millennials—and our Gen X friends too—are the children of Oprah. We grew up hearing and understanding the concept of "live your best life," and we are often working to put ourselves in a position to do so. We are a reflection of who and what we see, and Oprah, our guide, set us up to see putting ourselves first not only as totally acceptable but as absolutely necessary.

Oprah Winfrey, better known by all as just Oprah, changed the game when her namesake show debuted in 1986. Produced in Chicago, the iconic talk show broke every record possible, solidifying her position as the "Queen of Daytime TV." Not only did Oprah use her show to launch the careers of friends like Gayle King, she also can be linked to the rise of TV celebrities like Iyanla Vanzant, Suze Orman, and Dr. Phil, and the success of more than two decades worth of authors with books chosen for Oprah's Book Club. Though the show aired its final episode in 2011, it remains one of the highest-rated daytime talk shows in American television history.

There's a lot to remember about *The Oprah Winfrey Show*, a favorite being the "You get a car! You get a car! You get a car!" episode in which the entire studio audience of two-hundred-plus people got free brand-new cars. While episodes like that have now reached meme-level fame, those are not necessarily the ones I personally think of first. For me, the most memorable part of the show is the feeling that it gave me whenever I saw joy, or when I was encouraged to give to causes I cared about, or even when I simply was challenged to think of something different.

Thinking about Oprah as someone whose influence stretches far beyond the confines of a single TV show, what I learned from Oprah as I grew into my own as a full-fledged adult comes to mind. I learned how to meditate from an Oprah meditation challenge with Deepak Chopra; I found the courage to confront internal trauma listening to Iyanla Vanzant; I was inspired by the daily quotes I saw when I opened up my browser to the *O Magazine* website; I was reintroduced to Maya Angelou in a new way because her conversations expanded on the written work I'd loved for so long. And above all, in everything, in all things, I learned that being my best self can mean many different things, but that it takes a little work and a little focus to figure it out.

For some Oprah critics, the "live your best life" ideology could sound like a bunch of unrealistic talk. But essentially, the show exposed audiences to new ideas of what that type of care could look like, and for her viewers it was eye opening.

Oprah's focus on the idea of taking care of yourself first is essential for many reasons. But I see it as being a crucial part of normalizing activities such as rest, therapy, and physical activity. That's just not something everyone, especially low-income women and women of color, have always been afforded access to. It wasn't really until the late '80s and '90s, as reported by culture reporter Aisha Harris in her 2017 piece "A History of Self-Care," that the idea of wellness outside of traditional health care spread from a niche community to something seen as mainstream.[2]

Previously, we'd seen a shift in physical health care itself finally being seen for the political and societal issue it is: access to care in the US has never been equitable for people of color. But this new shift brought light to mental health inadequacies in particular, and cultivated the belief that caring for yourself, outside of just treating physical ailments, can be revolutionary. It is especially radical for Black people and those who are systemically affected by racism, classism, and all the other "-isms" to prioritize this type of care.

So we know that self-care as a concept cannot be defined as expensive products and massages, but it can be a radical exclamation of living life on your own terms. And the societal evolution from "I am a bad, selfish person if I don't put everyone else before me" to "I must be self-full and pour into myself before pouring into anyone else" is a norm that we all deserve.

24

THE OPRAH WINFREY SHOW

"When we went national, I remember at the time, Roger King [who distributed *The Oprah Winfrey Show* nationwide] told me that one station manager said that he'd rather put a potato in a chair in his market than have a big Black girl with a funny name. And in spite of that, from Memphis to Macon, from Pittsburgh to Pensacola, from New York to New Orleans, you all let me in."

—Oprah Winfrey on the *Oprah Winfrey Show* finale

WHEN A YOUNG JENN WHITE first saw *The Oprah Winfrey Show* in middle school, she noticed something: Oprah Winfrey looked like she could be someone she knew.

"I didn't really see myself on television," White told me while recalling her earliest memories of Oprah.[1] "Not really. And when she came on the TV, she looked like she could be my aunt, or my neighbor, or my big cousin. She looked accessible in this way that I hadn't experienced before. And it felt like when she was talking, even though it's in this talk show format, it always felt like she was talking to me.

"To have a Black woman in that space was pretty, pretty remarkable," White said. "And it wasn't just that she was Black—it was that she was, in her own words, overweight; she didn't look like other Black women on television in any space at that point and so she represented something different." Unlike the perfectly coiffed news anchors who all had a particular acceptable look, Oprah looked real. And her realness was inspirational for what a young girl growing up in Detroit could grow up to be.

"I was a really chatty kid, I think it's fair to say," White said. "And my mother would always tell me, 'You got the gift of gab, you can do something with that in your life, you have a gift.' And so when Oprah came on television, there was this person she could point to [and] say, 'This is what I'm talking about; you can do what she does.' And there was something really powerful about the example she pointed to being someone who looked like me."

In fact, Jenn White *did* grow up to be an Oprah of sorts. She's the host of *1A*, a national show on NPR, and she helped create a show called *Reset* on Chicago's local NPR station, WBEZ. She also was the host of award-winning WBEZ podcasts *16 Shots*, about the murder of Laquan McDonald, and *Making Oprah*, which looked at the mogul's rise in Chicago.

Black women like Jenn are breaking ground across media platforms, just like Oprah. Similar to television, public radio is notoriously slow in its efforts to diversify its workforce, both in hiring and retaining staff of color. This is because, as many educators believe, children become who they see. It's important for growth to see people who are mirrors—people that look like them—and people that are windows—people that give them a look into the outside world and, in this case, show what opportunities are possible.[2]

"[Oprah] was both a window and a mirror for me, because it was like this possibility of what was available," White said. "She was showing up as herself. She wasn't editing who she was for the audience. And that planted the seed in my head about what was possible for me."

In December 1983, Oprah was leaving Baltimore. The Mississippi native had arrived there from Nashville, where she'd spent her teenage years and had attended the HBCU Tennessee State University. She was a young and bright-eyed twenty-two-year-old who had excitedly moved there for a job at TV station WJZ as an anchor in 1976. But when she arrived, she found a coanchor who didn't want her there, instability as she was cycled through a number of different roles, and a barrage of harassment. That harassment, she says, was on top of the unprofessional requests she would be forced to handle, such as babysitting someone's kids or allowing a boss's girlfriend to move in with her rent-free.

And there, at WJZ, Oprah's look wasn't valued and leadership forced her to try to change it. "My boss informed me my hair was too thick for the green screen wall behind the news desk and I needed to change my style," she said in a press release announcing a new show with actor and entrepreneur Tracee Ellis Ross called *The Hair Tales.*[3] "So I was sent to a fancy salon in New York City and the stylist put a French perm on my hair. It burned so badly when he washed the perm out, my hair came out with it—and so did my identity and sense of self."

Even with all of the outrageousness of what was going on at WJZ, Oprah finally had some success when the station's show *People Are Talking* debuted in 1978 and she was paired with Richard Sher to host.[4] News leaders saw the move as a demotion for the young journalist, who was a shining light on camera but wrote too slowly for the fast-paced news. For Oprah, who was ready to leave the traditional confines of news journalism, it was a welcome change from the work that she says made her feel out of place. "Up until then, I'd been a news anchor and reporter," she wrote in her book *The Path Made Clear: Discovering Your Life's Direction and Purpose.*[5] "I knew I was not my authentic self. And my bosses certainly made no secret of their feelings. They told me I was the wrong color, the wrong size, and that I showed too much emotion."

On *People Are Talking*, audiences loved her and she got along well with her cohost, with whom she became close friends. On the show, Oprah says, she finally felt alive, like she'd finally found her life's calling. "My entire body told me this was what I was supposed to do," she also wrote. "As a reporter, I'd been exhausted all the time. I really had to drag myself in to work. But after one day on this local talk show, I was energized in a way that fueled every cell of my being."

But even as Oprah grew as a personality, her paycheck did not match that of her cohost. In 1980, she was making $22,000 while Sher was making $50,000. Years later, Oprah has often recalled the story of how she asked for pay equality and was unceremoniously denied. "You know how intimidating it is to go to the boss in the first place, but [I said to myself] I'm going to go and I'm going to stand up for myself," she told a group of business students at Stanford in 2014. "I said, 'Richard's making more money than I am and I don't think that's fair, because we're doing the same job, we sit in the same show.'"[6]

The station's general manager was not swayed by her courage—or by her very clear point that two employees who are doing the same job should be paid the same salary. He did not believe in pay parity for this situation and gave an absurd answer. "My general manager said, 'Why should you make as much money as him? He has children. Do you have children?' And I said no. He said, 'Well, he has to pay for college educations. He owns his own home. Do you own your home? . . . So tell me why do you need the same amount of money?'"

All this denial did was further fuel her. Recognizing that her employer did not see the value in her, Oprah set out to prove them wrong. Soon she'd be able to do just that.

Oprah brought that same personality with her to Chicago, joining a morning show on TV station WLS in 1984. At the time, *A.M. Chicago* was a short, half-hour show that struggled with poor ratings. The station's new general manager, Dennis Swanson, saw something special in Oprah after a former WJZ producer showed him her audition tape, and he wasn't wrong. Oprah turned the show around and made it into a ratings success, and the show was renamed *The Oprah Winfrey Show* in 1985.

It's not a coincidence, however, that Oprah ended up in Chicago. It was where she wanted to be. In an interview for *Making Oprah*, Oprah told Jenn White that she "manifested" moving to Chicago and making it the home for her show. Like other Black people in media who found success here, Oprah says she saw a unique opportunity to make a name for herself in this particular city. "As I was landing in the city, flying in on American Airlines and looking at the city, this feeling came over me—that I'm going to be here," she said. "And I remembered tearing up. It felt like, I used to say at the time, this will be my Tara, I will call it home. This will be my home. And I felt that way for years every time I would fly from anywhere and fly into O'Hare and see the city. I had that feeling of this is where I'm supposed to be."[7]

After the show officially became Oprah's, it continued to grow in popularity. Her realness and relatability were a hit with viewers, and the rest of the country wanted in on this success. After just one year, *The Oprah Winfrey Show* went into national syndication.

This expansion meant huge financial growth. Airing *The Oprah Winfrey Show* on various stations across the country meant rising ratings for whatever show was lucky enough to be slotted after it, so stations were willing to pay handsomely for the local broadcast rights. During its first two seasons of syndication, *The Oprah Winfrey Show* earned $115 million in revenue. By 1994, not even ten years later, Oprah herself was earning about $74 million, up from $72 million the year before, according to *Forbes*.[8] Even though she clearly wasn't the first host to have a successful daytime show, she quickly became the most influential. And soon everyone wanted to be Oprah.

"It's important to know how incredible she was as a presence on television," Jenn White said. "Because you had Phil Donahue, who really created this new genre of daytime talk show—he was the first person who really did it—but when she came on the scene, she was a Black woman in a space where there weren't really Black women in what was really an emerging genre in television."

Donahue was undoubtedly the king of daytime TV at this time, and it's arguable that decades after his last show aired in 1996, he still is. When *The Oprah Winfrey Show* first aired, his popular daytime talk show had been running since 1967 and been syndicated since 1970. But even as a legend in this industry, he recognized what Oprah brought to the table. "I interviewed Phil Donahue for the series too," Jenn added, "and he really acknowledges that while he sort of created [daytime talk, Oprah] was the one who took it to this really worldwide phenomenon that we came to know."

But before Oprah was known worldwide, like many young journalists, she had people who helped open doors for her. At her station in Baltimore, Oprah's uniqueness wasn't appreciated, but that changed when Swanson hired her for *A.M. Chicago*. "Dennis made a decision that has changed my life forever," Oprah said in a surprise appreciation segment she did for Swanson on her show in 1994. Remembering one of her first conversations with him, Oprah said his support gave her the freedom to be herself on-air. "I said to you, 'You know I'm overweight.' And you said, 'So what? So am I,'" she laughed.[9]

Oprah credits Swanson as the person who started her career. And in true proud mentor fashion, after she thanked him on-air, Swanson turned the credit right back to Oprah. "I remember the one piece of advice I gave you at the time," he said. "I don't know if you recall this, but I told you: Make sure your head always fits on your shoulders when all the awards and money and accolades came to you, and I give you credit because you've been able to do that."

It's clear that right from the start, Oprah's working relationship with Swanson was much different than with any of her bosses in Baltimore.

Instead of trying to unsuccessfully force Oprah into a mold that simply did not fit, Swanson saw her as television-ready exactly as she was, Jenn said.

"What he found in her was a certain authenticity and realness that he thought was going to resonate with audiences, especially with women," Jenn explained. "There was something about her and just her willingness to be open and transparent and herself, and he told her, 'I don't want you to change anything about yourself, I don't want you to lose weight, I don't want you to do any of that. I just want you to show up exactly as you are right now.'"

25

A SHIFT TO "LIVE YOUR BEST LIFE"

"When I came here, I was about to turn thirty years old. I didn't have a vision or a lot of great expectations. . . . I just wanted to do a good job and cause no harm."
—Oprah Winfrey on the *Oprah Winfrey Show* finale

ABOUT FIVE MONTHS AFTER becoming a nationally syndicated program, *The Oprah Winfrey Show* was up against a certain kind of pressure known to anyone who's ever worked in TV: sweeps. During certain months throughout the year, the Nielsen ratings service collects its most comprehensive data about what shows audiences across the country are watching, and these viewership numbers determine how much money a show can charge its advertisers. During sweeps periods, TV executives aim to keep viewership high, and this pressure can push shows to produce what they think is must-see TV.

It was during February 1987 sweeps that Oprah and her producers chanced a potentially dangerous show idea in the midst of a Georgia county seen as one of the most racist and dangerous places for Black people in the country. That year, Forsyth County was in the news as about twenty thousand civil rights marchers made their way into the city of Cumming to bring light to the area's past inflictions against Black people. They were met by racist counterprotesters, including Ku Klux Klan members and infamous former KKK leader David Duke.

The march included leaders such as Coretta Scott King, the Reverend Jesse Jackson, and Dick Gregory. It was one of the largest civil rights demonstrations since the 1965 rally in response to "Bloody Sunday," when racist law enforcement attacked activists Hosea Williams and John Lewis and a group of marchers they were leading across the Edmund Pettus Bridge in Selma, Alabama, to the state capital of Montgomery. The rally that followed had an estimated twenty-five thousand participants and was led by the Reverend Dr. Martin Luther King Jr.

Decades later, many of the same civil rights leaders were in Cumming to talk about the city's own history of racial intimidation. In 1912, a group of Black men were accused of the rape and murder of a white woman. One of the men was lynched, and white people drove out the area's other Black residents, numbered at approximately eleven hundred, setting fire to Black homes, churches, and businesses. Forsyth County had been a whites-only community ever since this racial cleansing.

The 1987 Brotherhood March was supposed to be a peaceful protest, but events quickly intensified as crowds of white supremacists infiltrated the scene with hateful messages, yelling, and jeering. "It really escalated into this violent scene, really ugly scene that was then broadcast all over the country," Patrick Phillips, author of *Blood at the Root*, told NPR's Terry Gross in 2016 about attending what he thought was a peace march that day. Phillips, who is white, lived in the area and went to the march with his parents as a sixteen-year-old.[1]

"And then at a certain point, you know, I heard a PA click on, and somebody screamed into a megaphone, raise your hand if you love white power, and all of these young men around me raised their fist and started screaming white power," Phillips added. "I saw a guy go by with a noose on his shoulder, and it was this horrifying moment where what had always been present in the county, but suppressed was suddenly very visible. And those images went all over the country, really all over the world."

Because of these events, Oprah and her producers saw a news value in going down to Forsyth County themselves to film a show right in the midst of where everything had taken place. The episode was full of tense moments, including a hostile white audience member explaining what he said was the "difference between a Black person and a nigger."[2] The show drew headlines and made for great, sensational TV. Oprah thought that perhaps this was an example of using her platform to get people talking, to expose harmful ideas, and to change minds.

During the next year's February sweeps period, Oprah and her team attempted to do another show about racism, but this time, things got out of hand and the episode marked a drastic turning point in the show's evolution. *The Oprah Winfrey Show* producers thought up the idea to produce an "edgy, controversial ratings booster" by inviting neo-Nazi skinheads onto the show to talk about why they were racist.[3] The show devolved into an outrageous disaster, with white supremacists talking over other people, ignoring Oprah's commands to sit down and listen to other people, and calling Black people "monkeys." It changed something in Oprah when, during a commercial break, she saw them signaling to each other and laughing. They were happy about what was going on: they were spreading the hate they'd come on the show to spread and causing the chaos they intended to cause. It wasn't what Oprah and her producers had wanted at all.

"I went, whoa! I think I'm doing one thing: I think I'm exposing them; I think I'm showing them and their vitriol and their dark side and trying to get them to see a different point of view," Oprah told Jenn White in their interview. "And they are using me."[4]

She didn't want to ever let people use her show to do harm again.

"She had this this moment of realization that shaped her," White told me. "Her intention had been to use the platform to illuminate the danger and the harm these neo-Nazi groups represented. But what happened instead was that they were using the platform to spread the word; she was giving them space to reach a broader audience with their message."

At this point, *The Oprah Winfrey Show* was a couple years old, but within that time, the show—and Oprah—had dramatically risen in notoriety. Being on the show was a huge deal, and she didn't yet realize that. "I think sometimes when you think about shows like hers, you don't necessarily grasp the power in reach until something like that happens," White added.

While Oprah was working on her commitment to lessen harm, other talk shows were imitating the very things she had vowed never to do again. In 1988, during November sweeps, Geraldo Rivera invited white supremacists and antiracist activists to come on his show together, and a huge fight broke out. John Metzger, a leader of the White Aryan Resistance Youth, used a racial slur against Jewish people, then called Roy Innis, then chairman of the Congress of Racial Equality, an "Uncle

Tom."[5] The fight became so violent Geraldo's nose was broken in the mayhem. Violence was still seen as a winning way to gain ratings during sweeps when Maury Povich and Jerry Springer launched their own racy talk shows in 1991.

Instead of trying to address the work of the imitators, *The Oprah Winfrey Show* kept moving forward in its mission of social responsibility. She explained this thinking in *Making Oprah*: "I learned the greatest lesson of any competitor, or anybody who's in business, and passed that on to the rest of my staff. And that is that you can only run your own race." She continued, "I was very clear when I started—I got clearer as I continued—but I was very clear that the purpose of this show was to be a light in the world and that the mission statement, 'We're here to uplift, enlighten, encourage, and entertain,' that that had to be real."[6]

In 1989, Oprah gave her team the following decree: *You can't bring me a show that doesn't fit the mission.* This decree was made after another upsetting incident that seemed to do more harm than good. "There was another incident where they had on a husband, a wife, and the husband's mistress," White told me. "And in that episode, the mistress reveals to the wife that she's pregnant. And the wife didn't know and was just understandably devastated. And that was another moment where [Oprah was] like, 'We can't blindside people like this. We can't allow the platform to be used to do harm.'"

26

OPRAH OWNS MEDIA

"What I learned in all of those thousands of interviews is that there is a common denominator in our human experience. Everybody wants to know: Did you hear me and did what I say matter?"

—Oprah at the *Forbes* 400 Summit in 2013

EVEN WITH ALL OF ITS SUCCESS at WLS, the TV station that first created and syndicated the show, *The Oprah Winfrey Show* had limitations. Oprah was the star of the show, but she wasn't the boss. WLS dictated what the environment would be like in the building, what salaries were, and all of the rules. It was those limitations that eventually pushed Oprah into ownership.

In 1986, Oprah started her own production company, Harpo Productions—Harpo is, of course, Oprah spelled backwards. Two years later, Harpo was at the helm of *The Oprah Winfrey Show*. Oprah had bought her own show, then purchased and renovated a $20 million facility on the Near West Side of Chicago to house Harpo Studios.

That power move proved fruitful, because Oprah was then able to create the kind of show she wanted: a bigger and bolder one.

Under Oprah's control, *The Oprah Winfrey Show* continued to grow. By the late 1990s, it had twenty million regular viewers, which meant more money for Harpo—$150 million in annual revenue—and about two hundred employees.[1] The show attracted celebrity guests ranging from superstar singers like Beyoncé and Tina Turner to almost every president and presidential nominee. Oprah became queen of the celebrity interview. (The infamous jumping-on-the-couch Tom Cruise interview became one to remember.)

On top of her out-of-this-world interviews, Oprah became known for her philanthropy. In 1998, she launched her own public charity, Oprah's Angel Network. With the support of her massive audience, it raised more than $80 million between its founding and when it closed in 2010. That money was used for scholarships and to establish sixty schools in thirteen countries, plus other projects such as women's shelters and youth centers.[2]

Oprah's philanthropy also extended to giving directly to those in her viewership who needed help. In 2004, as previously mentioned, Oprah famously gave her studio audience 276 cars—brand-new Pontiac G6 sedans, worth $28,500, each one with a huge red bow. Oprah's longtime friend, journalist Gayle King, had been on a plane next to a Pontiac executive and had been instrumental in making it happen.

Under Oprah's instruction, the show's production team sought out people to be in the audience who truly needed a car, asking slick questions such as "How do you get to work?" and, if they had their own vehicle, "How old is your car?"[3] The night before the surprise, Harpo employees stayed up all night tying a second much larger bow around each car. (Oprah had felt the first bows were too small and had asked for ones that were as large as the surprise itself.)

"Oprah is a girl who will tell you all the time, 'Love is in the details,'" King told *People* in 2022. "She wanted to make sure that every car had a bow, and not just a regular bow—it had to be an oversized jumbo red bow. I remember her looking at different shades of red to make sure it was the right shade of red. It was a whole big thing."[4]

The next day, during the surprise, Oprah asked the audience to open up the boxes being handed to them to see if they were the one person in the audience who would be winning a new car. And, of course, every single box had a car key. Oprah later explained that she repeated "You get a car!" so many times because people in the audience were just that shocked. "The reason why I was screaming the words is because other people were screaming so loudly, I thought they didn't understand or wouldn't understand what had just happened and what I was saying," she recalled. "What is just thrilling about that moment is you can see the wave of understanding hitting each person. . . . People at first didn't even understand what the prize was, what the joke was, what the fun of it was. And so that's why I was doing that."[5]

A note here to clarify a rumor about this giveaway: Pontiac paid the sales tax on each car, which was about $1,800, and licensing fees. But, as when someone wins the lottery, audience members who accepted the car had to pay a prize tax, and that tax could be up to $7,000 depending on a person's tax bracket. However, what is *not* often included in the many reports that misguidedly claim "Oprah didn't even pay the tax for the cars" is that *The Oprah Winfrey Show* also told audience members that if they didn't want to have to pay a gift tax, they could take cash for the car instead.

Nevertheless, and regardless of the press, two months later, Oprah's next big giveaway was set for teachers—those who work in what she called "the most honorable profession."[6] Each teacher received $20,000 worth of gifts such as TV sets, laptops, and washer-dryer sets—and checks for $2,500 for the taxes.[7]

While Oprah was working on her own show, though, she was simultaneously building an even larger empire. In 2000, she founded *O Magazine*, which eventually became OprahDaily.com during the pandemic. In 2003, she made *Forbes* magazine's list of billionaires with a net worth of $1 billion—just two years after Black Entertainment Television (BET) founder Robert Johnson became the first Black billionaire.[8] In 2007, she was one of the first investors in the Oxygen network, and in 2011, she launched OWN, the Oprah Winfrey Network, as a fifty-fifty partnership with TV giant Discovery.

Months after the launch of OWN, *The Oprah Winfrey Show* would ceremoniously end at the culmination of its twenty-fifth year. As she and her staff would later recall, they were running out of ways to top themselves. How do you get higher than giving everyone in your audience a car? They even thought about taking the show into outer space, they joked.

"*The Oprah Winfrey Show* would achieve a level of success no one could have predicted," Oprah wrote in *The Path Made Clear*. "It was an exhilarating experience. And yet, another little kernel of knowing was revealing itself to me. Even at the show's peak, I had a deep awareness that a supreme moment of destiny still awaited me. That's why, after twenty-five years, I trusted my instinct when it told me, *This isn't it. There's something else.* The show was my home, the audience was one of the great loves of my life, but I couldn't ignore the flicker of certainty telling me it was time to move on."[9]

OWN, however, had gotten off to a rocky start, and media reports were not very kind as the network struggled to find its voice and solid programming. "It felt like everywhere I looked, critics were taking me to task for OWN's performance. One of the toughest headlines announced, 'Oprah Winfrey Isn't Quite Holding Her OWN.' That one stung. I had enjoyed a long stretch at the top and was proud to be known as a powerful businesswoman. Now it felt like every decision I made ended up on the nightly news crawl."

But OWN did find its way, with programs such as *Greenleaf* and *Queen Sugar*, two NAACP Image Award–winning shows with stellar casts. And Oprah is still going strong. In 2020, she signed a deal with Discovery for a $35 million stake in their company in exchange for increasing Discovery's ownership in OWN to 95 percent.[10] Lately, audiences have enjoyed Oprah's intimate interviews in her garden in Montecito, California, like her bombshell 2021 sit-down with Prince Harry and Meghan Markle. In all of these moves, one thing is certain: Oprah is not a person to be slowed down or stopped.

"You don't have to be one thing—you can be everything," Jenn White told me. "You can be everything you want to be, and that continued to build over the course of her career, in launching a magazine and launching a cable network and she's like, 'I'm just gonna do all of it.'"

For many people, Oprah opened their eyes to a world of possibilities, and as she told her audience in that final episode, she showed us how to have influence in—and control of—our own lives. "Wherever you are, that is your platform, your stage, your circle of influence," Oprah told them. "That is your talk show, and that is where your power lies. In every way, in every day, you are showing people exactly who you are. You're letting your life speak for you. And when you do that, you will receive in direct proportion to how you give in whatever platform you have."[11]

Part X

SPORTS COOL

THE BEST. EVER. ANYWHERE.

Written while listening to "GO!" by Common

> "I wouldn't mind being the female MJ. I want to have major crossover appeal."
>
> —Candace Parker on ESPN in 2009

ON A SPRING SUNDAY NIGHT, in the middle of a global pandemic, over six million people were in their own homes but still connected. And not so surprisingly, it was Michael Jordan who brought us all together.

It didn't matter that it had been over two decades since Mike had stepped foot on a court. Or that most individual NBA teams of today could never play as strong of a role in our society's culture as the Chicago Bulls of the '90s did. Or even that many of us were barely even old enough to remember it all. None of it mattered.

What did matter, though, is that for two hours, instead of stressing and depressing about the doom and the gloom and the sadness in the world around us, COVID-19, or the 2020 we'd all hoped for but would never be, we were collectively throwing ourselves into a documentary about Mike's last season playing with our beloved Bulls, his *Last Dance*.

Last Dance was the most-viewed ESPN documentary ever, with over half of us hitting every advertiser's dream of the eighteen-to-forty-nine-year-old demographic. As we watched, we took our commentary to social media. And these numbers don't include the some three million others who would tune in later.

That era of Chicago Bulls championship wins was special not just because we won (note the intentional use of "we" here), and not just because we did so with remarkable playing by legendary players that the sport had not yet seen. What millions of us clearly understand—even the ones, like me, who weren't sports fans—is that this Chicago Bulls team was so unique that it changed how we watch and talk about the sport.

Michael Jordan became Michael Jordan right here in Chicago, and it was his all-star work with his Bulls teammates that changed not just sports culture but sports as a megaculture ingrained in what makes a city a city, what connects people across racial, ethnic, and sociocultural lines. Here in Chicago, there was nothing that brought people together more in the '90s than the team's repeated championship wins. During the championship Bulls' reign as a great NBA dynasty between '91 and '98, it was cool to be a fan—even if you knew nothing about the sport—because now it meant more than just a win. It represented who you were and what you supported.

I'm not sure how many Chicago Bulls shirts I had as a child or how often the number twenty-three was my chosen jersey number on teams. But I know that the Bulls are permanently part of how I dress. A Bulls jersey or shirt with some Jordans is often my uniform, one that shows just how deep fashion and sports are aligned, just as it's common to keep a black-and-white White Sox hat on hand.

And now Chicago has another championship team carrying on this legacy, but this time it's with the WNBA. Even before hometown hero Candace Parker returned home to play for the Chicago Sky and lead her team to its first championship in 2021, people had been asking the question: *Is Candace Parker the next Michael Jordan?*

Parker started off as a sports star when she won Rookie of the Year and MVP in the same year, making her the only WNBA player to have done so. In 2022 she was the first WNBA player featured on the cover of the video game NBA2K,[1] and she was voted AP Female Athlete of the Year—for the second time.[2] But it was her homecoming that had particular impact in Chicago, as the city seemed to have its eye on the Sky in a way it never had before.

"This is a woman playing for her hometown: choosing to come to Chicago, choosing to come to the Sky, who had not won a championship before, to win a championship and bring that to her city,"

Brandon Pope, an anchor and reporter at WCIU Chicago, told me in an interview.[3]

With the cultural impact Chicago sports has had, especially in basketball, I'm hoping to see the same support for the Chicago Sky while its players build their own dynasty as we've shown the Chicago Bulls. Although Candace Parker has moved on to another WNBA team, the Sky's talent and continuing influence on the city can't be denied.

"Chicago's had a basketball culture for decades," Pope said. "And it's been a training ground and, really, an incubator for some of the best basketball talent of all time—men's and women's—so it almost feels like Chicago needs to have a solid WNBA team."

Let's look back at those moments, when the legendary Chicago Bulls of the '90s reigned supreme, and when Chicago teams set the trend of more than just sports.

27

THREE-PEAT AFTER THREE-PEAT

"My heart, my soul, and my love has always gone to the city of Chicago."

—Michael Jordan in *The Last Dance*

CHICAGO KIDS IN THE '90S might have unknowingly taken for granted the fact they lived in a city with an extraordinarily great NBA team. Like Chris Herring, author of *Blood in the Garden: The Flagrant History of the 1990s New York Knicks*, many thought it was normal.

"I had mostly just kind of accepted that it was something that was just like the Bud Billiken Parade where it was like, 'Oh, we just get one of these every year,'" Herring told me in an interview. "I understood a little bit about how great the Bulls were; I certainly knew Michael Jordan was the greatest player in the league, and maybe the best player ever. I didn't realize how difficult [or] how easy it was for them, whatever it was, I didn't really understand the other dynamics that were at play."[1]

The sentiment makes sense. The Chicago Bulls won the NBA championship in 1991, 1992, and 1993, and then turned around and won it three more times: in 1996, 1997, and 1998. There was a "three-peat" and then another, and at the time many young people didn't realize how phenomenal that was. But these wins *were* phenomenal, and as the Bulls turned from simply a team to a dynasty, the league as a whole benefited from a newfound interest in the NBA.

"The numbers and the ratings are always up when you have a dynasty involved, when you have a team that is going to win six out of ten championships—in this case, six out of eight for the years that Michael was there," Herring explained. "And I think the closest we've really had since then, we've had maybe two teams: I would say the Lakers [with] Shaq and Kobe and they won three titles from '99 to 2003, and then you had the Warriors just the last few years with Steph Curry, Klay Thompson, Draymond Green, and then to some extent with Kevin Durant as well."

During the 1980s, global interest in the NBA had started to increase as international players started to join the league. And then during the 1992 Olympic Games, the US "Dream Team" traveled to Barcelona, Spain, and it changed how the world saw the NBA. The team, which included both Michael Jordan and Scottie Pippen of the Bulls, won all of its games. Media from around the world started to send reporters to cover NBA games in the States, and NBA viewership skyrocketed. The team everyone had their eye on was the team that was winning: the Chicago Bulls.

"People claim to hate that the league is ruled by one team, but that's when people that don't even have an interest in the sport will watch just to get a sense as to what everybody's talking about," Herring explained. "It's like anything else—a TV show that everybody's talking about. You have to see it. Even if you don't know what's going on, you want to be part of it somehow."

In the case of this Bulls team, it was not only about the game of basketball. These men, collectively, became a pop culture sensation. But undeniably, people were tuning in specifically to see Michael Jordan. "The numbers were just monstrous when you talk about Michael Jordan's involvement," Herring said. "He was in the finals every year. It was very similar to what we think about with regards to LeBron James now. He was just a singular talent, and if he was going to play and if he was healthy, you knew the Bulls were going to make it to at least the championship round, and probably win that as well."

Even with the many new NBA stars who have come into public appreciation over the years, Michael Jordan is still considered by many to be the NBA's all-time greatest player. Born in 1963 in New York, he grew up in North Carolina. He led a group of college basketball players to win the gold for USA at the 1984 Olympics in Los Angeles. (At the time, professional athletes weren't allowed to play.) That same year, he was drafted by the Bulls and was named Rookie of the Year. He was the league's Most Valuable Player five times.

Saying Jordan was a great player is an understatement. For people not old enough to remember seeing Jordan play in real time, *The Last Dance* documentary series wove together massive amounts of game footage to showcase why Jordan really was "His Airness"—nobody else, to this day, can fly like he did. "I know, for me, [*The Last Dance*] was really my first time seeing extended stretches, beside for maybe YouTube here and there, watching Michael Jordan play against competition from that era, and just watching the guy glide and soar through the air and looking as if he was almost from the future compared to everybody else," Herring said.

But, as amazing as Jordan was, he wasn't the only person with star power on the squad. And it's important to remember he wasn't alone in building the powerful dynasty. In the late '70s through the '80s, the Los Angeles Lakers famously won five NBA championships, and it was the duo of players Magic Johnson and Kareem Abdul-Jabbar that helped the team achieve them. Similarly, when the Chicago Bulls "three-peated" twice, it was Scottie Pippen who worked literally at Jordan's side.

Jacoby Cochran is host of the daily news podcast *City Cast Chicago* and was named a Chicago Bulls Culture Creator in the 2022–2023 season for his storytelling, which often centers on the city he loves. As a native Chicagoan, he says Pippen's extreme talent is sometimes overlooked. "While teams had dynamic duos before—your Magics, your Kareems— I think the Mike-Scottie dynamic of how multitalented Scottie Pippen was, I think more NBA players have games similar to Scottie Pippen's versus maybe Mike's, in a sense of now you see a better emphasis on ball handling, on passing, can you also defend, can you score when your best player's not on the floor," Cochran told me in an interview.[2]

Pippen was born in 1965 in Arkansas and was drafted to the Seattle SuperSonics and then traded to Chicago in 1987. His talent was immediately recognized and he became a huge asset to the team, even as a rookie. Like Jordan, he won Olympic gold medals, played on all-star teams, and was there for all six of the Bulls' championships. Not only was he a top player in the league at that time, but Cochran also described how Pippen's play style is still influential to this day. "I think the kind of Swiss army knife that Scottie Pippen was as a player is a real kind of model that modern players have built themselves to emulate and be more like," he explained.

The star players, the winning, the international media attention: all of this was part of a greater change that signaled to the world that Chicago was special, that it was—and still is—a world-class city. "You just see a kind of swagger about Chicago emerge during those years. Whether it's fashion, whether it's the growing influence [on] music, we're now an epicenter of culture," Cochran said.

During the period when the Bulls were on top, the city of Chicago was also aiming to become a tourist destination, one that would rival large cities around the world: New York, London, Paris. Part of that meant capitalizing on this culture that had spread from Chicago out to the corners of the world. "I also think that the '90s Bulls probably are when you think about [then Chicago mayor Richard M.] Daley's plan for transformation," Cochran said. "I think that success of the Bulls maybe created a desire to make Chicago this international city in a way: tourists from all over the world are coming here, people want to be here, Oprah is here, Mike is here."

Even today, decades later, what the Chicago Bulls gave to the city is still paramount. It's a level of pride that Cochran says you can feel throughout the city. "There's still this level of gratefulness," he explained. "And I don't think it holds us back, I don't think it holds us down, I don't think we're afraid to live up to our own history."

28

BE LIKE MIKE

"Michael Jordan, the man, will never be duplicated. The athlete will not be duplicated, but the mindset, work ethic, or sweat equity that he embodied and depicted are elements that other people can take. They can be the MJ of whatever. . . . That's just all internally from you. That goes into how much you work and how much you want it."

—Jasmine Jordan, field representative at the Jordan Brand and Michael Jordan's daughter

WITH MICHAEL JORDAN'S monstrous star power, he was big business. On top of his salary, which added up to $90 million throughout his basketball career, he earned $1.8 billion in corporate partnerships, according to *Forbes*. Even today, he is still worth $1.7 billion.[1]

After his first, brief retirement in 1993, Jordan returned to the NBA for the 1995–1996 season wearing number 45. His first game back was between the Bulls and the Indiana Pacers. That game was the highest-rated regular-season NBA game since 1973,[2] and this made Jordan-endorsed companies very happy. According to *Jet*, during that comeback season the stock of McDonald's, Sara Lee, Quaker Oats (which owned Gatorade), Nike, and General Mills—five companies Jordan endorsed—rose on Wall Street by a combined $23 million when he started practicing again.[3]

Jordan's famous 1992 Gatorade commercial was one that had people around the world singing, "If I could be like Mike." But out of all his endorsements and partnerships, one in particular stands out as the most influential on today's modern culture.

The Air Jordan.

The shoe that would change what is considered the ideal basketball shoe was birthed out of a shift in NBA culture and a desire to create more superstars. But at the time, Michael Jordan was not yet the kind of star player that companies would automatically expect to bring in high sales. "There was a transition from the '80s [into the '90s] to where the league was always trying to really establish tentpoles with star talent," Chris Herring, author of *Blood in the Garden*, told me. "In the '80s, it was mostly just Magic Johnson and Larry Bird, but you had this guy who started playing for Chicago, who I think some people saw potential in—certainly Nike and Adidas saw potential in Michael Jordan, but I think they were kind of taking a gamble."[4]

When Jordan joined the NBA in 1984, he wanted to sign a shoe contract with Adidas. But Nike, a much younger company, offered him a huge partnership: a five-year deal with base pay of $500,000 per year. This offer was three times as much as any other NBA sneaker deal at the time.[5] Jordan even went back to Adidas to see if they could compete with the offer, but they refused to match it.

Not all shoe executives could see the potential in Jordan, who stood at just six feet six. "At that time, you had shoe executives that were kind of thinking that seven-footers were going to be the most popular players in the game, because they'd always been the biggest difference makers," Herring said. "So all of a sudden you've got Michael Jordan, who's kind of this high-flying athlete."

Nike recognized the opportunity of Jordan's reputation, as a player who could jump so high he could practically ignore the laws of physics, and created the Air Jordan shoe and its now famous "Jumpman" logo. According to *The Last Dance*, Nike had hoped the Air Jordan line could make $3 million by year four of the contract. But in just the very first year, the shoe made $126 million.[6]

"The reason the shoe sales took off the way they did is because he was like nothing most people had seen before at the sport," Herring said. "So it obviously lifted the Bulls into a different stratosphere as far as how competitive they were, as far as how badly people wanted the merchandise, as far as how badly people needed to be at the games. And certainly, it kind of became the must-have shoe, when you talk about the culture specifically."

Before Jordan and his shoe took off in 1985, there were other shoes that were seen as the ideal. For years and years, that title went to Converse's Chuck Taylor All-Star. Then, in 1976, Julius "Dr. J." Erving created a Converse with his name in gold text called the Dr. J. Pro Leather. Nike, too, had created other shoes before the collaboration with Jordan—the 1978 Nike Blazer and the original Air Force 1—but it was the Air Jordan that took off in a way that not many would have predicted.

"People literally wanted to be like Mike," sneaker reporter Ticara Devone told me in an interview. "Little kids in that day and time, they wanted that shoe," she explained. "That marketing was great, because you felt like if you put that shoe on, you'll be like Mike on the court for sure."[7]

Even outside of the sport of basketball, the Air Jordan has become one of the most sought-after sneaker brands. New releases sell out in less than a second, people enter drawings just for the opportunity to get a spot in line to buy them, and there's an entire market for reselling them. The shoe's influence reaches deep into fashion and popular culture, twenty years after Jordan's final retirement after the 2002–2003 season.

"I think, even to this day, [Michael Jordan] is one of the most successful basketball players with a silhouette that has transcended him being in the NBA—it's cemented in multiple parts of culture, not just sneaker culture," Devone said. "The designs and all the elements of the Jordan Brand, it's just going to continue to transcend time."

In addition to the Air Jordan shoe getting better over time, Devone says the brand is continuing to innovate and stay relevant, building on the Jordan legacy but also creating collaborations with influential creators in younger generations. "It's amazing to see other artists and people embracing Jordan Brand," she explained. "So you have [music artist] Travis Scott, you have Nina Chanel [Abney], who is a multidisciplinary artist, you have all these different people who are part of this man's legacy. And I think they keep [the people who work at the Jordan Brand] continuing to reinvent themselves."

29

WHITE SOX HAT

"We not only changed music, we changed pop culture all over the world. We did that by making it all right for artists to be themselves. You no longer had to be squeaky clean. We opened the floodgates for artists who wanted to work on this side, artists who wanted to be raw."

—Ice Cube in *Billboard*

THE WHITE SOX HAT is a pop culture staple. It's gone through many forms throughout the years, with changes ranging from the colors to lettering. But it was in the 1990s that the distinctive black-and-white version worn today, with its strong hold on Black popular culture and coolness, came into existence. As essential to culture as the hat is, baseball historian and freelance columnist Shakeia Taylor is the first person to have reported a full analysis of its contribution. And there's a reason for that, she told me in an interview. "There's never really been anyone in baseball media who can tap into Black culture as it exists in the sport."[1]

Her story, "The White Sox Cap and Hip-Hop Culture," was the second piece in her residency at FanGraphs, a website that mostly publishes Major and Minor League Baseball statistical analysis.[2] The story behind the popularity of the White Sox hat involves both hip-hop and Blackness. The spread of the hat's popularity goes back to one rap group in particular: N.W.A. In 1991, group members Dr. Dre, Eazy-E, and Ice Cube started wearing it, and as Taylor reported in her piece, there's a clear reason why: colors.

On a July 2017 visit to Chicago, former Chicago Bulls star Kendall Gill interviewed Ice Cube for CSN Chicago. When Gill asked Cube why N.W.A wore this particular hat, Cube told him, "Chicago changed their colors to black and white. It was perfect for us."[3]

This change, which was announced in 1990 and implemented in 1991, was a nod to a previous White Sox hat and uniform designed in 1948. That earlier design featured the first S-O-X logo in Old English script, because the White Sox's recently appointed vice president, twenty-two-year-old Chuck Comiskey, wanted to make an impression by modeling the new Sox uniforms off those of the New York Yankees. "If I couldn't make the White Sox win," Comiskey told White Sox historian Rich Lindberg in the 1980s, "at least I would try to make them look like winners."[4]

Yet when the team returned to the 1948 design, its popularity and coolness stemmed not from its retro appeal but from Black '90s culture. As Taylor told me, the colors a person wore were extremely important in cities such as Chicago and Los Angeles where gangs were a major issue. Black and Brown young people, especially, knew what colors would be seen as gang colors and would think about their clothing choices to ensure that they came across as neutral. "The timeline [of the release of the new hat] lined up perfectly," Taylor said. "I think '90s culture is where you have to start. And for those of us who were Black and old enough to know what was going on, we remember that gangs were real.

"I remember not being able to wear my Georgetown jacket when I came to Chicago to visit because it was navy blue and had a big *G* on it," said Taylor, who moved to Chicago to attend Loyola University in 2001. "I think a lot of that informed the way we dressed at that time. Yeah, we had a lot of fun, girls wore baggy clothes, but at the same time, we needed [to wear] things that we wouldn't get shot for. And Ice Cube and N.W.A is the best example of that."

The popularity of the hat also spread because of who was now wearing it: one of the hottest rap groups in the country, with an outspoken, in-your-face attitude. "At that time, I would say that would have been considered counterculture, so it's rebellious," Taylor said. "You've got these guys talking about 'f— the police' and they wore White Sox hats. I think that's the biggest impact."

And when Black people embrace a piece of clothing, Taylor explained, we're going to make it into an entire look: "We're going to get a 'fit off." At the end of 1990, the White Sox were in eighteenth place out of twenty-six teams in product sales. The next year, after the launch of the new hat, the team was third—behind the Oakland Raiders and New York Yankees.[5]

More people have taken note of the hat's legacy in recent years, since the N.W.A biopic movie *Straight Outta Compton* was released in 2015. (Though some were quick to point out that a scene set in 1986 showed Eazy-E in the new design, which would not have been available until five years later.)

And the culture of hip-hop continues to work in tandem with sports, especially here in Chicago. In 2016, Chance the Rapper partnered with the apparel company New Era to redesign the White Sox hat, with his three new designs going on sale before that year's home opener.[6] However, the team never closed the official deal that would have made Chance the White Sox ambassador he always wanted to be. So instead he then designed his popular "3" hat, which he now generally wears *instead of* White Sox hats.

Looking at this history, it's clear that as Major League Baseball works to get Black viewers back to the sport,[7] fashion would be a strong way to do so. And that when major icons in hip-hop think something is cool, then it's cool.

"Hip-hop is fashion," Taylor said. "If art is fashion, fashion is art, and sports is a part of that for us. So that hat is a cool symbol; it probably went with whatever Mikes you were wearing that day. So N.W.A was the massive impact and then it filtered over into rap in general."

Part XI

THE ARTS

ART FOR THE PEOPLE

Written while listening to "VRY BLK" by Jamila Woods, featuring Noname

> "Every individual wants to leave a legacy; to be remembered
> for something positive they have done for their community."
> —Dr. Margaret T. Burroughs in *Ebony* in 1993

BEING ON A STAGE is exhilarating. Even as a kid, whenever I stepped out from behind a curtain, with a crowd full of people staring back, the anxiety hit then immediately filtered from fear to a feeling of pure happiness. My talent of choice? Oratory contests.

Really, I thought I was a performance princess, spending days and days memorizing pieces to perform. In them, I could be anyone. And to explore, I had endless options: a poem by Langston Hughes (*"Well, son, I'll tell you: Life for me ain't been no crystal stair"*), a speech by Sojourner Truth (*"Nobody ever helps me into carriages, or over mud-puddles, or gives me any best place! And ain't I a woman?"*), a monologue from Lorraine Hansberry's *A Raisin in the Sun* (*"I always thought it was the one concrete thing in the world that a human being could do"*).

Remembering each line I'd practiced tirelessly was another feat, one I'd accomplish by staring at different objects in my elementary school's auditorium instead of into the faces of those in the audience. A clock centered in the middle of the wall, a side-door exit, a wall sconce.

One thing that has never escaped me is how lucky I am to have been exposed to the arts at a young age. I was very young going to the

Art Institute to help "design" a new kids' exhibit; I was at the library diving into the minds of the greatest writers; I was at museums taking in all of the information my little head could hold.

When I think about the days I'm most curious about, it's what Black Chicago looked like in the 1930s and '40s. It's all I can ever think about when I pick up a book and imagine all of the literary and artistic bliss that was cultivated as Black folks began to congregate in and move in droves to Bronzeville.

A lot of love is given to Harlem and its renaissance—its place solidly formed in history as the home of all that is Black and cool. But what people fail to mention is that Black Chicago experienced its own renaissance in arts and literature. From writers like Gwendolyn Brooks and Richard Wright to artists like Archibald John Motley Jr. and Margaret Burroughs, Black folks living and working in Chicago's Black Belt supported the proud Black consciousness that was evolving while building the foundation of what has become one of the nation's strongest arts scenes.

A renaissance, by definition, is a revival of interest in something, so it's very fair to give credit to those in Harlem who shouldered such a strong intellectual explosion: the parties, the travel from Paris, the shows. But right here in Chicago, we had our own middle class, our own movement. And similarly, it was based on an increase in racial consciousness and what it meant to be Black in America at that time.

One thing that stands out to me, though, is that throughout the years, no matter the decade, Black art is so very celebratory of what it is to be Black. Too often, things that are Black and extraordinary are deemed important, when just our everyday existence is what really makes Black Chicago special. It's kids playing on the street, a group of church ladies heading into service, the older men who play chess at the coffee shop. These are the visual images that are imprinted in my mind when I think about Chicago, images of the people who make everything run, what makes a community a community.

Chicago artists did not shy away from the uncomfortable either: the struggle, and the ugly. And this precedent set up current artists to believe there is no limit to either their creativity or the activism that shines through it.

"In Chicago, when every building was boarded up, artists took over every block, every parameter that they could, to create art and beautify spaces that were in a time of despair," Angel Idowu, an arts reporter at Chicago's WTTW, told me. "When we didn't know what's going on with the pandemic, when we were protesting for George Floyd's life and Black Lives, Black Chicagoans continued to push a positive narrative like Black people always do in these sad moments."[1]

Here in Chicago, art is made both for and by the people.

30

BEING BLACK IS

"He apparently has undertaken to indicate the happy, light-heartedness characteristic of childhood and of the colored race and has accomplished his purpose admirably. His taste in choosing to depict modern life and his own people instead of borrowing from classic models caused approving comment on the part of visitors present."

—An article in the *Indianapolis Star* on
William Edouard Scott in 1913

IN A SPACIOUS GALLERY at the Chicago Cultural Center, images of the city's everyday Black life lined the white walls: a woman makes up a bed, a young boy listens to records, a duo of young girls play hand games through a shadowy window.

These photographs, captured by artist Cecil McDonald Jr., were part of his *In the Company of Black* exhibit and 2018 book of the same name. Writer Tempestt Hazel and poet avery r. young contributed to the book. The photos span almost a decade, include subjects McDonald knew personally and people he didn't, and show the beauty in life's small moments.

McDonald told me that the most common images of Black people in media depict extreme examples of what it means to be Black, like celebrities and marginalized or suffering people who represent the myths of "Black exceptionalism" on one hand and "Black misery" on the other. "I was thinking, well, where are people who teach eighth grade, where are the principals of a school, where are the people who drive the CTA bus?" McDonald said in an interview in 2019. "Those aren't thought of as exotic and/or interesting people to consider. And for me, they were ripe for consideration."[1]

In his photos, McDonald's subjects are doing housework, spending time with family, and taking part in what most consider day-to-day activities. Historically, McDonald said, this type of imagery of Black people has been missing from the history of photography. "To show the full breadth of the humanity of any group of people, you need to show everyone, not just a particular group of people," McDonald said.

Each image tells its own story, but Greg Lunceford, curator of exhibitions at the Chicago Department of Cultural Affairs and Special Events, decided to display most of the photos in clusters throughout the exhibit. In one grouping, the steam rises from a hot comb as a young girl gets her hair pressed, an old woman meticulously dusts a lampshade, and another woman—aged somewhere in between—sits on the couch with a pen in her mouth as she grips a piece of paper torn from the notebook lying next to her. Each scene is undoubtedly unique, but there's a sense of preparedness threaded through the separate but similar conversations.

The photos all say: *there's work to be done today.*

In another set of images, light from outside peeks through the windows in three different photos. A girl stares straight into the camera as light illuminates her eyes; a woman walks through a hallway in her home with her head held high as light bounces off her and her reflections in two surrounding mirrors; and a man reads a magazine as an angled window allows a prism of light to encompass him. The simple yet strong images evoke feelings of power and focus.

"All these little clusters of small vignettes for me, as a curator, are to try to pull the conversation out to a broader community because they were so singular and because there was kind of a conversation that was happening individually in each shot," Lunceford told me. "I wanted to disrupt them a little bit and I wanted to try to broaden the conversations. . . . In proximity, they become community."[2]

Although this exhibit closed in 2019, McDonald is not alone in his desire to celebrate the beauty in all Black people. Since the city's inception, Black artists have been doing this kind of work in an effort to change how Black people are seen. Art as an industry might often be seen as something in which only highbrow society people can take part.

But art is much more than fancy galleries and high price tags. Black art in particular has been a way to show the beauty, humanity, and wonderful brilliance of Black people.

Another artist who did just that was William Edouard Scott, a muralist, portraitist, and illustrator. Born in 1884 in Indianapolis, Scott graduated from the School of the Art Institute of Chicago in 1909, and much of his work revolved around the Black working class. During the Great Depression of the 1930s, Scott painted murals in parks all across Chicago as part of the Illinois Federal Art Project. He was extremely interested in history, and for the 1940 American Negro Exposition in Chicago, he painted a series of murals and portraits that portrayed the Black experience from the Revolutionary War era through the Great Migration. He would continue to create for the rest of his life, one of his last major murals being *The Negro in Democracy* in 1960. Scott died just a few years later in 1964.[3]

Archibald John Motley also chronicled twentieth-century Black life through his art. Like Scott, he was one of the first Black artists to attend the School of the Art Institute of Chicago, graduating in 1918. He was born in New Orleans in 1891 and moved to Chicago with his family when he was young. A modernist, Motley is known for his vibrant depictions of Black social life and jazz culture. Some of his most popular works are beautiful portraits of Black people just living: *Woman Peeling Apples* (1924), *Mending Socks* (1924), and *Old Snuff Dipper* (1928).[4]

A bit younger than both Scott and Motley, Eldzier Cortor also attended the School of the Art Institute of Chicago. These artists' schooling is important, because they were not only remarkable artists but also trailblazers who were able to attend the illustrious school at a time when it was extremely rare for a Black artist to be accepted. Cortor was born in 1916 in Richmond, Virginia, and then raised in Chicago. After receiving two fellowships from the Rosenwald Foundation in the 1940s, he traveled to the Sea Islands of Georgia and South Carolina, where he was inspired by the local Gullah community and wove that influence into his portraiture. Among all of his work, Cortor became known for how he celebrated Black women, believing "the Black woman represents the Black race."[5]

Dr. Margaret Taylor Burroughs was not only an artist but also someone who strongly championed supporting the arts, building multiple institutions in order to do so. Born in St. Rose, Louisiana, in 1915, Burroughs also moved to Chicago as a child. She received both her bachelor's and master's degrees from the Art Institute. She started her professional career as a high school teacher while also writing children's books. She also published poetry collections about Black life, including *What Shall I Tell My Children Who Are Black?* in 1968.[6]

As a visual artist, Burroughs explored many mediums, like sculpture and painting, but she often spoke about art in terms of being a prolific printmaker. She created prints for most of her life, including *Hop Scotch* (1991) and *Bill Broonzy—Me Folk Singer* (2006). She passed away in 2010.

Burroughs was also a trailblazer, spearheading multiple large-scale initiatives to support Black arts and culture. In the late 1930s, she, Cortor, and Motley, along with fellow artists Bernard Goss, Charles White, William Carter, and Joseph Kersey, came together to discuss what would become the South Side Community Art Center. As members of a group called the Arts Craft Guild, they wanted to create a space that supported the arts, with an artist- and community-centered approach. The center was officially founded in 1940, with First Lady Eleanor Roosevelt delivering the dedication speech the following year.[7] Other renowned artists at the time, such as Scott, also supported this center.

In the 1950s, Burroughs founded Chicago's Lake Meadows Art Fair to create more ways for Black artists to sell their art, since the galleries and other venues that invited Black artists to exhibit their work were limited. The fair ended in the 1980s but was resurrected by Helen Y. West in 2005.

In 1961, Burroughs pulled together a group of colleagues to found the Ebony Museum of Negro History and Art—the first independent museum celebrating Black culture in the United States—and in 1968, the museum was renamed the DuSable Museum of African American History after Jean Baptiste Point DuSable.[8] The museum, which started in Burroughs's South Side home, is likely her most recognized accomplishment.

The list of influential Black artists in Chicago is endless, and it's amazing to see how current artists, like *In the Company of Black* artist Cecil McDonald Jr., have continued this tradition. McDonald hoped those viewing his exhibit were "enchanted by what they see, that they can somehow see themselves, that they on some level gain a better appreciation for the everyday activities, and not take for granted the people we interact with on a regular basis."

31

CHICAGO'S OWN
LITERARY RENAISSANCE

"It had been only through books—at best, no more than
vicarious cultural transfusions—that I had managed to
keep myself alive in a negatively vital way. Whenever my
environment had failed to support or nourish me, I had
clutched at books."

—Richard Wright in *Black Boy*

POET AND PROFESSOR Nate Marshall's grandmother migrated to Chicago
from Alabama during the Great Migration. She was a librarian, and she
gave him both a story and a way to tell it. "I think I had this sense of story
or history," he told me in an interview.[1] "That for me is a lot of what I
think about when I think about poetry and my own relationship to it."

On top of family, there was also the impact of being exposed to
artistic leaders everywhere in the city, even in his neighborhood school.
When Haki Madhubuti, who was extremely influential in the Black Arts
Movement, came to Marshall's class, he told the nine- and ten-year-olds
something that always stuck with Marshall: "Y'all should do whatever
you want to do in life, but purport to be the best at it."

"I don't know if in other cities you have this ecosystem [of] Black
artistic history and lineage at your fingertips, before you even really
know what it is," Marshall said. What Marshall experienced—and what
so many other Black Chicago kids experience before they understand

it—is a complete immersion in a legacy of huge artistic movements that transformed our society.

"I think the thing about New York, as a place, it is special, there's nowhere like it," Marshall said. "But there's something about Chicago that feels both particular and special but also representative. If you can figure out how to make something work in Chicago, you could do it anywhere in the country. And that's not necessarily true of a city like a New York or L.A. that are more specific, that have more specific economies—there are factors that hold there that wouldn't hold in Middle America."

By most estimations, Chicago's Black artistic renaissance stretched from the 1930s to the 1950s. In addition to the visual artists who created work during this period, Chicago's Black literary movement grew along with the city's expanding Black population. Much of this development happened in Bronzeville.

In the 1930s, the name "Bronzeville" grew in popularity and became the common term for the neighborhood previously known as the Black Belt. White people had given the area derogatory names such as "Darkie Town" and the "Black Ghetto." But James J. Gentry, a theater editor at the *Chicago Bee* newspaper, suggested the name should be "Bronzeville," because Black people's skin is bronze in color. And after that, Gentry brought the idea to the *Defender*'s Robert Abbott, who helped popularize the name.

In and around Bronzeville were places, institutions, and initiatives where Black writers could gather. In 1932, the George Cleveland Hall Branch Library on Forty-Eighth and Michigan opened. It was there that Vivian Gordon Harsh, who was the first Black librarian at Chicago Public Library, started compiling a historical research collection that is still used today. The Hall Library's salons—meetings where people exchange ideas—were extremely popular. Black people from different backgrounds would meet to discuss things like literature and art. The salons were not seen as just being for a certain elite class; they were for everyone.

In 1940, the first and only American Negro Exposition was held in Chicago, celebrating Black achievement—just as the World's Columbian Exposition was supposed to celebrate achievement from people all over the world. This event was the first of its kind to ever occur, and it's considered the first time Black Americans could share their own stories on a large world stage. It showcased the great progress Black people had made in many industries, but so much of it was centered in the arts: poets Langston

Hughes and Arna Bontemps wrote a musical pageant called *Cavalcade of the Negro Theater*; Richard Wright's controversial novel *Native Son* was celebrated; artist William Edouard Scott painted twenty-four murals.

The exposition could display such work because this period provided key support for creative exploration in Chicago. From 1935 to 1943, as writers struggled to find work, the Illinois Writers Project hired artists and writers to do what they did best: create. The project was part of a national initiative by the Works Progress Administration (WPA). It opened doors not only for white authors like Nelson Algren, who was able to write his first novel, *Never Come Morning*, but also for Black writers like Richard Wright, who started work on *Native Son*.

After 1940 came the Parkway Community House, which had programming that included its own resident theater group, and also served as a place for writers like Bontemps, Hughes, and Wright to stay when they were in Chicago. There was also the South Side Writers Group, which was formed after a lecture Hughes and Wright gave at the National Negro Congress in 1936. For two years, writers in this group gathered weekly to read their work, including many writers who were also part of the Illinois Writers Project.[2]

This kind of inspiration that flows between people and spaces is something that's still alive in Chicago today. "[What] I think is vibrant about the city—and about the city as a cultural space—is that there are always people in that moment, that are making things who you're looking to as an inspiration," Marshall said.

Another writer who participated in the group was Margaret Danner, the first Black assistant editor at *Poetry* magazine—though Danner's contributions to the field of poetry have been somewhat overlooked. Her work is not as easy to find outside of library collections, and she didn't get the acclaim of her colleagues. It's one of the reasons why *Poetry* magazine wanted to do a special issue on her in 2022.

Danner was born in Kentucky in 1915 but claimed Chicago as her birthplace because her family moved to the city when she was very young and it's where she grew up. She won her first poetry prize in eighth grade and later studied at Loyola University, Roosevelt College, Northwestern University, and YMCA College.

"Reading through [Danner's] letters and her papers, which are stored at the University of Chicago Special Collections wing of [the Regenstein Library], you get [a] really clear feeling that she felt anxiety about . . .

not being seen by other writers and readers and publishers at the time," Srikanth Reddy, the issue's guest editor, told me in an interview.[3]

Danner started at *Poetry* as a reader who would review the submissions that came through the mailroom. In the hierarchy of a magazine, that means she literally started off at the bottom. But Danner developed a keen knack for finding new talent and giving them the opportunity to be highlighted.

She continued that work as a teacher. "All that time she was looking for new voices, new talent, new poets," Reddy said. "And I think there's something about her—I think it's maybe something that everyone feels who feels like they haven't been noticed or they've been overlooked—that you look harder when you feel that way. And that's why looking was so important to her as a writer."

Creativity can truly be a connector of people and generations. As a poet, Nate Marshall has been deeply interested in the work of Gwendolyn Brooks ever since he read her poem "Beverly Hills, Chicago" in high school. "I still love that poem, because it was the first time I'd ever really seen a poem written about a place that I had been," Marshall said.

Brooks was born in Topeka, Kansas, in 1917 but moved to Chicago when she was young and published her first poem when she was thirteen. By the time she was seventeen, she was publishing her poems in the *Defender*.[4] "Living in the city, I wrote differently than I would have if I had been raised in Topeka, Kansas," she said in a 1994 interview. "I am an organic Chicagoan. Living there has given me a multiplicity of characters to aspire for. I hope to live there the rest of my days. That's my headquarters."[5]

At this headquarters, Brooks became a Pulitzer Prize–winning writer whose poems often centered Black Chicago. She held the position of the Library of Congress consultant in poetry (now called the poet laureate) and stayed in Chicago, writing and teaching, until her death in 1990.

As for Chicago's place in the arts, Marshall admits he's "deeply biased" but sees his hometown as central to history and therefore a key influence in the art that stems from it. "If you're talking about labor history and how art intersects with activism and these ways that we envision a different world, there's no way to talk about that stuff and not talk about Chicago," he said. "And then certainly in terms of Black folks, I think that Chicago—as much as any other city or any other place in the country—I think really shaped America's vision for Black life in the twentieth century post–Great Migration."

32

TOUCH THE SKY

"It's about something that feels relatable, it's about your childhood, it's about imagination, it's about limitations or lack thereof. . . . So those who either grew up with heroes that were on baseball fields, football fields, basketball courts or heroes that were on comic book pages or in cartoon strips, it encapsulates a lot of that."

—Hebru Brantley on his *Nevermore Park*
exhibit in the *Chicago Tribune*

IN 2019, IN A ROOM IN Chicago's Museum of Science and Industry (MSI), guests lined tables filled with magazines to search for pictures and words they wanted to add to a "community collage." The collage quickly filled as they added photos of brown faces and words like "improve Chicago violence," "free," and "culture" that they felt represented the civil rights movement—both past and present.

On a large pane of glass, the artist leading the collaborative effort, Shala., sketched drawings he felt represented Martin Luther King Jr.'s legacy. "I wanted to create a piece that commemorated Dr. King," Shala. told me in a 2019 interview. "But in a new way, by saying the new Dr. Kings are [Black women]."[1]

For Shala., a first-generation Nigerian American who was born and raised in Chicago, when it comes to art and science, it's all connected. "It's all the same," said Shala., who's best known for his groundbreaking solar murals and sculptures. "Technology, art, culture, and music are all the same in my mind, and they all fuel each other. So it makes sense that I'm here, but I would've never seen myself here."

The next year, in 2020, little superheroes dashed through the Museum of Science and Industry on Martin Luther King Jr. Day, their capes blowing and badges glowing as they ran out of the Black Creativity Innovation Studio. On this museum family day, the studio was set up just for them. They picked their superpowers, determined their origin stories, and chose an identity. And then, of course, next up was building their gear.

The "Hero Lab" was a collaboration between the Innovation Studio and Jason Mayden, who was CEO and cofounder of the children's shoe company Super Heroic and one of that year's honored Black Creativity innovators. "A lot of kids who are coming here, they feel joy for a moment, but we want them to go home and have that joy be present in their everyday lives, so we wanted to give them something—an artifact of their heroism and their brilliance," Mayden told me.[2] "By them constructing their own cape, picking their superpowers, it gives them agency and we give them labels that help them, biased towards positive outcomes."

Every year, the Innovation Studio creates events like these to expose youth to careers and other opportunities in creative and STEM fields. Mayden, a former designer for Nike and the Jordan Brand, is a native South Sider and sees the opportunity to participate in Black Creativity as a way to fill the void left by the lack of representation in these fields. "By me being myself in these environments, it gives people permission to be themselves. And I think authenticity and access to authentic people is lacking in our community, because we often are told we have to switch our behaviors, switch our style of speech or dress in order to be deemed as innovative or deemed as intelligent," Mayden said. "But I think I've lived the life and have a career that reflects my true self. And if we can have kids feel like being who they are is enough, then that's a blessing."

The Innovation Studio events are part of MSI's annual Black Creativity program, which always officially kicks off with MLK Day. Since 1970, Black Creativity has drawn crowds to Chicago's Hyde Park neighborhood to celebrate the culture, heritage, and contributions of Black people in art and innovation. In 2020, all of these contributions were on display in a timeline of the program's fifty-year history, the Innovation Studio, and the Juried Art Exhibition—which is the longest-running exhibit of Black art in the country.

Black Creativity started as the Black Esthetics arts and culture festival, with a focus on emerging artists and performances in theater,
dance, and music. Among those influential in its creation were *Chicago
Defender* publisher John H. Sengstacke, photographer Bobby Sengstacke,
fine arts editor Earl Calloway, history professor and MSI trustee John
Hope Franklin, and South Side Community Art Center members such as
artist Douglas R. Williams. At the inaugural event in 1970, the "Queen
of Gospel" Mahalia Jackson performed.

In 1984, the museum worked with the *Defender* to rethink the overall program of the exhibition, deciding to add science, technology, and
history to its focus and change its name to Black Creativity. It also added
a fundraising gala, supported by Johnson Publishing Company founders
Eunice and John Johnson, that was attended by Oprah. And in 1988,
MSI featured one hundred Black scientists, engineers, and inventors in
Black Achievers in Science.

"We added science and technology, but always kept the art," Angela
Williams, deputy creative director at MSI, told me. "And really, in a
way, we were ahead of the curve in terms of a larger global thinking.
Now, STEAM [science, technology, engineering, art, and math] is part
of educational thinking in terms of what students need to be looking
at towards the future."[3]

Williams took the lead on the *Black Creativity: 50 Years* exhibit in
2020, and said one of her favorite highlights from the program's history was a 2007 exhibit called *Design for Life* that featured industrial
designer Charles Harrison. Harrison was responsible for redesigning the
3-D View-Master and soon after became the chief of design at Sears,
Roebuck & Co.—the company's first Black executive. "He spent many,
many years at Sears and lived right here in Chicago," Williams said.
"The bios [in the exhibit] are really hyperfocused on Chicago stories,
and he's one of those stories."

Since its inception, Black Creativity has championed established
Black artists and innovators while launching the careers of emerging
talents. Artists such as Hebru Brantley, Harmonia Rosales, Theaster
Gates, and Amanda Williams were featured in Black Creativity before
their rise to wide acclaim.

In the broader art world, according to a 2018 Artnet analysis, the
number of exhibitions focusing on Black artists had jumped to record-
breaking numbers in recent years but Black art still accounted for less

than 3 percent of museums' acquisitions. In some museums, it was less than 1 percent.[4] The Juried Art Exhibition has been an antidote to the industry's lack of Black representation for more than fifty years.

But flying high, without a ceiling on ambition, has been a staple of Chicago's modern art scene. And if there's an artist who has made art cool, it's Hebru Brantley. The Bronzeville-bred art superstar is referenced in songs, such as Chance the Rapper's "Angels," and is a celebrity favorite. Especially now, Brantley's work is not relegated to art galleries and fancy museums. His work centers around the iconic characters he's created, influenced by the South Side of Chicago's AfriCOBRA movement of the 1960s and '70s. These characters can be found in murals across the city—their first public wall was inside the store of a Chicago streetwear brand named Leaders 1354.

"We have this idea of [Brantley's characters] FlyBoy and Lil Mama just literally flying all over the city," arts reporter Angel Idowu told me. "And before you knew it, they're flying over . . . all of these spaces, and [Brantley] was able to really build a brand off of that. I think that that speaks to Chicago's culture and influence: We really see the sky as the limit."[5]

In 2019 Brantley, who started out as a graffiti artist when he was a teen, created a truly immersive version of the world of his characters in the exhibition *Nevermore Park*. Walking through Nevermore feels like traveling through time and space, an out-of-this-world continuum that is undoubtedly Chicago but a version never before seen.

Newspapers seemingly fly around the entrance: It's a newsstand that could be straight out of an old superhero TV show. But the magazines that line it are familiar archival copies of *Ebony* and *Jet* magazines from over the years. Just feet away, old TVs with staticky screens blink on and off as a jacket belonging to one of the Tuskegee Airmen—who Brantley sees as the original "fly boys"—hangs on a chair. And then there's a train car that also seems to physically and metaphorically be part of both today and the past. Although it looks like a CTA car from the outside, the back is a small but elegant and elaborately decorated Pullman car.

"Nevermore is a (fictional) area on the Southeast Side of Chicago that's a bit overly stylized and hyper-embellished, and that's the stomping ground of our main characters and that's where our stories take place," Brantley told culture writer Darcel Rockett in the *Chicago Tribune*. "The installation is just putting the audience, submerging them in that world for however long that they want to get pictures, stand and travel through and engage in that space."[6]

The Afrofuturist experience of Nevermore pushed its attendees into a world that does not yet exist, while at the same time nodding to history. What has to happen inside a mind to be able to dream up such a world? How often can an exhibition truly take people somewhere else?

Or as Angel Idowu marveled, "Who would have thought creating these characters—to create this world just simply for your murals—and then to take it a step further and create . . . tangible, physical FlyBoys and Lil Mamas that kids could play and run around with and then thinking about how that went to Nevermore Park. That was a full experience, to step into this world that he's been giving us little dips and drops of for however many years beforehand, and so I think that that just speaks to the Chicago influence, being really encouraged to do anything."

Being in this city, with its rich cultural history and some of the world's greatest cultural institutions, has shaped the way its residents think about what is possible. Just like the young kids seen flying around MSI, older generations of Black Chicagoans, too, have created limitless attitudes. To them, art is in everything and it's found everywhere, but especially inside of them.

"Chicago really fuels our movement and our creativity and our expression," Idowu said. "Those spaces have allowed us to understand that the sky is the limit. And we don't have to be traditional in the ways that we are telling our stories."

EPILOGUE

The End Is Just the Beginning

Written while listening to "Home" by BJ the Chicago Kid

"Write about *our people*: tell their story. You have something
glorious to draw on begging for attention. Don't pass it up."
—Lorraine Hansberry in her "To Be Young, Gifted, and Black"
speech to *Readers Digest* / United Negro College Fund creative
writing contest winners

LOOKING BACK THROUGH photos of me growing up, there are parts of
Chicago culture sprinkled throughout those memories: a little me point-
ing to Chicago on a huge world map; the '90s Bulls T-shirts I wore
proudly like they were name-brand; CDs of the house music I danced
to like nobody was watching. And it's not hidden either. On the wall at
my daddy's house, there's a copy of an article I wrote for the *Chicago
Defender*'s youth column in high school—long before I ever really knew
what journalism was.

I did know, though, that there was so much I could learn about
Black history, about Chicago history, about *my* history. My seventh-
grade social studies teacher, Mrs. Marcia Arrington, always gave us
assignments that pushed us toward this kind of thing. We spent hours at
Carter G. Woodson Library researching all of the things that we could be
proud of but that she wanted us to learn how to discover for ourselves.

I had already learned from my mama a lot about Black history, the names and basic facts of people who I could be proud of. And my elementary school teachers, who were mostly Black women, had made sure their classes containing all Black children understood the beauty of Blackness just as much as we knew reading, writing, and arithmetic. They taught us hymns and spirituals to sing during assemblies and how to up our Black History Month projects: my personal favorite was making a papier-mâché sculpture of eighteenth-century writer Phillis Wheatley and then showing it off during an in-school "parade."

But it was Mrs. Arrington who taught us how to really research, drawing up a new question in our young minds: Now, what are *we* going to do next? And now, decades later, I'm still happily putting together some of those very important pieces that Mrs. Arrington was laying out: our past is just as much of our today as it ever was; the end is just the beginning.

But it's true that, in many ways, Chicago does look different than it did just a few decades ago. Articles and studies describe what is now seen as a strong Black migration away from Chicago, considered a mass exodus of the very families who helped build and create the city's culture. Between 2010 and 2020, Chicago lost eighty-five thousand of its Black residents, an almost 10 percent decline.[1] One inequity cited as a cause of this population decline, especially in some neighborhoods, is a loss of affordable housing, sparked by the demolishing of the city's public housing developments between 1995 and 2010, which displaced many families who lived in those almost twenty-two thousand units.[2]

As Dr. Eve L. Ewing says in her book *Ghosts in the Schoolyard* about the failure of those developments, "From former residents to journalists, everyone seemed to have a theory."[3] But regardless of why, this major action pushed Chicago to start losing many of its Black residents, as did other factors such as disinvestment in Black communities, an unemployment rate that remains intolerably higher for Black residents, mass incarceration, and predatory housing contracts.

And yet, despite these inequities, Black Chicago continues to persevere—just as we have in the past. And friends, Black Chicago, the love of my life, never loses its sparkle. Even when we need to shine a dull veneer back to its glory days, its value and potential don't change. A real diamond never loses its luster. And for me, that potential is rooted in the hearts, minds, and creativity of our youth.

The heartbeat of Black Chicago is so strong that every year, when the snow melts and the cold winds finally decide to soften their blows a bit, we are still strong. As I'm writing this, it's springtime, which means prom and graduation season. On Friday evenings especially, as I drive through my beloved South Side, almost every other block has a house filled with balloons, yard signs, and enlarged photos of beautiful, young, Black people. It's a season of celebrating new milestones and accomplishments, but also growth. There is so much ahead for them, and for those of us who love them. It's both a duty and an honor to support that.

What I want for my son and the next generation of Chicagoans is clear: I want them to know their power, I want them to know this is *their* city too, and I want them to know that everything they see is theirs for the taking. It's like that scene in *The Lion King*: as they hang out, go to school, play, laugh, and love, I want them to know that "everything the light touches" is theirs.

To me, that sense of pride and push toward empowerment is essential because, like in other cities, the push toward equality can be a slow and strenuous process. But as we work to make Chicago a fairer, more welcoming place for everyone, they need to know they aren't forgotten. And they aren't. Everywhere I look, I see amazing young creatives putting in the work to make sure the world knows they are here.

There are artists still in their teens who submit their work to the Museum of Science and Industry's Black Creativity competition, art that both stuns judges every year and expresses what's in their hearts. The city's young performers have created a vibrant scene for open mics, often integrating their social justice work because they know what their voices can do. I cry at watching Deeply Rooted Dance Theater's Youth Ensemble perform. The beauty and intensity in their movements tell stories that run deep through generations of Black folks and connect us to the past just by us watching. And there are young actors, like those on Showtime's *The Chi*, that make the series with their wit, comedic timing, and ability to emote.

They are young. They are gifted. *They are Black.*

But even as amazing as they are, I want to make sure that our generation does its part in helping them to become even greater, to accomplish even more than any of us ever did. And if we really want them to be able to stand on our shoulders, as we stand on those of our ancestors, we need to ensure that they live in a Chicago that they know is theirs—one that looks like them and tells their stories, one that gives them the space for creative ownership, one that helps them bloom.

But I don't see this as a problem. Thankfully, as journalist, I get to play the amateur historian, paying close attention to everything around me. And the more I look through Black Chicago's past, the more excited I am for the future. And that's exactly what I had to do to write this book. I had to get back outside, take a ton of trips to Woodson Library, and take my city back in. And as I did, I noticed more and more that the line between what was and what is has blended, leaving a city where there isn't a single corner that can be explained with broad brushstrokes—only tiny, intricate marks that tell stories so deep they absorb you.

In the most gorgeous way, Chicago is starting to look more and more like the Black people who made it great, and many of the things that have left are coming back into view. I can drive on Jean-Baptiste Pointe DuSable Lake Shore Drive to get downtown to Ida B. Wells Drive. I can visit a new monument to learn more about Pullman porters or admire the Johnson Publishing Company building, which has been renovated into something new but is thankfully still there.

It's time to use our past to look toward our future. And from what I can tell, it's going to be even more beautiful.

ACKNOWLEDGMENTS

THIS LOVE LETTER to the place that raised me was an honor to write and wouldn't have been possible without the support of my family and friends, who made sure I ate meals, calmly accepted my declined event invites, and always pumped me up every step of the process. My "Work Like Beyoncé" group was along with me for this entire ride. I wrote almost the entire book while coworking with them on Zoom: early mornings, late nights, and marathon sessions on the weekends. This book is just as much theirs as it is mine, and I'm so grateful they were there.

My editor, Alicia C. Sparrow, taught me how to move from journalistic writing to standing on my thoughts in book form. "Say it with your chest," she would write in my notes. She guided me from an idea to an entire book and I could not have done this without her. And thank you to managing editor Devon Freeny for the meticulous copyedits—not only the ones that would have left me seriously embarrassing myself but also those that made me think deeply about what I wanted certain lines to truly say. Copyediting is like tying the big red bow on the brand-new car, and I'm thankful this one is ready to drive off the lot.

To my many interviewees, I am honored you shared your expertise with me, for this book specifically and in past reporting: Danielle Robinson Bell, Joy Bivins, Mary Brooks, Toronzo Cannon, Jacoby Cochran, Ayana Contreras, Cheryl Corley, Mary Datcher, Ticara Devone, Charla Draper, Dr. Allyson Nadia Field, DeJuan C. Frazier, Chris Herring, Angel Idowu, Alan King, Greg Lunceford, Adeshola Makinde, Nate Marshall, Jason Mayden, Cecil McDonald, Sergio Mims (rest in power), Scarlett

Newman, Dometi Pongo, Brandon Pope, Srikanth Reddy, Dr. Mark A. Reid, Monique Rodriguez, Shala., Melody Spann Cooper, Richard Steele, Shakeia Taylor, Dr. Elizabeth Todd-Breland, Charles Whitaker, Jenn White, David Whiteis, and Angela Williams. It is a privilege that I don't take for granted.

And to Chicago, my first love, thank you for making me who I am. Let's keep showing the world how we do it. South Side, worldwide, baby! XO.

NOTES

Introduction: From Chicago with Love

1. "The History of Bronzeville," Chicago Studies, University of Chicago, accessed August 22, 2022, https://chicagostudies.uchicago.edu/bronzeville/bronzeville-history -bronzeville.
2. Christopher Robert Reed, "Beyond Chicago's Black Metropolis: A History of the West Side's First Century, 1837–1940," *Journal of the Illinois State Historical Society* 92, no. 2 (Summer 1999): 125, JSTOR, http://www.jstor.org/stable/40193212.
3. Danielle Gray, "Kim Kardashian Slammed for Calling Cornrows 'Bo Derek Braids,'" *Allure*, January 29, 2018, https://www.allure.com/story/kim-kardashian-called -cornrows-bo-derek-braids-lol-come-on-girl.
4. Tiana Randall, "The Problem with TikTok's 'Clean Girl' Aesthetic," i-D, *Vice*, July 12, 2022, https://i-d.vice.com/en_uk/article/epzna7/tiktok-clean-girl-aesthetic.
5. "Carter G. Woodson," NAACP, accessed January 31, 2022, https://naacp.org/find -resources/history-explained/civil-rights-leaders/carter-g-woodson.
6. "Our History," Association for the Study of African American Life and History, accessed February 14, 2022, https://asalh.org/about-us/our-history/.
7. Kenton Bell, ed., "Popular Culture," Open Education Sociology Dictionary, accessed June 27, 2023, https://sociologydictionary.org/popular-culture/.

Homecoming

1. Gwendolyn Brooks and Elizabeth Alexander, *The Essential Gwendolyn Brooks* (New York: Library of America, 2005), 113–114.

1. Black Journalism Pushes for Progress

1. Donald L. Grant and Mildred Bricker Grant, "Some Notes on the Capital 'N,'" *Phylon* 36, no. 4 (1975): 436, https://doi.org/10.2307/274643.

2.   Communication Research Institute of William Penn University, "Alexander Clark
      Becomes an Attorney, Newspaper Publisher and Ambassador," Iowa PBS, 2012,
      https://www.iowapbs.org/iowapathways/artifact/1547/alexander-clark-becomes
      -attorney-newspaper-publisher-and-ambassador.

3.   "Why Colored Men Should Subscribe for a Paper Published by His Own Race,"
      Conservator, December 18, 1886, Library of Congress, https://chroniclingamerica
      .loc.gov/lccn/sn84024048/1886-12-18/ed-1/seq-1/.

4.   Ellen Shubart, "5 Fun Facts About the World's Columbian Exposition of 1893,"
      Chicago Architecture Center, accessed June 27, 2023, https://www.architecture
      .org/news/historic-chicago/5-fun-facts-about-the-worlds-columbian-exposition
      -of-1893/.

5.   Ida B. Wells, *Crusade for Justice*, 2nd ed. (orig. publ. 1970; Chicago: University of
      Chicago Press, 2020), 56.

6.   "Southern Violence During Reconstruction," *American Experience*, PBS, accessed
      August 9, 2023, https://www.pbs.org/wgbh/americanexperience/features
      /reconstruction-southern-violence-during-reconstruction/.

7.   "Southern Horrors: Lynch Law in All Its Phases" (New York: New York Age Print,
      1892), Schomburg Center for Research in Black Culture, New York Public Library,
      https://digitalcollections.nypl.org/items/634281e0-4abc-0134-346c-00505686a51c.

8.   Frederick Douglass, Irvine Garland Penn, Ferdinand Lee Barnett, and Ida B. Wells,
      The Reason Why the Colored American Is Not in the World's Columbian Exposition
      (Chicago: Miss Ida B. Wells, 1893), https://digital.library.upenn.edu/women/wells
      /exposition/exposition.html.

9.   Douglass et al., *Reason Why*.

10.   Wells, *Crusade for Justice*, 101.

11.   "Early Chicago: The 1893 World's Fair," WTTW Chicago, September 11, 2018,
      https://interactive.wttw.com/dusable-to-obama/1893-worlds-fair.

2. The Making of the Man

1.   "History," Hampton University, accessed September 10, 2022, https://home.
      hamptonu.edu/about/history/.

2.   Roi Ottley, *The Lonely Warrior: The Life and Times of Robert S. Abbott* (Chicago:
      H. Regnery, 1955), Kindle ed., chap. 1.

3.   Abbott-Sengstacke Family Papers, Vivian G. Harsh Research Collection of Afro-
      American History and Literature, Woodson Regional Library, Chicago Public
      Library.

4.   Abbott-Sengstacke Family Papers.

5.   Ottley, *Lonely Warrior*, chap. 1.

6.   Kai El'Zabar, "Today . . . Yesterday," *Chicago Defender*, May 6, 2015, Issuu, https://
      issuu.com/chidefender/docs/binder3/6.

7.   Ottley, *Lonely Warrior*, chap. 5.

3. A Great Migration

1.   Ottley, *Lonely Warrior*, chap. 6.

2. Elaine Thatcher, "Julius Taylor and the Broad Ax," Utah Stories from the Beehive Archive, Utah Humanities, 2008, https://www.utahhumanities.org/stories/items /show/162.

3. Brian Dolinar, ed., *The Negro in Illinois: The WPA Papers* (Urbana: University of Illinois Press, 2013), 117.

4. Abbott-Sengstacke Family Papers.

5. Robert S. Abbott, "Looking Back . . . ," *Chicago Defender*, May 4, 1935, ProQuest, https://www.proquest.com/historical-newspapers/looking-back/docview/492447998 /se-2.

6. Emmett J. Scott, "Letters of Negro Migrants of 1916–1918," *Journal of Negro History* 4, no. 3 (1919): 327, https://doi.org/10.2307/2713780.

7. David Blatty, "W.E.B. Du Bois and Booker T. Washington Had Clashing Ideologies During the Civil Rights Movement," Biography.com, February 9, 2021, https://www .biography.com/news/web-dubois-vs-booker-t-washington (page discontinued).

8. Abbott-Sengstacke Family Papers.

9. "American Race Prejudice Must Be Destroyed!," *Chicago Defender*, August 11, 1928, ProQuest, https://www.proquest.com/historical-newspapers/other-21-no-title /docview/492208914/se-2.

10. Isabel Wilkerson, "The Long-Lasting Legacy of the Great Migration," *Smithsonian Magazine*, September 2016, https://www.smithsonianmag.com/history/long-lasting -legacy-great-migration-180960118/.

11. Ethan Michaeli, *The Defender: How the Legendary Black Newspaper Changed America* (Boston: Houghton Mifflin Harcourt, 2016), Kindle ed., chap. 4.

12. James Grossman, "Great Migration," Encyclopedia of Chicago, 2005, http://www .encyclopedia.chicagohistory.org/pages/545.html.

13. "Quickfacts: Chicago City, Illinois," US Census Bureau, accessed September 11, 2022, https://www.census.gov/quickfacts/chicagocityillinois.

14. "U.S. Enters World War I," Library of Congress, accessed June 27, 2023, https://www .loc.gov/item/today-in-history/april-06/.

15. "Immigration and the Great War," National Park Service, accessed June 27, 2023, https://www.nps.gov/articles/immigration-and-the-great-war.htm.

16. Sean J. LaBat, "World War I," Encyclopedia of Chicago, 2005, http://www .encyclopedia.chicagohistory.org/pages/1383.html.

17. Daniel Hautzinger, "How World War I Transformed Chicago," WTTW Chicago, April 10, 2017, https://interactive.wttw.com/playlist/2017/04/07/how-world-war-i -transformed-chicago.

18. Larry Tye, interview by Steve Inskeep, "Pullman Porters Helped Build Black Middle Class," *Morning Edition*, NPR, May 7, 2009, https://www.npr.org/transcripts /103880184.

4. News in Times of Turmoil: Black Nuance, Black Perspective

1. Robert Loerzel, "Blood in the Streets," *Chicago*, July 23, 2019, https://www .chicagomag.com/chicago-magazine/august-2019/1919-race-riot/.

2. Dr. Elizabeth Todd-Breland (associate professor of history at the University of Illinois Chicago), in discussion with the author, November 2020.

3. Daniel Hautzinger, "'We're Still Here': Chicago's Native American Community," WTTW Chicago, November 8, 2018, https://interactive.wttw.com/playlist/2018/11/08/native-americans-chicago.

4. Daniel Hautzinger, "The Horrific Violence and Continuing Legacy of Chicago's 1919 Race Riot," WTTW Chicago, July 26, 2019, https://interactive.wttw.com/playlist/2019/07/26/chicago-1919-race-riot.

5. Robert Loerzel, "Blood in the Streets," *Chicago*, July 23, 2019, https://www.chicagomag.com/chicago-magazine/august-2019/1919-race-riot/.

6. "The History," Chicago Race Riot of 1919 Commemoration Project, accessed June 14, 2021, https://chicagoraceriot.org/history/the-riot/.

7. Julius L. Jones, "The Red Summer of 1919," *Chicago History Museum Blog*, July 26, 2019, https://www.chicagohistory.org/chi1919/.

8. "Chicago Race Riot of 1919," Encyclopedia Britannica, August 19, 2020, https://www.britannica.com/event/Chicago-Race-Riot-of-1919.

9. Amisha Padnani and Jessica Bennett, "Remarkable People We Overlooked in Our Obituaries," *New York Times*, March 8, 2018, https://www.nytimes.com/interactive/2018/obituaries/overlooked.html.

10. DeNeen L. Brown, "For Scores of Years, Newspapers Printed Hate, Leading to Racist Terror Lynchings and Massacres of Black Americans," Printing Hate, Howard Center for Investigative Journalism, October 18, 2021, https://lynching.cnsmaryland.org/2021/10/12/printing-hate-newspapers-lynching/.

11. "Coded Language," EdJustice, National Education Association, November 2, 2018, https://neaedjustice.org/social-justice-issues/racial-justice/coded-language/.

12. "Report Two Killed, Fifty Hurt, in Race Riots," *Chicago Daily Tribune*, July 28, 1919, ProQuest, https://www.proquest.com/historical-newspapers/report-two-killed-fifty-hurt-race-riots/docview/174434441/se-2.

13. "I. W. W. and Race Prejudice," *Chicago Daily Tribune*, July 28, 1919, ProQuest, https://www.proquest.com/historical-newspapers/i-w-race-prejudice/docview/174477491/se-2.

14. "Reaping the Whirlwind," *Chicago Defender,* August 2, 1919, ProQuest, https://www.proquest.com/docview/493425434.

15. Ottley, *Lonely Warrior*, chap. 1.

16. Wells, *Crusade for Justice*, 306.

17. Dolinar, *Negro in Illinois*, 117.

18. "About the Chicago Illinois Idea," Library of Congress, accessed February 19, 2022, https://chroniclingamerica.loc.gov/lccn/sn90053126/.

19. "When You Need Money: $25,000 Concern Financed by Colored Men Does a General Brokerage Business," *Chicago Defender*, May 21, 1910, ProQuest, https://www.proquest.com/docview/493150349/5A2C8C95EB964939PQ/1.

20. "The Broad Ax," Illinois Digital Newspaper Collections, accessed February 19, 2022, https://idnc.library.illinois.edu/?a=cl&cl=CL1&sp=TBA&e=-------en-20--1--txt-txIN----------.

21. Roscoe C. Simmons, "Author of a Civilization," *Chicago Defender*, Abbott-Sengstacke Family Papers.

Cadillac Baby's Show Lounge

1. David Whiteis (author of *Chicago Blues: Portraits and Stories*), in discussion with the author, March 2019.
2. Sebastian Danchin, *Earl Hooker, Blues Master* (Jackson: University Press of Mississippi, 2001), 130.

5. Mississippi Mud Music

1. David Evans, "The Birth of the Blues," in *American Roots Music*, ed. Robert Santelli, Holly George-Warren, and Jim Brown (New York: Harry N. Abrams, 2001), 41.
2. "Phonograph," Encyclopedia Britannica, October 16, 2022, https://www.britannica .com/technology/phonograph.
3. Nellie Gilles and Mycah Hazel, "Radio Diaries: Harry Pace and the Rise and Fall of Black Swan Records," *All Things Considered*, NPR, July 1, 2021, https://www.npr.org /2021/06/30/1011901555/radio-diaries-harry-pace-and-the-rise-and-fall-of-black -swan-records.
4. "Rock & Roll Hall of Fame Announces 2021 Inductees," Rock & Roll Hall of Fame, accessed August 9, 2023, https://www.rockhall.com/rock-roll-hall-fame-announces -2021-inductees.
5. Howlin' Wolf, interview by Chris Strachwitz, April 20, 1967, Arhoolie Foundation, https://arhoolie.org/howlin-wolf-interview-2/.

6. An Urban Chicago Style

1. Whiteis, in discussion with the author.
2. Cheryl Corley (national correspondent at NPR), in discussion with the author, April 2019.
3. Toronzo Cannon (blues musician), in discussion with the author, April 2019.

On My Radio

1. Tiffany Walden, "Mike Love and the Dizz on the Rise and Fall of WGCI's Bad Boy Radio and the Birth of the Birthday Line," *Chicago Reader*, April 26, 2017, https:// chicagoreader.com/blogs/mike-love-and-the-dizz-on-the-rise-and-fall-of-wgcis-bad -boy-radio-and-the-birth-of-the-birthday-line/.
2. Richard Steele (radio host), in discussion with the author, March 2022.
3. Herb Kent and David Smallwood, *The Cool Gent: The Nine Lives of Radio Legend Herb Kent* (Chicago: Chicago Review Press, 2009), 285.

7. The Voice of Chicago

1. Melody Spann Cooper (chairman of Midway Broadcasting Corporation), in discussion with the author, January 2022.
2. "Pervis Spann," HistoryMakers, February 8, 2002, https://www.thehistorymakers.org /biography/pervis-spann-39.
3. Kent and Smallwood, *Cool Gent*, 82.

4.   Howard Reich, "A Chicago Voice That Echoes Nationwide: As WVON Celebrates 50 Years, the People Who Know It Best Take Stock of Its Unparalleled Legacy," *Chicago Tribune*, March 31, 2013, ProQuest, https://www.proquest.com/docview/1321665451 /8CA2C2833028489EPQ/.

8. Rise of the Black Radio Star

1.   Ryan Ellet, "'Destination Freedom': 'A Garage in Gainesville' and 'Execution Awaited' (September 25; October 2, 1949)," Library of Congress, accessed March 7, 2022, https://www.loc.gov/static/programs/national-recording-preservation-board /documents/DestinationFreedom.pdf.

2.   "Jack Gibson Recalls the First All-Negro Radio Soap Opera, 'Here Comes Tomorrow,'" Smithsonian Productions, April 9, 1991, Archives of African American Music and Culture, Google Arts & Culture, https://artsandculture.google.com/asset /jack-gibson-recalls-the-first-all-negro-radio-soap-opera-here-comes-tomorrow -smithsonian-productions/WgETN0qPK11VRw.

3.   "Jack Gibson Discusses Al Benson's Popularity in Chicago," n.d., Indiana University Archives of African American Music and Culture, YouTube, December 4, 2015, https://www.youtube.com/watch?v=0Y2su0MguUE.

4.   "Golden Age of Black Radio—Part 1: The Early Years," Archives of African American Music and Culture, Google Arts & Culture, accessed February 23, 2022, https:// artsandculture.google.com/story/golden-age-of-black-radio-part-1-the-early-years -archives-of-african-american-music-and-culture/3wUxRMZB2RIOIQ.

5.   Kent and Smallwood, *Cool Gent*, xiii–xiv.

6.   Kent and Smallwood, xv.

7.   Lynn Van Matre, "Daniels Before Dawn," *Chicago Tribune*, December 30, 1973, ProQuest, https://www.proquest.com/historical-newspapers/daniels-before-dawn /docview/171015071/se-2.

8.   Dan Kening, "Yvonne Daniels, 'First Lady of Radio,'" *Chicago Tribune*, June 23, 1991, https://www.chicagotribune.com/news/ct-xpm-1991-06-23-9102250399-story.html.

9. The Chicago Sound

1.   Mary Datcher (founder of Global Mixx Media Group), in discussion with the author, April 2020.

2.   Barbara Sherlock, "E. Rodney Jones, 75," *Chicago Tribune*, January 9, 2004, https:// www.chicagotribune.com/news/ct-xpm-2004-01-09-0401090092-story.html.

3.   Forrest Wickman, "How a Black-Owned Label Brought the Beatles to America," *Slate*, January 10, 2013, https://slate.com/culture/2013/01/the-beatles-and-vee-jay -records-how-it-took-a-black-owned-label-to-bring-the-beatles-to-america.html.

4.   Dave Hoekstra, "Chicago's Dreamgirls," *Chicago Sun-Times*, December 19, 2006, author's personal website, https://www.davehoekstra.com/wp-content/uploads/2021 /11/Opals-Chicagos-Dreamgirls.pdf.

Dancing Down

1.   Alan King (Chosen Few Picnic cofounder), in discussion with the author, May 2019.

10. The Scene That House Built

1. DeJuan C. Frazier (founder of House Arrest Dance Team), in discussion with the author, February 2022.

2. Datcher, in discussion with the author.

11. "It's a Drill"

1. Ciaran Thapar, "From Chicago to Brixton: The Surprising Rise of UK Drill," *Fact*, April 28, 2017, https://www.factmag.com/2017/04/27/uk-drill-chicago-brixton/.

2. Sam Davies, "The Controversial Music That Is the Sound of Global Youth," BBC, June 7, 2021, https://www.bbc.com/culture/article/20210607-the-controversial -music-that-is-the-sound-of-global-youth.

3. Dometi Pongo (journalist), in discussion with the author, March 2020.

4. DJ Vlad, "King Louie on Pac Man Inventing 'Drill,' Doesn't Want to Speak About His Murder (Part 3)," YouTube, August 26, 2021, https://youtu.be/H4KOX0XsIrM.

5. Jeanita W. Richardson and Kim A. Scott, "Rap Music and Its Violent Progeny: America's Culture of Violence in Context," *Journal of Negro Education* 71, no. 3 (Summer 2002): 175–192, https://doi.org/10.2307/3211235.

6. Joe Coscarelli, "Hologram Performance by Chief Keef Is Shut Down by Police," *New York Times*, July 26, 2015, https://www.nytimes.com/2015/07/27/arts/music /hologram-performance-by-chief-keef-is-shut-down-by-police.html.

7. Coscarelli, "Hologram Performance by Chief Keef."

Black Excellence, Baby

1. Jeffrey Gottfried and Michael Barthel, "Black, Hispanic and White Adults Feel the News Media Misunderstand Them, but for Very Different Reasons," Pew Research Center, August 20, 2020, https://www.pewresearch.org/fact-tank/2020/06/25/black -hispanic-and-white-adults-feel-the-news-media-misunderstand-them-but-for-very -different-reasons/.

12. If I Were a Negro

1. "John H. Johnson," HistoryMakers, November 11 and December 16, 2004, https:// www.thehistorymakers.org/biography/john-h-johnson-40.

2. Eleanor Roosevelt, proposed article for *Negro Digest*, 1948, Eleanor Roosevelt Papers, vol. 1, Encyclopedia.com, https://www.encyclopedia.com/politics/news-wires-white -papers-and-books/proposed-article-negro-digest.

3. Alexis Clark, "Black Americans Who Served in WWII Faced Segregation Abroad and at Home," History.com, August 5, 2020, https://www.history.com/news/black -soldiers-world-war-ii-discrimination.

4. "Negro Digest," Highlights from the Gates Collection of African American History and Culture, Portland State University Library, accessed February 25, 2022, https:// exhibits.library.pdx.edu/exhibits/show/gates/jimcrow/negro-digest.html.

5. Ed Gordon, "'Ebony,' 'Jet' Founder John H. Johnson," *News & Notes*, NPR, August 9, 2005, https://www.npr.org/templates/story/story.php?storyId=4792165.

6. Jonathan Fenderson, *Building the Black Arts Movement: Hoyt Fuller and the Cultural Politics of the 1960s* (Urbana, IL: University of Illinois Press, 2019), Kindle ed., introduction.
7. Steve Johnson, "'Johnson Publishing' Exhibit Shows Off Company's Design Flair—Without a Plexiglass Museum Case," *Chicago Tribune*, July 5, 2018, https://www.chicagotribune.com/entertainment/museums/ct-ent-johnson-publishing-exhibition-theaster-gates-0705-story.html.
8. Adeshola Makinde (artist), in discussion with the author, February 2022.

13. The JPC Launching Pad

1. Charles Whitaker (dean of Northwestern University's Medill School of Journalism), in discussion with the author, February 2022.
2. Wendy Goodman, "The Black Media Mogul Who Changed History," Curbed, *New York Magazine*, June 13, 2020, https://www.curbed.com/2020/06/see-the-ebony-magazine-offices-in-their-former-glory.html.
3. Lakeidra Chavis, "The Fading Extravagance of the Johnson Publishing Building," WBEZ Chicago, November 14, 2017, https://www.wbez.org/stories/the-fading-extravagance-of-the-johnson-publishing-building/dd598c81-ed3c-4560-b2cc-32922f4f6316.
4. Matt Crawford and Melanie Bishop, *Landmark Designation Report: Johnson Publishing Company Building* (City of Chicago, October 5, 2017), https://www.chicago.gov/content/dam/city/depts/zlup/Historic_Preservation/Publications/Johnson_Publishing_Co_Bldg.pdf, 4.
5. Crawford and Bishop, 9.
6. "New JPC Building Dedicated," *Jet*, June 1, 1972, Google Books, https://books.google.com/books?id=pbEDAAAAMBAJ&pg=PA10.
7. Brent Staples, "The Radical Blackness of Ebony Magazine," *New York Times*, August 11, 2019, https://www.nytimes.com/2019/08/11/opinion/ebony-jet-magazine.html.
8. E. R. Shipp, "Ebony, 40, Viewed as More than a Magazine," *New York Times*, December 6, 1985, https://www.nytimes.com/1985/12/06/us/ebony-40-viewed-as-more-than-a-magazine.html.
9. "Lerone Bennett, Former Editor for 'Ebony' and 'Jet,' Dead at 89," TheGrio, February 15, 2018, https://thegrio.com/2018/02/15/lerone-bennett-editor-dead-at-89/.
10. E. James West, *Ebony Magazine and Lerone Bennett Jr.: Popular Black History in Postwar America* (Urbana: University of Illinois Press), Kindle ed., chap. 1.

14. What's Happening in Black America

1. Whitaker, in discussion with the author.
2. Farrell Evans, "Why Harry Truman Ended Segregation in the US Military in 1948," History.com, November 5, 2020, https://www.history.com/news/harry-truman-executive-order-9981-desegration-military-1948.
3. Exec. Order No. 9,981, July 26, 1948, General Records of the United States Government, RG 11, National Archives.

4. Simeon Booker, "30 Years Ago: How Emmett Till's Lynching Launched Civil Rights Drive," *Jet*, June 17, 1985, Google Books, https://books.google.com/books?id =R7MDAAAAMBAJ&pg=PA13.

5. Danielle Robinson Bell (assistant professor at Northwestern University), in discussion with the author, February 2022.

6. "Ebony," Encyclopedia Britannica, August 27, 2020, https://www.britannica.com /topic/Ebony-American-magazine.

7. Avis Weathersbee, "Did I Really Just Buy Ebony?," *Ebony*, March 2, 2021, https:// www.ebony.com/good-question/were-back-for-good/.

15. Celebration of Black Cuisine

1. UChicago Dining, "The Connection Between Food, Art, and Culture: A Conversation of Black Culture, the Past, Present, and Future" (panel, University of Chicago, Chicago, IL, February 28, 2022).

2. Whitaker, in discussion with the author.

3. Jessica B. Harris, *High on the Hog : A Culinary Journey from Africa to America* (New York: Bloomsbury, 2012), 195.

4. Freda DeKnight, *A Date with a Dish: Classic African-American Recipes* (Mineola, NY: Dover, 2014), 6.

5. Charla Draper (former *Ebony* food editor), in discussion with the author, February 2022.

6. "Dr. Jessica B. Harris on the Ebony Test Kitchen," Museum of Food and Drink, YouTube, March 2, 2022, https://www.youtube.com/watch?v=2SIY58_zUF4.

First Taste of Beauty

1. "How Did I Get Here? Desirée Rogers," Bloomberg Businessweek, 2016, https://www .bloomberg.com/features/2016-how-did-i-get-here/desiree-rogers.html.

2. Lauren Valenti, "Naomi Campbell's Guide to a Glamorous 10-Minute Beauty Routine," *Vogue*, June 15, 2020, https://www.vogue.com/article/naomi-campbell -beauty-secrets.

16. Making Fashion Fair for Ebony Skin

1. Joy Bivins (director of the Schomburg Center for Research in Black Culture and former director of curatorial affairs at the Chicago History Museum), in discussion with the author, January 2022.

2. André Leon Talley, *The Chiffon Trenches: A Memoir* (New York: Ballantine, 2020), 74.

3. Talley, *Chiffon Trenches*, 72–73.

4. "Jessie C. Dent, 96, New Orleans Pianist, Teacher and Community Leader Who Inspired Creation of the Ebony Fashion Fair Dies," *Jet*, April 2, 2001, Google Books, https://books.google.com/books?id=8cMDAAAAMBAJ&pg=PA55.

5. Talley, *Chiffon Trenches*, 73.

6. Dennis Hevesi. "Eunice Johnson Dies at 93; Gave Ebony Its Name," *New York Times*, January 9, 2010, https://www.nytimes.com/2010/01/10/business/media/10johnson .html.

7. "50 Years of Ebony Fashion," WTTW Chicago, May 1, 2013, https://news.wttw.com /2013/05/01/50-years-ebony-fashion.

8. Treonna Turner, "The Ebony Fashion Fair," Fashion and Race Database, July 23, 2021, https://fashionandrace.org/database/the-ebony-fashion-fair/.

9. "The History of a Chicago-Based Cosmetics Company Made for Women of Color," WGN-TV, February 21, 2020, https://wgntv.com/hidden-history/the-history-of-a -chicago-based-cosmetics-company-made-for-women-of-color/.

10. Lindsay Peoples Wagner, "Desiree Rogers Has Been Celebrating Black Beauty Since Before It Was a 'Trend,'" The Cut, *New York Magazine*, February 23, 2022, https://www .thecut.com/2022/02/in-her-shoes-desiree-rogers-on-revamping-fashion-fair.html.

17. The Limitless Art of Fashion

1. Makinde, in discussion with the author.

2. Andrew Connor, "Remembering Alumnus Virgil Abloh, a Pioneering Designer Inspired by Architecture," Illinois Tech, December 16, 2021, https://www.iit.edu/news /remembering-alumnus-virgil-abloh-pioneering-designer-inspired-architecture.

3. Doreen St. Félix, "Virgil Abloh, Menswear's Biggest Star," *New Yorker*, March 11, 2019, https://www.newyorker.com/magazine/2019/03/18/virgil-abloh-menswears -biggest-star.

4. Carrie Shepherd, "Virgil Abloh's First Exhibit Is at His Home Base," WBEZ Chicago, June 11, 2019, https://www.wbez.org/stories/chicago-fashion-designer-virgil-abloh -gets-first-museum-exhibit/02316722-3772-40a4-bbb0-59c1974bc70c.

5. Scarlett Newman (fashion journalist), in discussion with the author, February 2022.

6. Robin Givhan, "Virgil Abloh's Wondrous Success," *Washington Post*, November 29, 2021, https://www.washingtonpost.com/nation/2021/11/29/virgil-abloh -appreciation/.

The Shine of a Crown

1. "About," The Official CROWN Act, accessed July 17, 2023, https://www.thecrownact .com/about.

2. Monique Rodriguez (founder and CEO of Mielle), in discussion with the author, February 2019.

18. From Respectability to Black and Proud

1. Kathy Peiss, *Hope in a Jar: The Making of America's Beauty Culture* (Philadelphia: University of Pennsylvania Press, 1998), 67.

2. Ayana D. Byrd and Lori L. Tharps, *Hair Story: Untangling the Roots of Black Hair in America*, rev. ed. (New York: St. Martin's, 2014), 74.

3. Moriah James, "Sizzle: Annie Turnbo Malone, Madam C.J. Walker, and the Complicated History of the Hot Comb," National Museum of African American History & Culture, January 10, 2019, https://nmaahc.si.edu/explore/stories /collection/sizzle.

4. Gerald Horne, *The Rise & Fall of the Associated Negro Press: Claude Barnett's Pan-African News and the Jim Crow Paradox* (Urbana: University of Illinois Press, 2017), 35.

5.   "Mende" (pamphlet), National African Language Resource Center, accessed June 28, 2023, https://nalrc.indiana.edu/doc/brochures/mende.pdf.

6.   "Annie Malone and Madam C.J. Walker: Pioneers of the African American Beauty Industry," National Museum of African American History & Culture, accessed June 28, 2023, https://nmaahc.si.edu/explore/stories/annie-malone-and-madam-cj -walker-pioneers-african-american-beauty-industry.

7.   Horne, *Rise & Fall of the Associated Negro Press*, 35.

8.   "Poro College Moves Plant to Chicago," *Afro American* (Baltimore, MD), August 2, 1930, Google News, https://news.google.com/newspapers?id=m6A9AAAAIBAJ& pg=838,1763641.

9.   Peiss, *Hope in a Jar*, 113.

10. Byrd and Tharps, *Hair Story*, 78.

11. Ayana Contreras (author of *Energy Never Dies: Afro-Optimism and Creativity in Chicago*), in discussion with the author, January 2022.

19. At the Root of Change

1.   Mary Brooks (former Soft Sheen employee), in discussion with the author, April 2020.

2.   Veronica Anderson, "Soft Sheen Thinks Sale; Family Firm Has Retained First Boston," *Crain's Chicago Business*, May 27, 1995, https://www.chicagobusiness.com /article/19950527/ISSUE01/10009551/soft-sheen-thinks-sale-family-firm-has -retained-first-boston.

3.   Jennifer White and Colin McNulty. "Obama 2: Chicago Politics Ain't Beanbag," WBEZ Chicago, February 15, 2018, https://www.wbez.org/stories/obama-2-chicago -politics-aint-beanbag/92ffe0ce-cdfc-4650-baf7-3138b44d780a.

4.   "Bettiann Gardner," HistoryMakers, August 22, 2002, https://www.thehistorymakers .org/biography/bettiann-gardner-39.

Black and White and Technicolor

1.   Sergio Mims (film critic and cofounder of the Black Harvest Film Festival), in discussion with the author, September 2021.

2.   Dr. Allyson Nadia Field (University of Chicago professor and author of *Uplift Cinema: The Emergence of African American Film and the Possibility of Black Modernity*), in discussion with the author, September 2021.

3.   Lonnae O'Neal, "Hair Care Pioneer Joan Johnson Made 'Ultra Sheen, Afro Sheen and Ultra Sheen Cosmetics' a Feature of Black Identity," Andscape, September 10, 2019, https://andscape.com/features/hair-care-pioneer-joan-johnson-made-ultra -sheen-afro-sheen-and-ultra-sheen-cosmetics-a-feature-of-black-identity/.

20. Silence and the Silver Screen

1.   Lee Pfeiffer and Dick Lehr, "The Birth of a Nation," Encyclopedia Britannica, March 23, 2020, https://www.britannica.com/topic/The-Birth-of-a-Nation.

2.   Dr. Mark A. Reid (University of Florida professor and author of *Redefining Black Film*), in discussion with the author, September 2021.

3.   Field, in discussion with the author.

4. Untitled article, *Chicago Defender*, August 30, 1913, ProQuest, https://www.proquest
.com/docview/493229859.

5. Jacqueline Najuma Stewart, *Migrating to the Movies: Cinema and Black Urban
Modernity* (Berkeley: University of California Press, 2005), 186.

6. Juli Jones, "Moving Pictures Offer the Greatest Opportunity to the American Negro
in History of the Race from Every Point of View," *Chicago Defender*, October 9, 1915,
ProQuest, https://www.proquest.com/historical-newspapers/moving-pictures-offer
-greatest-opportunity/docview/493287793/se-2.

7. "Ebony Film Cancelled: Phoenix Theatre Manager Refuses to Use Degrading Movie,"
Chicago Defender, May 12, 1917, ProQuest, https://www.proquest.com/historical
-newspapers/ebony-film-cancelled/docview/493518458/se-2.

21. Talkies

1. David Pierce, *The Survival of American Silent Feature Films: 1912–1929* (Washington,
DC: Council on Library and Information Resources and the Library of Congress,
September 2013), 25, https://www.loc.gov/static/programs/national-film
-preservation-board/documents/pub158.final_version_sept_2013.pdf.

2. "Black Silent Film Then and Now," Academy Museum of Motion Pictures, accessed
January 5, 2022, https://www.academymuseum.org/en/black-silent-film-then-now.

3. Field, in discussion with the author.

4. Mims, in discussion with the author.

5. Oscar Micheaux, *The Conquest: The Story of a Negro Pioneer* (New York: Washington
Square Press, 2003).

6. "Oscar Micheaux (U.S. National Park Service)," National Park Service, accessed
January 9, 2022, https://www.nps.gov/people/oscar-micheaux.htm.

7. Oscar Micheaux, *The Homesteader: A Novel* (orig. publ. 1917; Lincoln: University of
Nebraska Press, 1994).

8. Erin Blakemore, "Watch the Oldest-Known Surviving Film by an African-American
Director," *Smithsonian Magazine*, February 23, 2017, https://www.smithsonianmag
.com/smart-news/watch-oldest-known-surviving-film-african-american-director
-180962035/.

9. Stewart, *Migrating to the Movies*, 244.

10. "Oscar Micheaux," Turner Classic Movies, accessed January 9, 2022, https://www
.tcm.com/tcmdb/person/131052%7C119611/Oscar-Micheaux.

22. Singing Cowboys

1. Micheaux, *The Homesteader*, 39.

2. "Star Herb Jeffries in Western Picture," *Chicago Defender*, October 23, 1937,
ProQuest, https://www.proquest.com/historical-newspapers/star-herb-jeffries
-western-picture/docview/492500371/se-2.

3. "'Herb' Jeffries Goes Temporarily Blind," *Chicago Defender*, July 31, 1937, ProQuest,
https://www.proquest.com/historical-newspapers/herb-jeffries-goes-temporarily
-blind/docview/492465344/se-2.

4. Blake Allmendinger, *Imagining the African American West* (Lincoln: University of Nebraska Press, 2005), 68.

5. "New Motion Picture Company Enters Negro Field in the South; To Make Eight Pictures," *New York Age*, March 9, 1940.

6. Michael K. Johnson, *Hoo-Doo Cowboys and Bronze Buckaroos: Conceptions of the African American West* (Jackson: University Press of Mississippi, 2014), 102.

7. Julia Leyda, "Black-Audience Westerns and the Politics of Cultural Identification in the 1930s," *Cinema Journal* 42, no. 1 (Autumn 2002): 47–48, JSTOR, http://www .jstor.org/stable/1225542.

8. "Herbert Herb Jeffries," Hollywood Walk of Fame, October 25, 2019, https:// walkoffame.com/herbert-herb-jeffries/.

9. "Herb Jeffries 100th Birthday! Herb Talks About Duke Ellington and Jump for Joy," Symphonic Swing, YouTube, September 7, 2013, https://www.youtube.com /watch?v=mNlaV5i6i88.

10. "Herb Jeffries 100th Birthday!," Symphonic Swing.

11. William Yardley, "Herb Jeffries, 'Bronze Buckaroo' of Song and Screen, Dies at 100 (or So)," *New York Times*, May 26, 2014, https://www.nytimes.com/2014/05/27/arts /music/herb-jeffries-singing-star-of-black-cowboy-films-dies-at-100.html.

23. Dancing, Afros, and a Whole Lotta Soul

1. Michael Miner, "An Early Glimpse of Don Cornelius," *Chicago Reader*, August 19, 2021, https://chicagoreader.com/blogs/an-early-glimpse-of-don-cornelius/.

2. Neil Strauss, "You Say 'Soul Train' Is How Old?," *New York Times*, December 31, 1995, https://www.nytimes.com/1995/12/31/tv/cover-story-you-say-soul-train-is -how-old.html.

3. Aida Chapman, "Soul Train," *Billboard*, September 28, 1974, Google Books, https:// books.google.com/books?id=twcEAAAAMBAJ&pg=PT14.

4. Contreras, in discussion with the author.

5. "Our Legacy," Afro Sheen, accessed March 5, 2022, https://www.afrosheen.com/our -legacy (site discontinued).

6. Bell, in discussion with the author.

A Full Cup

1. "Why You Should Put Yourself First," *Oprah's Lifeclass*, OWN, YouTube, March 28, 2012, https://www.youtube.com/watch?v=ZhqokZF5OFU.

2. Aisha Harris, "A History of Self-Care," *Slate*, April 5, 2017, http://www.slate.com /articles/arts/culturebox/2017/04/the_history_of_self_care.html.

24. The Oprah Winfrey Show

1. Jenn White (journalist and host of *Making Oprah*), in discussion with the author, January 2022.

2. S. R. Toliver, "Imagining New Hopescapes: Expanding Black Girls' Windows and Mirrors," *Research on Diversity in Youth Literature* 1, no. 1 (2018): https://sophia .stkate.edu/rdyl/vol1/iss1/3.

3. "OWN, Onyx Collective and Hulu Announce Unprecedented Partnership to Simultaneously Premiere Original Docuseries 'The Hair Tales,'" Discovery Press Web, June 24, 2021, https://press.discovery.com/us/own/press-releases/2021/own -onyx-collective-and-hulu-announce-unprece-5499/.

4. David Zurawik, "Oprah—Built in Baltimore," *Baltimore Sun*, May 18, 2011, https:// www.baltimoresun.com/entertainment/bs-xpm-2011-05-18-bs-sm-oprahs -baltimore-20110522-story.html.

5. Oprah Winfrey, *The Path Made Clear: Discovering Your Life's Direction and Purpose* (New York: Flatiron, 2019), 14.

6. "Oprah Winfrey on Career, Life, and Leadership," Stanford Graduate School of Business, YouTube, April 28, 2014, https://www.youtube.com/watch?v=6DlrqeWrczs.

7. "Oprah 1: No Strategy, No Plan, No Formula," WBEZ Chicago, November 10, 2016, https://www.wbez.org/stories/oprah-1-no-strategy-no-plan-no-formula/4ae62e92 -647c-42df-88f2-4c3cdb89e284.

8. Robert La Franco and Josh McHugh, "How Oprah Went from Talk Show Host to First African-American Woman Billionaire," *Forbes*, October 1995, https://www .forbes.com/sites/jennifereum/2014/09/29/how-oprah-went-from-talk-show-host -to-first-african-american-woman-billionaire/.

9. "Oprah Thanks the Man Who Started Her Career," Oprah.com, November 26, 2010, https://www.oprah.com/own-oprahshow/oprah-thanks-the-man-who-started-her -career-video.

25. A Shift to "Live Your Best Life"

1. Terry Gross, "The 'Racial Cleansing' That Drove 1,100 Black Residents out of Forsyth County, GA," *Fresh Air*, NPR, September 15, 2016, https://www.npr.org/2016/09/15 /494063372/the-racial-cleansing-that-drove-1-100-black-residents-out-of-forsyth -county-ga.

2. "Oprah Visits a County Where No Black Person Had Lived for 75 Years," *The Oprah Winfrey Show*, 1987, YouTube, January 2, 2015, https://www.youtube.com/watch ?v=WErjPmFulQ0.

3. "How a Gang of Skinheads Forever Changed the Course of *The Oprah Winfrey Show*," Oprah.com, January 1, 2015, https://www.oprah.com/own-oprahshow/how -a-gang-of-skin-heads-changed-oprah-show-history-video.

4. "Oprah 2: Skinheads and Scented Candles," WBEZ Chicago, November 17, 2016, https://www.wbez.org/stories/oprah-2-skinheads-and-scented-candles/56cc04d7 -c516-4c3b-b72e-3f1dc797f140.

5. "Geraldo Rivera Breaks Nose During Melee on His TV Talk Show," Associated Press, November 4, 1988, https://apnews.com/article/734658f0e6401b1d42cb9a2e5a11 7b17.

6. "Oprah 2," WBEZ Chicago, https://www.wbez.org/stories/oprah-2-skinheads-and -scented-candles/56cc04d7-c516-4c3b-b72e-3f1dc797f140.

26. Oprah OWNs Media

1. Mark R. Wilson, Stephen R. Porter, and Janice L. Reiff, " Harpo Productions Inc.," Encyclopedia of Chicago, 2005, http://www.encyclopedia.chicagohistory.org/pages /2693.html.

2. "About Us," Oprah Winfrey Charitable Foundation, accessed January 8, 2021, https:// www.oprahfoundation.org/about-charity.

3. "Oprah 3: YOU GET A CAR!," WBEZ Chicago, November 22, 2016, https://www .wbez.org/stories/oprah-3-you-get-a-car/a10ded30-5eac-49c9-bfaf-4db65df8e71a.

4. Glenn Garner, "Oprah's Best Friend Gayle King Reveals the Unique Way She Was Behind the 'You Get a Car' Giveaway," *People*, January 28, 2022, https://people.com /tv/oprah-best-friend-gayle-king-was-behind-you-get-a-car-giveaway-exclusive/.

5. Brad Witter, "Why Oprah's Car Giveaway Is the Most Epic Talk Show Moment Ever," Biography.com, May 29, 2020, https://www.biography.com/news/oprah-car -giveaway.

6. Al Lowe, "Oprah Winfrey Honors Good Teachers with Luxury Gifts," *Pittsburgh Post-Gazette*, December 29, 2004, https://www.post-gazette.com/local/west /2004/12/29/Oprah-Winfrey-honors-good-teachers-with-luxury-gifts/stories /200412290265.

7. "Oprah Gives Away Nearly 300 New Cars," History.com, January 27, 2010, https:// www.history.com/this-day-in-history/oprah-gives-away-nearly-300-new-cars.

8. "Forbes Magazine: Fewer Billionaires, but Winfrey on List," *Chicago Tribune*, February 28, 2003, https://www.chicagotribune.com/news/ct-xpm-2003-02-28 -0302280385-story.html.

9. Winfrey, *Path Made Clear*, 15.

10. Elaine Low, "Discovery Increases Stake in Oprah Winfrey's OWN to 95%," *Variety*, December 23, 2020, https://variety.com/2020/tv/news/discovery-stake-oprah -winfrey-own-harpo-1234872374/.

11. "*The Oprah Winfrey Show* Finale," Oprah.com, May 25, 2011, https://www.oprah .com/oprahshow/the-oprah-winfrey-show-finale_1/all.

The Best. Ever. Anywhere.

1. Annie Costabile, "Watch: Candace Parker Shares Personal TED Talk on Demolishing Limitations," *Chicago Sun-Times*, January 15, 2022, https://chicago.suntimes.com /chicago-sky-and-wnba/2022/1/14/22883784/watch-candace-parker-shares -personal-ted-talk-on-demolishing-limitations.

2. Doug Feinberg, "Candace Parker Voted AP Female Athlete of Year for 2nd Time," *U.S. News & World Report*, December 29, 2021, https://www.usnews.com/news /sports/articles/2021-12-29/candace-parker-voted-ap-female-athlete-of-year-for-2nd -time.

3. Brandon Pope (reporter/anchor at WCIU Chicago), in discussion with the author, August 2022.

27. Three-Peat After Three-Peat

1. Chris Herring (author of *Blood in the Garden: The Flagrant History of the 1990s New York Knicks*), in discussion with the author, February 2022.
2. Jacoby Cochran (host of *City Cast Chicago*), in discussion with the author, November 2022.

28. Be Like Mike

1. "Profile: Michael Jordan," *Forbes*, December 8, 2022, https://www.forbes.com/profile/michael-jordan/.
2. Alex Wong, *Cover Story: The NBA and Modern Basketball as Told Through Its Most Iconic Magazine Covers* (Chicago: Triumph, 2021), 63.
3. "Michael Jordan Worth His Weight in Gold—and Then Some," *Jet*, April 10, 1995, Google Books, https://books.google.com/books?id=_zgDAAAAMBAJ&pg=PA56.
4. Herring, in discussion with the author.
5. Kurt Badenhausen, "Michael Jordan Has Made over $1 Billion from Nike—the Biggest Endorsement Bargain in Sports," *Forbes*, June 28, 2021, https://www.forbes.com/sites/kurtbadenhausen/2020/05/03/michael-jordans-1-billion-nike-endorsement-is-the-biggest-bargain-in-sports/.
6. Jason Guerrasio, "Michael Jordan Wanted a Shoe Deal with Adidas So Badly That He Went Back to the Company Before Signing with Nike to See If It Could Match the Deal," *Insider*, May 6, 2020, https://www.insider.com/michael-jordan-almost-ditched-his-nike-deal-for-adidas-2020-5.
7. Ticara Devone (sneaker reporter), in discussion with the author, November 2022.

29. White Sox Hat

1. Shakeia Taylor (sports journalist), in discussion with the author, February 2022.
2. Shakeia Taylor, "The White Sox Cap and Hip-Hop Culture," FanGraphs Baseball, April 13, 2018, https://blogs.fangraphs.com/the-white-sox-cap-and-hip-hop-culture/.
3. "Express Yourself: Ice Cube Explains White Sox Cap Significance in N.W.A.," NBC Sports Chicago, July 19, 2017, https://www.nbcsports.com/chicago/chicago-white-sox/express-yourself-ice-cube-explains-white-sox-cap-significance-nwa.
4. Jesse Dukes, "Who Came Up with the Iconic White Sox Look?," WBEZ Chicago, October 11, 2017, https://www.wbez.org/stories/who-came-up-with-the-iconic-chicago-white-sox-look/d6cae5bb-ed65-4ed0-bb87-b0bb288252e4.
5. Cathy Horyn, "White-Hot Sox Cap," *Washington Post*, August 15, 1991, https://www.washingtonpost.com/archive/lifestyle/1991/08/15/white-hot-sox-cap/4888f4b0-7ff3-44d7-8bfe-baa122ad4605/.
6. Ben Cosman, "Check Out the New White Sox Hats Designed by Chance the Rapper," MLB.com, April 7, 2016, https://www.mlb.com/cut4/chance-the-rapper-designs-white-sox-caps c170980006.
7. David Waldstein, "Baseball, Popular but No Longer Dominant, Seeks to Reclaim Its Cool," *New York Times*, October 25, 2021, https://www.nytimes.com/2021/10/25/sports/baseball-popularity-black-participation.html.

Art for the People

1. Angel Idowu (arts reporter), in discussion with the author, January 2022.

30. Being Black Is

1. Cecil McDonald (artist), in discussion with the author, February 2019.
2. Greg Lunceford (curator), in discussion with the author, February 2019.
3. "William Edouard Scott Papers," Chicago Public Library, accessed March 4, 2022, https://www.chipublib.org/fa-william-edouard-scott-papers/.
4. "Archibald Motley: Jazz Age Modernist," Whitney Museum of American Art, accessed March 4, 2022, https://whitney.org/exhibitions/archibald-motley.
5. "Eldzier Cortor," Smithsonian American Art Museum, accessed March 4, 2022, https://americanart.si.edu/artist/eldzier-cortor-1000.
6. "Margaret Burroughs," Poetry Foundation, accessed March 4, 2022, https://www.poetryfoundation.org/poets/margaret-burroughs.
7. "About Us," South Side Community Art Center, accessed January 20, 2021, https://www.sscartcenter.org/about-us/.
8. "About Us," DuSable Museum of African American History, accessed January 28, 2022, https://www.dusablemuseum.org/about-us/.

31. Chicago's Own Literary Renaissance

1. Nate Marshall (poet and professor), in discussion with the author, June 2020.
2. Heidi Sperry, Susan Perry, and Terry Tatum, "Chicago Black Renaissance Literary Movement," ed. Brian Goeken, Heidi George Cleveland Hall Branch of the Chicago Public Library, the Richard Wright House, and the Gwendolyn Brooks House, accessed March 7, 2022, https://www.chicago.gov/content/dam/city/depts/zlup/Historic_Preservation/Publications/Chicago_Black_Renaissance_Literary_Movement_Report.pdf.
3. Srikanth Reddy (writer and author), in discussion with the author, February 2022.
4. "Gwendolyn Brooks," Poetry Foundation, accessed March 6, 2022, https://www.poetryfoundation.org/poets/gwendolyn-brooks.
5. "Gwendolyn Brooks: Chicago's Poet," Chicago Public Library, June 1, 2017, https://www.chipublib.org/blogs/post/gwendolyn-brooks-chicagos-poet/.

32. Touch the Sky

1. Shala. (artist), in discussion with the author, January 2019.
2. Jason Mayden (CEO and cofounder of Super Heroic), in discussion with the author, January 2020.
3. Angela Williams (director at the Museum of Science and Industry), in discussion with the author, January 2020.
4. Julia Halperin and Charlotte Burns, "African American Artists Are More Visible than Ever. So Why Are Museums Giving Them Short Shrift?," Artnet News, September 20, 2018, https://news.artnet.com/the-long-road-for-african-american-artists/african-american-research-museums-1350362.
5. Idowu, in discussion with the author.

6.   Darcel Rockett, "Hebru Brantley's Aviator-Goggle-Wearing 'Flyboy' Gets His Own
      Park, Neo-futuristic Art Installation in Pilsen This Fall," *Chicago Tribune*, July 30,
      2019, https://www.chicagotribune.com/entertainment/ct-ent-hebru-brantley
      -nevermore-park-0730-20190730-osqcrv4ugvdx5l56u24fvhknra-story.html.

Epilogue: The End Is Just the Beginning

1.   Elvia Malagón, Andy Boyle, and Rachel Hinton, "Chicago Population Up 2% over
      the Past Decade as City Keeps Title of Third-Largest City in U.S.," *Chicago Sun-
      Times*, August 12, 2021, https://chicago.suntimes.com/2021/8/12/22622062/chicago
      -census-2020-illinois-population-growth-decline-redistricting-racial-composition.
2.   Dimitri Nesbitt, "Engineered Displacement," University of Illinois Chicago, July 6,
      2021, https://storymaps.arcgis.com/stories/90057aec5418495ebee90d427f493f98.
3.   Eve L. Ewing, *Ghosts in the Schoolyard: Racism and School Closings on Chicago's South
      Side* (Chicago: University of Chicago Press, 2018), 85.

INDEX

Black Esthetics arts and culture
    festival, 220
Black filmmakers, xiv, 148,
    151–155, 156–158, 161
Black Harvest Film Festival, 157
Black Hawk War, 25
Black history, xiii–xiv, 223–224
Black History Month, xiv, 224
Black Opal, 114
Black Power, 91, 136–137
Black pride
    art and, 208, 210–212
    Chicago and, 224–225
    Durham and, 59
    Ebony and, 97–99
    hair and, 136–137, 140
    identity and, ix–xii
    Makinde and, 93–94
    Soul Train and, 165–166
Black Swan Records, 40, 57
Black World (a.k.a. *Negro Digest*),
    88, 91–92
blackface, 150–151, 162–163
Black's View of the News, A, 164
Blood at the Root (Phillips), 182
*Blood in the Garden: The Flagrant
    History of 1990s New York
    Knicks* (Herring), 194, 199
blues music, xii, xiv, 35–37,
    39–42, 43–45, 57
Bontemps, Arna, 216
Booker, Simeon, 103
Boyd, Eddie, 38
Bracken, Jimmy, 64
branding, 198–200

Brantley, Hebru, 218, 220–221
Bridgeport, Chicago, 26
*Bright Moments, Memories of the
    Future*, 143
Brillare, Selyna, 129
Broad Ax, 17, 30
Bronze Buckaroo, The (Jeffries),
    161
Bronzeville, Chicago, x, xii, 23,
    142, 215. *See also* Black Belt
    (Chicago region)
Bronzeville Life, 31
Brooks, Gwendolyn, 5, 208, 217
Brooks, Mary, 138–141
Brotherhood of Sleeping Car
    Porters, 102
Brown, James, 123
Brown v. Board of Education,
    102–103
Bryant, Kobe, 195
Bud Billiken Parade, 31, 194
Building the Black Arts Movement
    (Fenderson), 92
Bump J, 80
Bunch, Lonnie G., II, 149
Buol, Mark, 79
Burnett, Chester "Howlin' Wolf,"
    39, 41–42, 43–45, 53
Burrell, Tom, 166
Burrell Advertising, 166–167
Burrell McBain, 166–167
Burroughs, Dr. Margaret T.,
    207–208, 212–213
Butler, The (Foster), 153
Byrd, Ayana D., 134–136